Moving Frames

Film Europa: German Cinema in an International Context
Series Editors: **Hans-Michael Bock** (CineGraph Hamburg); **Tim Bergfelder** (University of Southampton); **Barbara Mennel** (University of Florida)

German cinema is normally seen as a distinct form, but this series emphasizes connections, influences, and exchanges of German cinema across national borders, as well as its links with other media and art forms. Individual titles present traditional historical research (archival work, industry studies) as well as new critical approaches in film and media studies (theories of the transnational), with a special emphasis on the continuities associated with popular traditions and local perspectives.

Recent volumes:

Volume 26
Moving Frames: Photographs in German Cinema
Edited by Carrie Collenberg-González and Martin P. Sheehan

Volume 25
Peter Lilienthal: A Cinema of Exile and Resistance
Claudia Sandberg

Volume 24
Rethinking Jewishness in Weimar Cinema
Edited by Barbara Hales and Valerie Weinstein

Volume 23
Sensitive Subjects: The Political Aesthetics of Contemporary German and Austrian Cinema
Leila Mukhida

Volume 22
East German Film and the Holocaust
Elizabeth Ward

Volume 21
Cinema of Collaboration: DEFA Coproductions and International Exchange in Cold War Europe
Mariana Ivanova

Volume 20
Screening Art: Modernist Aesthetics and the Socialist Imaginary in East German Cinema
Seán Allan

Volume 19
German Television: Historical and Theoretical Perspectives
Edited by Larson Powell and Robert R. Shandley

Volume 18
Cinema in Service of the State: Perspectives on Film Culture in the GDR and Czechoslovakia, 1945–1960
Edited by Lars Karl and Pavel Skopal

Volume 17
Imperial Projections: Screening the German Colonies
Wolfgang Fuhrmann

Volume 16
The Emergence of Film Culture: Knowledge Production, Institution Building, and the Fate of the Avant-Garde in Europe, 1919–1945
Edited by Malte Hagener

For a full volume listing, please see the series page on our website: http://www.berghahnbooks.com/series/film-europa

Moving Frames

Photographs in German Cinema

Edited by
Carrie Collenberg-González and Martin P. Sheehan

berghahn
NEW YORK • OXFORD
www.berghahnbooks.com

First published in 2022 by
Berghahn Books
www.berghahnbooks.com

First paperback edition published in 2026

Library of Congress Cataloging-in-Publication Data

Names: Collenberg-Gonzalez, Carrie, editor. | Sheehan, Martin P., editor.
Title: Moving frames : photographs in German cinema / edited by Carrie Collenberg-Gonzalez and Martin P. Sheehan.
Description: New York : Berghahn Books, 2022. | Series: Film Europa : German cinema in an international context ; volume 26 | Includes bibliographical references and index.
Identifiers: LCCN 2021040515 (print) | LCCN 2021040516 (ebook) | ISBN 9781800733763 (hardback) | ISBN 9781800733770 (ebook)
Subjects: LCSH: Motion pictures—Germany—History. | Photography in motion pictures.
Classification: LCC PN1993.5.G3 M68 2022 (print) | LCC PN1993.5.G3 (ebook) | DDC 791.430943—dc23
LC record available at https://lccn.loc.gov/2021040515
LC ebook record available at https://lccn.loc.gov/2021040516

British Library Cataloguing in Publication Data

A catalogue record for this book is available from the British Library

EU GPSR Authorized Representative

LOGOS EUROPE, 9 rue Nicolas Poussin, 17000, LA ROCHELLE, France

Email: Contact@logoseurope.eu

ISBN 978-1-80073-376-3 hardback
ISBN 978-1-80758-073-5 paperback
ISBN 978-1-80758-550-1 epub
ISBN 978-1-80073-377-0 web pdf

https://doi.org/10.3167/9781800733763

Contents

Illustrations

Acknowledgments

We are especially grateful to everyone who took part in our discussions of these ideas that began at a seminar on photographs and German cinema at the 2017 German Studies Association conference and are also indebted to the authors in this book for their ideas, patience, efficiency, and senses of humor. Our deepest gratitude to our team of editorial assistants from Portland State University and California State University, Long Beach: Dan Baliban, Christine Claringbold, Josephine Claus, Kimberly Moisan, Johanna Morris, Shayna Snyder, Courtney Yamagiwa, and especially, Emily Wysocki. For everything else we thank our families, friends, and colleagues who supported us through the process and offered ideas, advice, and support, particularly Aldo González and Mari Ramler.

Introduction

Photographs as Rupture and Affect in German Film

Carrie Collenberg-González and Martin P. Sheehan

As the building blocks of moving pictures, still photographs have been integral to cinema since its inception, and the relationship between these visual media has only grown more connected and complicated over time. Photographs have countless manifestations and connotations because the social relationship—the interaction between photographic practice, world, image, and user—represents what John Roberts calls "an endlessly englobing and organizational process in which representations of self, other, 'we,' and the collective are brought to consciousness as part of everyday social exchange and struggle."[1] The act of making a photograph, viewing it, or placing it into a new context (especially into a filmic context) has the potential to bring to "consciousness" certain "representations" of aesthetic, epistemological, and cultural realities that might otherwise go unnoticed.

Given this potential, photographic images often take on a disruptive function when encountered within a film's narrative. As artifacts outside cinema and the cinematic realities of film, photographs can function as visual representations of past realities that are reinserted into the present, thereby bringing attention to these past realities. As formal ruptures, photographs have an affective function that prompts action, thought, or emotion in a way that can inspire the construction (or destruction) of meaning, understanding, or feeling. When bodies encounter photographs in film, an intensity seems to pass into those bodies and inspire in them emotional, mental, or physical movement. This affective dimension can register as corporeal senses (vision and touch), memory, a recognition of the uncanny, a source of information or evidence—not one more than the other but, rather, all at once and with infinite hermeneutic potential determined not just by subjective approaches, but also by the encounter between a subject and an object and the contexts in which they are viewed and by whom.

Photographic theory and film theory have a kind of sibling relationship: they share parts of their DNA and inform one another at times, yet they exist independently and sometimes clash. Emerging in the modern period, both media prompted similar concerns about form, content, affect, and representation, as evident in the work of prominent early twentieth-century philosophers and critics like Walter Benjamin and Siegfried Kracauer. Enlightenment and modern philosophy about aesthetics and representation, in turn, informed the work of midcentury and postmodern critics, including André Bazin, Roland Barthes, Susan Sontag, David Campany, Gilles Deleuze, Kaja Silverman, and others. Yet, despite this shared critical heritage, the relationship between photography and film and, in particular, photographs *in* film diverge in two crucial areas—a photograph's status as evidence and the stillness of photographic images. Campany, for example, argues that examples of photography in cinema most often concern the photograph's "complex status as evidence" because "the 'proof' of photography as memory or history is nearly always at stake."[2] He posits that viewing a photograph in film differs greatly from viewing that same photograph in real life: "Film tends to overstate the photograph's difference, while presenting that difference as if it were essence. We see the photograph exaggerated by those qualities that distinguish it from film: its stillness, its temporal fixity, its objecthood, its silence, its deathliness, even."[3] Campany's neat distinction echoes the concerns of his critical predecessors and suggests that the relationship between photographs *in* film hinges on the notion of rupture: that is, photographs in film disrupt foundational beliefs about as well as desires for truth, time, space, life, and death.

A prominent debate in the scholarly literature on photography and film concerns the relationship between stillness (photographs, stills, freezeframes) and motion (film).[4] Even the term *moving pictures* implies such a differentiation, which has only grown more fraught with the ascent of digital technologies. Eivind Røssaak established the stillness/motion distinction as a defining feature of photography in film in his 2011 volume of collected essays covering what he identifies as three phases in which this distinction developed and how it can be observed over time: "a turn to the *in-between*, a turn to history, and a turn to algorithms."[5] Other volumes explore the stillness/motion dynamic as well. Laurent Guido and Oliver Lugon, for instance, posit that much twentieth-century scholarship on film and photography was informed by this dynamic even as "the two media ceaselessly crossed the boundary and blended these categories."[6] Similarly, Karen Beckman and Jean Ma argue "for the impossibility of watching the movement without simultaneously watching the stasis and the media that produce these effects."[7] "The hesitation between stasis and motion," Beckman and Ma observe, "actually produces an interval in which rigorous thinking can emerge."[8] The present volume also acknowledges the critical potential of stillness/motion, and many of the chapters in this volume rely on arguments defined by this distinction.

However, the critical power of stillness/motion seems to be located in the rupture of one or the other—that is, stillness is defined by its disruption of motion, just as motion is defined by its disruption of stillness. Photographic theory often deals in such binaries—not just stillness/motion, but also life/death, truth/fiction, past/present—and their inherent tensions that only become more compounded in film. But the critical moment is located in the disruption of the aforementioned binaries and the assumptions, beliefs, and dreams associated with them. Defining the use of photographs in film (and in general) as a rupture enables us to accept what we already know and what has captured our imagination since the beginning of their interaction—that is, despite representing radical breaks that mark the sudden end of one condition (i.e., motion) and the beginning of another (i.e., stillness), photographs problematize the borders that seem to separate the binaries, thereby bringing attention to these borders.

While the notion of rupture can also be applied to the transnational potential of cinema, it is central to a specifically German cinema and cultural history. For example, the numerous, radical breaks in German political history serve as the organizing principle of Sabine Hake's *German National Cinema*.[9] To be sure, in several contributions in this volume, the photographs in a particular film are explored in terms of their relationship to the film's historical, cultural context. Although a specifically "German" approach to photographs in film does not emerge across the volume, what the analyzed films do have in common is that the ruptures they depict are analogous to the historical and social context they represent that is itself defined by ruptures. The sudden disjuncture of time, space, memory, and narrative represented by photographs draw our consciousness and curiosity, but it is only in context that one can begin to make meaning from these frames and the ruptures they represent. Taking into account the reception of photographs, photographs in film, and the diegetic and national contexts of the films analyzed, the social relations created by these ruptures are also significant. Several chapters in this volume explore how ruptures in assumptions of truth, time, life, and death are connected to (and impacted by) the body and inform specifically German relationships to understanding the past and resisting or accepting hegemonic narratives.

If we understand *affect* to mean the impact of an encounter between one body and another, then in the case of this volume, it can also refer to the encounter between a photograph and a film, between a photograph and those within the filmic reality, and between a photograph on film and its viewers. The role played by the spectator's body and mind is essential to understanding how cinema and photography intersect because the reception of both media depends on the aesthetic, cultural, social, and productive contexts in which they are deployed. "The body," Røssaak argues, "is not just the carrier of a personal history, but a storage site and an intensified receptive surface in a media-saturated society. Thus, the body belongs to a history of media and mediations."[10] How the meaning associated with these practices is constructed depends both on the mind and body, as well as their relationship to history. Because the acts of touching, looking at, creating, displaying, using, distributing, or manipulating photographs are often physical in nature, these acts necessarily engage the spectator's body.

Acknowledging the interaction between photographs and the spectator's body (including their experience and memory) paves the way for understanding the wide-ranging affective register of photographs in film. The body as a site of a personal connection to images must also be understood within the larger political context, which determines how images are used and received. Photographs *move* us, and while the viewer makes sense of the photograph, the photograph, in a way, also makes sense of the viewer and the contexts in which they encounter the image.

By exploring the use of photographs in German cinema from Expressionism to the Berlin School, this volume addresses the shifting formal and narrative roles that photographs can play in films. Each chapter investigates what is suggested within diegetic and extra-diegetic contexts when photographs are encountered in German films. Together, the chapters in this volume engage with and build on a multidisciplinary scholarship to demonstrate the effects of photographic rupture and affect in German cinema.[11] Hake defines German cinema itself as "a site of crises, ruptures, and antagonisms, but also of unexpected influences, affinities, and continuities."[12] These historical ruptures are analogous to the act of making a photograph and represent ruptures of continuity on a number of levels, which are also related to established concepts in media studies like stillness/motion and to German cultural history that has itself been defined in terms of rupture over the years. When photography was invented, Susie Linfield asserts, the medium almost immediately "inspired a host of conflicts and anxieties in participants, critics and onlookers."[13] Given the tumultuous and violent record of twentieth-century German history, how it exploited representation for ideological violence, and the ethical and moral dimensions of creating images in general, it is hardly surprising that German films have a cautious relationship to images and photographs in particular. And yet, despite the photograph's ability to bear witness to history, their use in German film also transcends the confines of national cinema and culture and tells us more about the human condition in general.

***

Other edited volumes address the relationship between photography and cinema—or how photographs function within cinema—but none investigate this topic within a specifically German context. To address this gap in scholarship, we convened a seminar at the 2017 German Studies Association conference, where many of these contributions were first discussed. Although not exhaustive, the eleven chapters in this volume present diverse perspectives about how photographs work in both the most canonical and less well-known films throughout the last one hundred years of German film history. They are just as likely to share overarching trends about the multidimensional potential of photographs and their relationship to rupture, affect, memory, and the politics of representation as they are to contradict each other and to raise more questions. To be sure, this volume is not attempting to present a diachronic exploration of photographs in German film. We have arranged the chapters chronologically for the sake of convenience and to situate them within their historical moments that correspond to general eras of German national cinema. Like photographs themselves, the essays refer to specific historical moments while simultaneously inhabiting multiple temporalities that resist such categorization. If it were possible to achieve, we would have them all exist at once.

The first chapter highlights the significance of photographs in Zille films, an understudied yet popular genre in Weimar cinema that attempted to emulate the milieu and visual style of Berlin illustrator and photographer Heinrich Zille. Jason Doerre's "Layers of Exposure: The Photographic Approach in Gerhart Lamprecht's Zille Film *Slums of*

Berlin (1925)" examines *Slums of Berlin*, the first Zille film that is based on the artist's biography, features Zille himself in the opening scenes, and dissolves his illustrations into moving pictures. By drawing upon archival sources and the work of Siegfried Kracauer, Doerre argues that Lamprecht employs a photographic approach that merges the naturalism of Zille's work with strategies of New Objectivity in film. *Slums of Berlin* relies on the evidentiary quality of photographs to depict the faces and places of the urban poor in Berlin but offers no explicit solution to the problems that plague this milieu—struggles that the characters and Zille himself experienced. Born into the fifth estate, these figures also used photography as a means to a higher station, a vantage point from which they could critically examine, reflect upon, and share their experience. In a similar fashion, *Slums of Berlin* uses photographic dimensions to represent the lives of these characters and provide the viewer with the opportunity to inhabit and reflect upon the social conditions of Weimar Berlin between 1918 and 1933.

Josef von Sternberg's film *The Blue Angel* is one of the most well-known films of the late Weimar period that produced some of the most beloved and influential films in international cinema history. In "Objecting Objects: Photographs and Subjectivity in *The Blue Angel* (1930)," Martin P. Sheehan provides a new take on the film in his exploration of how photographic postcards exert an increasingly disruptive force throughout Sternberg's film. Drawn toward the tantalizing promotional photographic postcards of Marlene Dietrich's character, Lola Lola, numerous male figures assert a sense of agency and superiority over the images. However, Sheehan examines how the film juxtaposes instances of assumed control with assertive chaos that feature the photographs to challenge the ostensible subjectivity and upper-class hegemony of men. The images unravel the prevailing order or presumed reality and gain the upper hand by disrupting several aspects of the film's visual and narrative space: the presumed sanctity of the classroom, Professor Rath's superiority, and the conventional power dynamics between teacher and student and man and woman. In so doing, *The Blue Angel* illuminates what Siegfried Kracauer terms the "flood of images" (*Bilderflut*)—that is, the rapid increase of printed photographs in mass media periodicals that began to impact the social and political order during the Weimar period by threatening perceived notions of power, gender, and representation.

In the wake of World War II, so-called "Adenauer films" continued to display the acute understanding of the potentially persuasive and pernicious effects that still and moving images had during the National

Socialist period under the direction of Reich Minister of Propaganda Joseph Goebbels. Adenauer films—that is, postwar films produced between 1949 and 1963 when Konrad Adenauer served as the first Chancellor of the Federal Republic of Germany—attempted to navigate a post-National–Socialist world by delineating a path to normality while calling to bear witness. In "Before- and Afterlives: On the Stillness of Photographs at the Outset of Adenauer Cinema," John Davidson examines postwar films that use photographs to seek a mode of redemption through Christianity and reflect the attempts of Christian institutions that sought to refashion their role as moral arbiters in Germany. Examining films that reflect this attempt through their intermedial treatment of photographs and the formal problem of stillness posed in their relationship to finitude and death, his chapter argues that these films forecast a Barthesian understanding of photographs as both witnesses of lives that went before and vessels of death in a postreligious society. According to Davidson, these films employ dialogue and animation to combat the photograph's stillness and visually reassert the religious in the form of a cinematic afterlife. Davidson's analysis illuminates an important transition in this understudied period of German film history before the 1962 Oberhausen Manifesto that launched the New German Cinema.

The New German Cinema (1962–81) is known for departing radically from film conventions, for being concerned with and interrogating the past, and for refusing to accept the image of Germany as portrayed by the mainstream media in Germany and abroad. Stefanie Harris draws on this context in "Filming after Walker Evans: Wim Wenders' 'American Photographs' in *Kings of the Road* (1976)" by analyzing how Wenders' film incorporates the material and aesthetic structures of Evans' photobook *American Photographs* (1938). Translating Evans' photographic record of Americans during the Great Depression to his film, Wenders documents Bruno Winter and Robert Landers as they travel through border towns in West Germany and visit various movie theaters along the way. From the composition of the shots to their serial organization, Wenders creates a visual catalog of the everyday. He documents the film industry's decline as well as generational and technological change while simultaneously presenting and thus tenderly preserving the German postwar social condition. By reframing how photographs represent reality in a society flooded with commercial and industrial imagery, Harris argues that Wenders' incorporation of Evans' documentary style functions as a metaphor for critical inquiry and a model for criticism during a distinct political and cultural moment in postwar West Germany that resists and reflects the American colonization of the West German psyche during this period.

In 1946, just one year after the end of World War II, the film studio DEFA (*Deutsche Film-Aktiengesellschaft*) was founded in the Soviet-Occupied Zone in East Germany. This studio became responsible for all East German films until it was officially dissolved in 1992 after the fall of the Berlin wall and Germany's reunification. Although films produced by DEFA are often understood to correspond to the studio's attempt to reeducate Germans and convey a unified image of East Germany that corresponded to the tenets of Socialist Realism, the DEFA Studio for Documentary Films (*DEFA-Studio für Wochenschau und Dokumentarfilme*) also produced experimental films by Jürgen Böttcher. In "The Transgression of Overpainting: Jürgen Böttcher's Radical Experiments with Intermediality in *Transformations* (1981)," Matthew Bauman outlines how Böttcher's trilogy of nonnarrative films uses photographs to provide a rare East German commentary on the intersection of painting, photography, film, identity, and resistance. Bauman argues that Böttcher's documentation of his artistic process—overpainting and reframing photo-postcards of art historical images that he then rephotographs and projects as diapositive slides onto various surfaces—challenges the perceived authority of representation in a repressive state. At the same time, Böttcher uses his role as a filmmaker to document (and thus reassert) his identity as his anarchic alter ego Strawalde, whose work was rejected by the state apparatus. By using photography as a bridge between his painter and film-maker personalities, Böttcher engages with and challenges Western conceptions of visual media and provides thoughtful responses to foundational texts of the field that challenge the orthodoxies imposed on the East German artistic community as much as they inspired avant-garde artists and filmmakers to follow in his footsteps.

German film history changed radically after the reunification of East and West Germany in 1990 and brought forth a new style of filmmaking, which Eric Rentschler dubbed the "cinema of consensus."[14] Rentschler uses the term disparagingly to lament the decline of the New German Cinema strategies in exchange for popular and conventional approaches to filmmaking and national identity. Although Rentschler locates these films between 1985 and the late 1990s, they were produced well into the twenty-first century. In "The Promise of Agency: Photographs and Value in *Tattoo* (2002)," Cynthia Porter outlines the conventional uses of photographs to drive the narrative and contribute to character development in Robert Schwentke's crime-thriller. Set in the wake of the body art renaissance of the 1990s, *Tattoo* follows two Berlin homicide detectives as they investigate a series of crimes that are linked by one primary detail: each dead body they discover is missing a large swath of tattooed skin. Porter also delineates how digital photographs of the tattoos in the film respond to the value consideration of tattoos as art objects that can be viewed, bought, and sold. Her chapter is an example of the unwieldy potential of photographs that, on the one hand, comply with generic conventions of consensus films that audiences have come to expect and, on the other hand, speak to cultural practices that question boundaries and the politics of representation through photographs, in films, or on skin.

Rentschler's cinema of consensus also encompasses heritage films—lavish period films that draw their power by creating consumable pasts that ensnare the audience in the film's world through a spectacular mise-en-scène. While Lutz Koepnick's seminal article on German heritage films about the Holocaust anchored them in the 1990s, they continue well into the twenty-first century.[15] This volume includes two chapters that examine the use of photographs in German heritage films from different angles. The first, Reinhard Zachau's "Curating the Image: Visual Intertextuality in *The Baader Meinhof Complex* (2008)," investigates the intermedial references to literary and cinematic texts within the larger film about the early history of Germany's radical leftwing terrorist organization, the Red Army Faction (RAF). Zachau illustrates how the film broadens conventional limits of the heritage film genre by documenting strategies throughout the film to recall iconic press photos, nouvelle vague films, and paintings from Gerhard Richter's cycle *October 18, 1977*. The images examined in this chapter and their cinematic, literary, and aesthetic resonance subsequently blur any semblance of truth or history of the group, except the one that exists in the image itself and its exchange with the viewer. As such, *The Baader Meinhof Complex* can be understood as a heritage film that reminds and reinitiates a multigenerational and international audience into a complex visual heritage located at the convergence of violence, ideology, and representation and initiates a post-RAF mourning process for subsequent generations.

The second examination of heritage films investigates the photographic character of memory in three separate German films that respectively address the Holocaust, the GDR, and the Gastarbeiter period. Carrie Collenberg-González's "Re-Presenting German Heritage Films: Photographic Memory in *Aimée & Jaguar* (1999), *Good Bye, Lenin!* (2003), and *Almanya: Welcome to Germany* (2011)" shows how the story of each film creates a self-enclosed world that is structured by photographs—either by reanimated flashbacks in *Aimée & Jaguar* that present Lilly Wust's memory of Felice Schragenheim, by the chiastic strategies employed with moving and still images of Berlin and Christiane Kerner in *Good Bye, Lenin!* that highlight Alex's coming of age and coming to terms with the death of his mother and the GDR, or through optically unconscious elements of family photographs and postmemory in *Almanya: Welcome to Germany*. Extending the work of Ulrich Baer, Collenberg-González shows how the structural similarities between photographs and trauma relate to German heritage films by using consensus-driven strategies to represent significant (and marketable) historical periods in twentieth-century Germany. The photographs in these films can thus also serve as an analogy for the representation of history and a processing of trauma that is specific to German national cinema.

In stark contrast to market-driven consensus films, the slower-paced Berlin School films of the early twenty-first century embrace a new film aesthetic that challenges conventional modes of seeing and interpreting the past, thereby evincing an embrace of transnational cinema. In "Imaging the 'Good Life': Destabilizing Subjecthood and Conceptions of the Normative Family in *Ghosts* (2005)," Simone Pfleger employs the work of Queer theorist Lauren Berlant to explore the role computer-generated photographs play in the film. Pfleger examines how director Christian Petzold challenges the fantasy of a "good life" depicted in a photograph—a life of connection for the film's protagonist within a nuclear family unit, grounded in cisgender heteronormativity. According to Pfleger, the film resists a redemptive reading of the images and thus critiques the oppressive presence (and persistence) of heteronormative familial structures, which reflect larger transnational and universal struggles that can certainly be found within German society but are not limited to it. As Pfleger concludes, the film encourages the audience to become active, critical participants in the viewing experience while negotiating their own investment in "good life" fantasies.

From Wiene's *The Cabinet of Dr. Caligari* (1920) to Jörg Buttgereit's *Nekromantik* series, the history of the horror film genre in Germany reflects the cultural anxieties that rose in response to national traumas. Although German horror did not develop at the same rate as the horror genre internationally, the global, environmental, and political crises since the turn of the twenty-first century have initiated an increased production in these types of films. In "Violence, Death, and Photographs: Capturing the (Un)Dead in *Rammbock* (2010)," Melissa Etzler illuminates the complex relationship that the use of photographs, cameras, and flash units have within the zombie horror genre. Applying ideas by Roland Barthes, Friedrich Kittler, and Walter Benjamin, Etzler demonstrates how the instances of photography (both in analog and digital formats) elevate the film from a generic zombie tale about undying love to a critical and darker social commentary on German culture. Photographs, she argues, are used to manipulate memory, dominate others, control identity, and rewrite or immortalize the past in a desperate attempt to anchor the present. In this manner, *Rammbock* can be read allegorically as a commentary on modern warfare, violence, and *Vergangenheitsbewältigung* (coming to terms with the past).

In "Possible Archives: Encountering a Surveillance Photo in *Karl Marx City* (2016)," Anke Pinkert investigates the complex role photography plays in mediating personal and public memory. The intermedial relations between still and moving images throughout the film reveal how the indeterminacy of the archive destabilizes the self-legitimizing notion of the Stasi Records Agency (*BStU-Der Bundesbeauftragte für die Unterlagen des Staatssicherheitsdienstes der ehemaligen Deutschen Demokratischen Republik*) as the sole authority on East German life. *Karl Marx City* documents Petra Epperlein (the film's codirector and autobiographical subject) as she returns home to former East Germany and explores the Stasi Records Agency to determine whether her late father had served as a government informant. This chapter argues that the handling and placement of archival photographs demonstrate how photography in the film moves beyond the evidentiary in the production of personal and public memory, thereby illuminating slippages in the hegemonic control of visual records in the aftermath of historical erasure. Like many of the chapters presented in this volume, Pinkert questions the form, content, and context of images and raises questions about where and how memory is stored and the tension between personal and public memory.

As demonstrated above, many of the chapters in this volume explore the ruptures that photographs cause in the cinematic time of the film, the narrative, and the character and viewer's experience of time and memory. The characters and audience experience the use of photographs in film on an affective spectrum that *moves* them on various analytical, psychological, and corporeal registers. The chapters examine the role of photographs in German film from different perspectives—they cite their use to relate the viewer to the characters, to disrupt personal and political hegemonies and heteronormative paradigms, to represent fantasies of cultural or national identity, and to serve as structural analogies for trauma, violence, and *Vergangenheitsbewältigung*. In the conclusion to the volume, "Toward a *Camera Ludica*: Agency and Photography in Videogame Ecologies," Curtis L. Maughan examines the various and ever-multiplying processes of photography that shape gaming culture in and beyond videogame worlds. In a discussion that links player agency to the 2017 game *Attentat 1942*, theoretical considerations of Game Studies scholars Sebastian Möring and Marco de Mutiis, and the works of media artist Thomas Hawranke, Maughan shows how the procedural and participatory essence of photography in gaming provides helpful footholds as photography and film become ever more complicated by digital media ecologies. Maughan's conclusion outlines the potential of video game studies to help imagine new perspectives that illuminate the role agency plays in the discussion of photographs and cinematic and digital media.

As the first study of photographs in German film, this volume inevitably cannot claim to be exhaustive in terms of its contribution to debates on photography and cinema, in the conclusions that are drawn from examining photographs and their use in German cinema in the aforementioned chapters, nor in the analyses of German films that employ photographs. For example, it does not address some of the most iconic German films well known for their use of photographs, like *People on Sunday, The Legend of Paul and Paula, Redupers, Alice in the Cities, Run Lola Run*, and many others. It also does not include chapters that address the use of photographs in storyboards, promotional materials, and the distribution of German films, which would also be relevant. Nonetheless, we hope that the films analyzed in this volume demonstrate the significance of this formal question, and we are certain that the chapters herein promise to be a significant contribution to visual studies that will initiate further explorations of the photographs and German cinema.

***

Although our initial task was to locate what is specifically "German" about the use of photographs in the films discussed in this volume, ascribing a national character to the diverse and multidimensional cultural work of photographs in German film remains a challenge. As Andrés Mario Zervigón writes in *Photography and Germany*, it is "just as difficult to designate a distinctly German photography as it is to define German identity as a whole."[16] Like Zervigón, we recognize the "problem of designation"[17] inherent in a project that attempts to draw connections between a nation and photographic media, or, in our case, its intersection with national cinema. However, if Zervigón is correct that "photography as both an innovation and a way to make innumerable images helped construct notions of Germany and the German in the modern age,"[18] it has been productive to explore how photographs in German films are entangled within the inextricable relationship between identity and representation in the twentieth and early twenty-first centuries, even if the conclusions do not yield definitive results.

Germany's founding as a cohesive, modern nation and its subsequent grappling with identity coincide with the development of photographic and film technologies. Despite the illusion of stability and unity created by the unification of Germany into the German empire under Otto von Bismarck in 1871, the nation has over the years undergone volatile changes in its form (leadership, borders, political systems) and content (citizens, cultural production). From its inception in 1839, photography took on the role of documenting German nationalist fantasies in 1871, a role that continues today.[19] In 1895, almost twenty-five years after the 1871 unification of Germany, German brothers Max and Emil Skladanowsky presented their films at the Wintergarten Ballroom in Berlin, and French brothers Auguste and Louis Lumière projected their ten short films in Paris—marking what David Campany has called, "the first meeting of photography and cinema."[20] These dates serve to anchor the intersection of photography, film, and Germany in an origin story that began in the nineteenth-century and continued throughout the twentieth century. This intersection has subsequently informed modernity in historically specific ways that align with and reflect rapid technological changes in visual media, politics, and society.

Films are cultural products, and, as such, context is paramount. In *German National Cinema*, Sabine Hake explains that German films were created in a specific social, historical, and cultural context that absolutely must be acknowledged: "Thus positioned between the national and transnational, and the local and the global, film must be seen as an integral part of social and cultural history, with the myriad stories, characters, places, lineages, and sounds amounting to an imaginary archive of hopes, desires, ambitions, joys, anxieties, resentments, and what Siegfried Kracauer calls the 'daydreams of society.'"[21] Following Hake's assertion "that film must be seen as an integral part of social and cultural history," this volume does consider specific motifs in German film as responses to and reflections of their national context. However, whereas Hake approaches German film through a primarily historical lens, the chapters in this volume instead have the intermedial phenomena—the photographs and the films they appear in—at their core. Also, while Hake follows a diachronic approach that "remains committed to the conceptual and didactic advantages of a master-narrative,"[22] this volume offers readers numerous case studies (of both canonical films and lesser-known works) to illuminate the myriad ways photographs in film might offer insight into German cultural products at critical points in the country's history from the Weimar Republic to a unified twenty-first century Germany.

Photographs in film pose a formal rupture that often initiates debate regarding stillness and motion. Consequently, this rupture creates an encounter with the viewer who reacts to the image and its formal constellations. This reaction, or affect, can take infinite forms and is dependent on the viewer, context, and history of the image and its use. As a tool employed in various genres to specifically German forms of *Vergangenheitsbewältigung*, photographs serve as ruptures that initiate moments of contemplation that show a character's complicit hand in using images to construct memory and how the character interacts with those photographic objects. How a character interacts with a photograph can suggest a conscious attempt to create (and thus control or combat) the past in the creation of a photograph. Alternatively, characters might dovetail a photograph's associative potential with manageable narratives that fit into desires of those characters while also reflecting the desire for a moment, if one is willing to accept that films reflect the culture in which they arise. In summary, the chapters as individual parts work together and demonstrate the significance of rupture and affect; they serve as analogies that allow us to imagine larger conclusions about the use of photographs in German cinema and their employment in the construction of meaning. In analyzing how photographs in film reflect concerns with historical and cultural ruptures, memory, and representation, we learn how these concerns can in turn inform our understanding of the image and celebrate the diverse approaches and conclusions drawn. Oliver Wendell Holmes called photographs a "mirror with a memory," and the use of photography in commemorative contexts is a trend that has survived the digital transition.[23] In many ways, the premise of the volume itself is part of a larger body of memory work that arises at a crucial moment in the gradual departure of analog photography in favor of the digital—that the work of art, the body, and the reception are also historically determined.

The twentieth century has brought forth generations of people and media that rely upon photographs to document, represent, tell stories, and remember—practices that connect and distinguish the twentieth century from preceding centuries. With time, we suspect that we will gain more critical distance from the photographic practices of this period that will cast these photographic idiosyncrasies into relief. The widespread use of the Internet and digital photography have significantly altered photographic practices in the early twenty-first century. Given this break, even the contributions in this volume must be understood as timepieces that, like photographs themselves, maintain referents in the real but also reflect nostalgic tendencies to fetishize the photograph. As a type of magic object, the photograph allows us to transcend time, to inhabit multiple worlds and dimensions, and to create narratives that define the human condition, eternally caught up in the wake of revolutionary technological change. The focus on photographs and cinema in this volume might therefore also respond to the unconscious recognition that these two inextricably linked forms of visual media more clearly represent the past than they do the present. Ultimately, the chapters in this volume demonstrate that the use of photographs in German national cinema cannot be prescribed with any finality; instead, the contributions here limn the contours of German cinema at specific historical moments while simultaneously reflecting larger transnational trends that resonate across cultural and global lines, thereby telling us more about humanity's desire for agency than the media forms themselves.

Carrie Collenberg-González is Assistant Professor and Section Head of German and Director of the *Deutsche Sommerschule am Pazifik* at Portland State University. She has published on Heinrich von Kleist, German cinema, immersion instruction, and the aesthetics of terrorism. Her most recent articles include "Rape Culture and Dialectical Montage: A Radical Reframing of *People on Sunday* (1930)" in *Feminist German Studies* (2020) and "The Daisy Oracle: A New *Gretchenfrage* in Goethe's *Faust*" in the *Goethe Yearbook* (2021). She is coauthor of *Cineplex: German Language and Culture Through Film* (2014), and her coedited volume *Heinrich von Kleist: Artistic and Philosophical Legacies* is forthcoming.

Martin P. Sheehan is Interim Chair of the Department of Foreign Languages and Associate Professor of German at Tennessee Tech University. His research on dramatic form, performance, and photography has been featured in *Seminar*, *Archiv*, *Colloquia Germanica*, *Interdisciplinary Humanities*, and *Studia Neophilogica*. A member of the digital humanities research collective at Vanderbilt University since 2016, his current projects explore visual culture, disability in German dramatic comedy, and social network analysis.

Notes

1. John Roberts, *Photography and Its Violations* (New York: Columbia University Press, 2014), 5.
2. David Campany, *Photography and Cinema* (London: Reaktion Books, 2008), 95.
3. Ibid., 96.
4. The emphasis on the relationship between stillness and motion is evident in the titles of many of the few available volumes on the subject, including *Between Stillness and Motion; Still Moving;* and *Between Still and Moving Images*. See Laurent Guido and Oliver Lugon, eds., *Between Still and Moving Images* (New Barnet, Hertz: John Libbey Publishing, 2012); Eivind Røssaak, ed., *Between Stillness and Motion: Film, Photography, Algorithms* (Amsterdam: Amsterdam University Press, 2011); Karen Beckman and Jean Ma, eds., *Still Moving: Between Cinema and Photography* (Durham: Duke University Press, 2008). See also Garrett Stewart, *Between Film and Screen: Modernism's Photo Synthesis* (Chicago: University of Chicago Press, 1999). Tom Gunning, "The 'Arrested' Instant: Between Stillness and Motion," in *Between Still and Moving Images*, ed. Guido and Lugon, 30.
5. Røssaak, *Between Stillness and Motion*, 14.
6. Guido and Lugon, *Between Still and Moving Images*, 3.
7. Beckman and Ma, *Still Moving*, 5.
8. Ibid.
9. Sabine Hake, *German National Cinema* (Hoboken, NJ: Taylor and Francis, 2013).
10. Røssaak, *Between Stillness and* Motion, 11.
11. It must be noted, however, that the chapters in this volume do not deliberately or directly examine rupture and affect; rather, when compounded and viewed in conversation with extant scholarship, their individual arguments and points of departure demonstrate the significance of these terms as a whole.
12. Hake, *German National Cinema*, 1.
13. Susie Linfield, *The Cruel Radiance: Photography and Political Violence* (Chicago: University of Chicago Press, 2012), 13.
14. Eric Rentschler, "From New German Cinema to the Post-Wall Cinema of Consensus," in *Cinema and Nation*, ed. Mette Hjort and Scott MacKenzie (London: Routledge, 2000), 260–77.
15. Lutz Koepnick, "Reframing the Past: Heritage Cinema and the Holocaust in the 1990s," *New German Critique* 87 (2002): 47–82.
16. Andrés Mario Zervigón, *Photography and Germany* (London: Reaktion Books, 2017), 8.
17. Ibid., 9.
18. Ibid., 11.
19. For a more thorough account of the relationship between the German empire and photography, see Zervigón, "Photography and Nation, 1871–1918," in *Photography and Germany*, 47–81.
20. Campany, *Photography and Cinema*, 8.
21. Hake, *German National Cinema*, 1.
22. Ibid., 2.
23. Oliver Wendell Holmes, "The Stereoscope and the Stereograph," in *Soundings from the Atlantic* (Boston: Ticknor and Fields, 1859), 129.

Bibliography

Beckman, Karen, and Jean Ma, eds. *Still Moving: Between Cinema and Photography*. Durham: Duke University Press, 2008.

Campany, David. *Photography and Cinema*. London: Reaktion Books, 2008.

Guido, Laurent, and Oliver Lugon, eds. *Between Still and Moving Images*. New Barnet, Hertz: John Libbey Publishing, 2012.

Gunning, Tom. "The 'Arrested' Instant: Between Stillness and Motion." In *Between Still and Moving Images*, edited by Laurent Guido and Oliver Lugon, 23–31. New Barnet, Hertz: John Libbey Publishing, 2012.

Hake, Sabine. *German National Cinema*. Hoboken, NJ: Taylor and Francis, 2013.

Holmes, Oliver Wendell. "The Stereoscope and the Stereograph." In *Soundings from the Atlantic*, 124–65. Boston: Ticknor and Fields, 1859.

Koepnick, Lutz. "Reframing the Past: Heritage Cinema and the Holocaust in the 1990s." *New German Critique* 87 (2002): 47–82.

Linfield, Susie. *The Cruel Radiance: Photography and Political Violence*. Chicago: University of Chicago Press, 2012.

Rentchler, Eric. "From New German Cinema to the Post-Wall Cinema of Consensus." In *Cinema and Nation*, edited by Mette Hjort and Scott MacKenzie, 260–77. London: Routledge, 2000.

Roberts, John. *Photography and Its Violations*. New York: Columbia University Press, 2014.

Røssaak, Eivind, ed. *Between Stillness and Motion: Film, Photography, Algorithms*. Amsterdam: Amsterdam University Press, 2011.

Stewart, Garrett. *Between Film and Screen: Modernism's Photo Synthesis*. Chicago: University of Chicago Press, 1999.

Zervigón, Andrés Mario. *Photography and Germany*. London: Reaktion Books, 2017.

Figure 1.1. *Slums of Berlin* (*Die Verrufenen*). Directed by Gerhard Lamprecht. Berlin: National-Film AG, 1925. Screen capture by Jason Doerre.

Chapter 1

Layers of Exposure

The Photographic Approach in Gerhart Lamprecht's Zille Film *Slums of Berlin* (1925)

Jason Doerre

The first Zille film, Gerhard Lamprecht's 1925 film *Slums of Berlin* (*Die Verrufenen*), opens up with the sketch artist, Heinrich Zille, in his atelier. A prolonged take shows his leathery, worn face gazing directly at the camera as billows of smoke from his thick cigar envelop his figure. Slowly, he places his spectacles upon his face as the frame fades out, and a medium shot of him before his easel fades in. Around him one can see the somewhat disheveled state of the atelier, with folders and papers strewn about his desk. Zille begins his work at the easel, and the frame cuts to an iris shot of the sketch—men in 1920s-style newsboy hats around a table drinking and smoking. The hand of the artist continues working while the frame dissolves to a scene showing a tableau composition of Zille's sketch that introduces the main narrative. The transition from the drawing to film photography suggests a link to reality, as Zille's sketch comes to life.

Slums of Berlin is based on a true story that Heinrich Zille told about the fate of an acquaintance.[1] Robert Kramer, the main character, is released from prison after being sentenced for perjury, which he committed to protect his former fiancée, Gerda. After his release the stigma of having been convicted of a crime spells his expulsion from the comforts of the bourgeoisie and casts him into the dire straits of society's undesirables, or fifth estate (*fünfter Stand*).[2] This fall shows Kramer navigating the seas of destitution, as he futilely searches for work while the curse of his criminal record lingers. Abandoned by his former fiancée and father, living in an asylum for the homeless, and without prospects to find honest work, he is saved from taking his own life by a young prostitute named Emma. With the help of Emma and photographer Rottmann, Kramer is eventually able to regain a dignified existence. Trouble, however, befalls Emma when her brother involves her in a botched robbery and they must flee. While Emma is on the run from authorities, Kramer finds work in a factory, where he is able to climb the social ladder and eventually reenter the bourgeoisie by marrying the factory owner's sister.

While Heinrich Zille had worked for decades photographing and sketching the so-called *Milljöh* (milieu), or the impoverished sections of Berlin, his work soared in popularity throughout the 1920s, making his name synonymous with lifelike depictions of the urban poor. Other artists had for years celebrated his artistic talents, but Zille, who thought himself a commoner, did not strive for fortune and fame.[3] Gerhard Lamprecht's foundational Zille film, *Slums of Berlin*, is a tribute to Zille but also an attempt at creating a film form with an appeal to authenticity by invoking the artist's name. In adapting Zille's work for the cinema, Lamprecht connects the naturalism[4] of the older artist with the New Objectivity[5] of the Weimar Republic by bringing to life Zille's milieu in motion pictures. Through its photographic documentation of impoverished neighborhoods around Berlin, Lamprecht's Zille film offers bourgeois viewers a glimpse into the world of the so-called "fifth estate" and demands from them a sense of empathy.

Heinrich Zille, Film, and Photography

In a 1965 radio interview with Gero Gandert, Lamprecht recounts details about the origin and production of *Slums of Berlin*.[6] According to the director, when he first pitched the concept of making a motion picture based on Heinrich Zille's work, he found little interest from the likes of Erich Pommer at Decla Bioskop.[7] Eventually, the smaller company, National Film, accepted the proposal and agreed to produce the film. Lamprecht's idea of a Zille film was bolstered by his direct contact to Zille through a friend. This connection helped procure the cooperation of Heinrich Zille, who agreed to make a brief appearance in the first scene and gave permission to adapt directly from his work. This, of course, added considerable credibility in advertising it as a Zille film, but it also placed pressure on the production to make the film as lifelike as possible, spurring Lamprecht and his film crew to seek out real places and people that would emulate the works of Heinrich Zille.

At the time of its release, critics overwhelmingly deemed *Slums of Berlin* a rousing success. The film premiered on 28 August 1925 with much anticipation, no small thanks to an aggressive advertising campaign. In addition to the usual avenues of publicity, it was preceded by a radio broadcast conversation with Heinrich Zille, who provided listeners with salient anecdotes from his years documenting Berlin's poor.[8] As was often the case, prominent guests were invited to the premiere in order to bolster its release, including, among others, Zille's friend and fellow artist Käthe Kollwitz. Reporting on the premiere, *Deutsche Filmwoche* magazine noted the jubilant applause for a film that "typifies Berlin, that inartificially and authentically construes the Berlin of the fifth estate, everything true the whole way through up to the end."[9] The young film critic, and later publisher of books about the medium of photography, Andor Krazna-Krauz proclaimed the film to be the greatest success early in the film season.[10] Although the film had some difficulty with the Berlin Board of Censors on account of the title and the language in several of its intertitles, the Central Institute for Education and Classroom Instruction in Weimar Germany recognized the educational merits of *Slums of Berlin*, which meant that cinema owners received a tax reduction for showing it. This, of course, ensured that the film would circulate longer in the theaters and thereby generate more revenue, but it also showed that the film satisfied the progressive spirit in the golden years of the short-lived Weimar Republic.[11]

The use of Heinrich Zille's name was an important part of the film's advertising campaign and success. Although it provided occasion to bring the film into the limelight, the wave of sudden attention, including questions about the film directed at Zille, prompted him to issue a public statement to the press that makes clear his role in the production. He writes:

> After the first advertisements of the film *Slums of Berlin (The Fifth Estate)* from the National Film Corporation, and whose production I assisted, there are so many inquiries coming to me from the public that I'm not in a position to answer them individually. I would be gratefully obliged if you would make it clear by including it in the lines of your esteemed publication that the manuscript of the film does not originate from me. The plot of the film, however, is derived from an actual experience from my early days. Apart from that the film attempts to bring my drawings to life on screen in its reproduced milieu of the fifth estate.[12]

Interestingly, Zille here seems to lay partial claim to the film's authorship, while simultaneously distancing himself. This statement does not exactly exude disappointment in the film, but rather it appears that

Zille generally had a positive opinion of it and saw the opportunity that the medium of film offered to continue his artistic project into the future. In 1927, two years before his death, Zille recounted his first experience with film in *Slums of Berlin* and his resistance to further film collaborations. Zille notes, "I actually swore off wanting to have anything more to do with film after *Slums of Berlin*. No, not that the film wasn't good! I wish I could draw scenes such as those that Lamprecht filmed . . . and the screenplay (that's what it's called, right?) was also good, 'twas a true experience."[13] Even though the artist puts on an air of coyness when talking about his work in concert with film, it is not difficult to discern that the aging artist derived a degree of pleasure in the prospect of the younger generation continuing his work with the still nascent medium of cinema. The care that Lamprecht and his crew took to film on location and seek out living members of the fifth estate, not just creating a studio replica of the slums of Berlin, clearly made a favorable impression on Zille.[14]

Lamprecht's use of film to capture images of daily life in Berlin's poorer neighborhoods is reminiscent of how Zille had experimented with the medium of photography to do the same. The photographic work of Heinrich Zille is unique because it stands as one of the first instances of the proletariat using the medium to depict itself.[15] His photographs show the same sentimentality for his subjects as can be found in his more famous sketch work depicting Berlin's denizens in bar scenes, tenement courtyards, streets, trash heaps, at work, and at leisure. Born in 1858 to an impecunious proletarian family, Zille intimately knew the urban poor and their spaces, having lived during his youth in the slum neighborhood around the *Schlesischer Bahnhof* in Berlin. As a young man, Zille avoided being fully entrenched in the proletariat by receiving training as a lithographer, which enabled his social climb into the petite bourgeoisie. This profession offered the young man the opportunity to expand his technical and aesthetic horizons, learning new methods of artistic representation, such as drawing as well as the nascent field of amateur photography. That Zille had experimented artistically with the medium of photography was not considered until Friedrich Luft's 1967 book on this work.[16] While working as a lithographer for his employer, the *Photographische Gesellschaft* in Berlin, Zille gained technical experience with the medium of photography, as well as access to equipment from the late 1880s to about 1910.[17] A look through some of the available editions of Zille's photography shows an experimenting amateur photographer documenting the same milieu depicted in his sketch work. In some lighthearted photographs he captures moments of leisure, while in others Zille attempts to capture the essence of Berlin's tenement milieu.

Heinrich Zille's artistic project was altogether photographic, both in content and perspective. Despite the fact that he maintained a deep affection for the subjects of his work, Zille did not attempt to glorify them or beautify the spaces they inhabited, making these images more poignant and real than the work of many contemporaries. Siegfried Kracauer tells us that photography's first impulse, "that the photographer must indeed reproduce, somehow, the objects before his lens; that he definitely lacks the artist's freedom to dispose of existing shapes and spatial relationships for the sake of his inner vision," originates from the era of realism in which the medium was born in the nineteenth century.[18] This instinct—that of following realistic tendencies—has born into the world, according to Kracauer, a photographic approach which has shaped our understanding of the world and how we engage with it. He continues, "All in all, the realists among the modern photographers have done much to synchronize our vision with topical experiences in other dimensions. That is, they have made us perceive the world we actually live in—no mean achievement considering the power of resistance inherent in habits of seeing."[19] The perspective of photography informs other artistic mediums, which is readily apparent in the documentary-like sketches of Heinrich Zille that function as snapshots of daily life in rear courtyards, barrooms, and streets of Berlin. Many of these same spaces can be found in Zille's early photographic work, which certainly informed many of his later sketches. Through these sketches and photographs the spectator is led into the lives of Berlin's urban poor so intimately that one's other senses are stimulated by the sights. In a drawing of a crowded Berlin apartment, one imagines with ease the sounds of the children packed into a single room as well as the smells and stuffiness of the air. In a crowded barroom scene, one is immediately struck by the suffocating billows of cigar smoke, and in the scenes of children playing in a tenement courtyard, the foul smells of the less-than-hygienic conditions come to life.

Slums of Berlin, Weimar Cinema, and Weimar Society

A superficial glance at scholarship concerning Weimar cinema will show that the *Zeitfilm* genre and its Zille films are by no means a secret.[20] Nevertheless, there is only a scant amount of recent work that gives this genre consideration. This attests not to a glaring omission on the part of works that attempt to provide a nuanced picture of Weimar cinema, away from the singular focus on a select few films, but rather to the magnitude and diversity of filmmaking in this era. Film journals from the 1920s and early 1930s often mention the Zille film, as if the label were common terminology.[21] Today, many films remain relatively obscure in comparison to those considered classic Weimar films, but this does not mean they were any less meaningful to contemporary cineastes. A film such as *Slums of Berlin*, while familiar to contemporary consciousness with its cast and documentation of a temporally specific social condition, as well as specific spatial locations that were largely destroyed some decades later in the war, did not have the enduringly familiar referents for later audiences to grasp. The photography of Berlin's slums and their denizens in the 1920s seems in many respects more otherworldly than the fantasy realms of some more popular Weimar films. Still, the social conditions displayed in *Slums of Berlin* were replaced in rapid succession in the immediate decades to follow, which can explain why this and other similar films did not endure.

Despite the relative obscurity of Zille films in comparison to other genres, some, such as *Slums of Berlin*, still find mention in current scholarship. Recent DVD releases of several such titles increase the likelihood that subsequent attention to Weimar Cinema will be more attuned to these films. More recent studies of the Zille film typically employ it as an example of the film industry's failed attempt to combine social critique and entertainment.[22] Other studies of the *Zeitfilm* genre focus exclusively on Phil Jutzi's 1929 film *Mother Krausen's Journey to Happiness* (*Mutter Krausens Fahrt ins Glück*), which was the final Zille film. This production of the Prometheus Film Corporation is typically considered an example of the Weimar proletarian film along with other productions from the same company such as Slatan Dudow's 1932 film *Kuhle Wampe*.[23] Perhaps the most detailed engagement with the Zille film can be found in Bruce Murray's *Film and the German Left in the Weimar Republic*.[24] In his analysis, Murray credits *Slums of Berlin* as the pioneering title. Like others, he highlights the confused message in the narrative, but he also finds significance in the visual aspects, taking note of the reduced reliance on intertitles to narrate.[25] Likewise, Peter Jelavich gives Lamprecht recognition for the social criticism inherent in the many scenes that depict the misery of Berlin's denizens, despite the tacked-on happy ending.[26] While these scholars do place emphasis on the depiction of Berlin's impoverished classes, they make no more than a descriptive account of these depictions. The task of this chapter, therefore, is to provide a more detailed analysis of scenes that emulate

Zille's works and the interplay between the mediums of film, photography, and Zille's sketch art.

Even if the films regarded as "expressionist" are those most remembered today, there is no doubt that Weimar cinema was vastly more diverse than that. The *Zeitfilm* genre, for instance, stood in stark contrast to many of the more notable films from the era. These films were occupied with depicting contemporary social problems for which they sought to heighten public awareness.[27] *Slums of Berlin* ushered in a new level of class consciousness in cinema by making the lower classes its focal point, while Lamprecht's subsequent films continued this tradition. His two other Zille films followed *Slums of Berlin* in 1926, completing a trilogy that addresses the social problems that affected the impoverished areas of the Weimar Republic. *Children of No Importance* (*Die Unehelichen*) tells the story of three illegitimate children who are raised by abusive foster parents in a tenement apartment. After one child dies from neglect, the remaining children are placed in homes with upstanding bourgeois families. The plot of the film was based on an official report in the Weimar Republic concerning the welfare and protection of children. *People to Each Other* (*Menschen untereinander*) explores the lives of an apartment building's inhabitants, each of whom represents a section of Weimar society. With the milieu of the Berlin tenement building being the central focus of the film rather than the story of any one of the figures, it is less socially conscious than the other two Zille films. Still, the admixture of pitiable living conditions and joviality does not fail to echo Heinrich Zille's humorous but affecting social criticism by depicting the good along with the bad in his milieu.

Through his juxtaposition in these films of different social classes and the environments they inhabited, Gerhard Lamprecht provides a picture of society at a historical moment. Around the same time that Lamprecht was making these films, figures such as August Sander were doing much the same with photography. One of the leading photographers in the era of New Objectivity, Sander is known for his documentation of society through photographic portraits. This is most apparent in his now classic 1929 photobook *Face of Our Time* (*Antlitz der Zeit*), which includes portraits taken from members of different classes of Weimar society that work together to provide a statement about social relations at the time. Lamprecht picks up on these contemporary trends in photography that were apparent in Zille's work but also in the context around him.

Slums of Berlin reflects both the social conditions and the aesthetic directions of its time. Despite its appeal to empathy at the end regarding the dreadful plight of the urban poor in the Weimar Republic, *Slums of Berlin*, as well as the *Zeitfilm* genre altogether, is more in tune with the currents of New Objectivity. Emulating the trends in photography at the time, cinematic New Objectivity assumed a documentary quality. While this new artistic direction had its filmic breakthrough with G. W. Pabst's 1925 star-studded film *Joyless Street* (*Die freudlose Gasse*), it should be noted that *Slums of Berlin* appeared less than half a year later. Accordingly, Lamprecht's Zille film can be thought of as a pioneering example of New Objectivity in the cinema. The rise of this stylistic direction perhaps also accounts for the increased appeal of Zille's work in the 1920s—as well as his admission to the *Akademie der Künste* (Academy of the Arts)—with the demand for more objectivity, sobriety, and simplicity with regard to depiction. While Zille's sketches have an undeniably sentimental quality—especially those with captions written in dialect—a look at some of his photographic work from the turn of the century shows a more aloof artist capturing the essence of objects, not unlike the New Objectivity photographers of the 1920s such as Albert Renger-Patzsch and August Sander. *Slums of Berlin* is then a telling document of the early twentieth century with its multivalence of artistic mediums and styles.

The Photographic Nature of *Slums of Berlin*

By showing a drawing transposed onto moving photographic images, the film's opening scene reveals a connection to the work of Heinrich Zille, thereby inviting the viewer to identify other scenes adapted from the artist's work. These scenes, while not always essential to the plot, flavor the film with Zille's famous milieu. One scene captures children playing within the squalid confines of a building's back courtyard.[28] With the opening shot, Kurt Hasselmann, the cinematographer, places the camera in a neutral, seemingly unsuspecting position. The low-placed, medium–long-range shot emulates the distance a photographer would use to document the atmosphere of the courtyard and the child subjects in a candid fashion. This acquaints the viewer with the Zille milieu: four children are playing innocently in the foreground, while the camera captures this genuine scene of a Berlin *Hinterhof* (back courtyard). The walls surrounding this space frame the courtyard, while the existence of a background space is revealed with the tops of buildings that protrude over the walls. The depth of space provides the impression that the confines of the courtyard within the confines of the frame are merely a single instance of a larger whole. It is one small fragment of many such spaces that make up the slums of Berlin.

This opening shot momentarily blurs the line between the mediums of photography and cinema before the narrative disturbs the natural setting, when Gustav, Emma's small-time criminal brother and Robert's former cellmate in prison, enters the scene. In some respects, this disruption echoes the fade from Zille's drawing to the opening shot, which transitions from the medium of sketch art to cinema, while this scene seemingly transitions from a photographic approach to a cinematic one. After Gustav's entry, the realism of the take transitions to a medium shot that is more in line with the conventions of cinema than photography, as Gustav interacts with the children, thereby disturbing the serenity of the moment and interpolating them into the narrative. After they show him a dead rat, the film cuts to an intertitle written in heavy dialect, "We didn't do anything to it, but it's so damp in our apartment."[29] The pathos evoked by this statement, and its kitschy content, produce a kind of naïve sentimentality that contrasts with the aloof view of the scene's first shot. This reflects the captions that Zille includes with his sketches that add sentimentality. The use of dialect in this scene and in the captions of Zille's drawings harkens back to the era of naturalism when authors attempted to emulate the phonetic sounds of specific dialects in their written texts.

The subject matter of Zille's drawings, when coupled with lighthearted captions, have provoked a certain degree of ambiguity regarding Zille's reception. His aspiration to depict the poor as they were gained him a considerable degree of credibility with the political left in Weimar Germany. Nevertheless, the entertainment factor regarding his sketches depicting humorous moments in the lives of Berlin's impoverished classes raised the ire of some critics who believed it trivialized poverty.[30] Perhaps this is why Rudolf Arnheim, writing in *Das Stachelschwein*, maintains that the photography in *Slums of Berlin* adapted from Zille's sketches is more effective in evoking a sense of naturalism than are the artist's drawings.[31] The limitations of drawings, he argues, take away from the power of Zille's subject matter. With the camera, an optimal degree of realism is achieved when the art becomes the observation of reality itself rather than a depiction thereof.[32]

Gustav's significance in the narrative is minimal until the end of the film, when an ill-planned, petty scam results in homicide and forces him to flee the slums with Emma. Until this point, however, he functions as a kind of guide, leading the self-restrained camera through Berlin's downtrodden milieu. Directly off the courtyard where the children are at play, the viewer is led down some stairs into an abode resembling a *Berliner Zimmer*, the typical living space of the poor in tenement apartment blocks. While the middle- and lower middle-class families inhabited the spacious apartments facing the street, the dark and dank rooms facing the courtyard were reserved for the classes at the bottom of the social spectrum. Following Gustav's entry into the room, the camera documents the interior of this space as well as its inhabitants. The scene immediately cuts to a medium shot of Gustav's mother arduously washing clothes at a rickety washtub. The shot of her laboring holds for several seconds; the aged and weatherworn face of the tired woman tells the story of a life filled with hardships. A shot reverse shot of her and Gustav sutures him into the scene before another medium shot captures the wash lady and her son together in a frame that reveals the atmosphere of the apartment. This tightly packed frame suggests the cramped conditions of the room with several items hanging on the wall and a small window as the only source of light in the background. Gustav inquires of his mother about his father, who points to a bed in the one-room apartment where he is sleeping. When Gustav awakens him, his father's first reaction is to extend his hand, as if asking for a handout, before he recognizes his son. His worn and somewhat emaciated appearance suggests a life of hard knocks and hard living. These figures embody much of what Kurt Tucholsky said about the appearance of some people who so well represent their social class that the individual can stand for the group.[33] Much like the photographic work that August Sander did in the era of New Objectivity, the facial images captured by the cinematographer Kurt Hasselmann reveal the essence of society's undesirables. The naturalistic tendency of the film is heightened by the fact that many of the characters were given no makeup at all, which for the silent film era was quite a rarity.[34]

"Nourishment forms the person," writes Alfred Döblin, "the air and light in which he moves, the work that he does or doesn't do, after that the particular ideology of his class."[35] If man is a product of his environment, it was important for Lamprecht to provide a compelling picture of the atrocious living conditions in Berlin's slums. Lamprecht's decision to film on location in poor neighborhoods found a chorus of praise in the media. *Kinematograph*, in its review of *Slums of Berlin*, writes, "The pictures from the asylum for the homeless, the basement washroom, the dismal courtyards of the poor districts, all of that is not only produced with directorial skill, but also with genuine humanity."[36]

The scene filmed at an actual asylum for the homeless is especially telling of the quality of life for Berlin's denizens. The scene begins with an intertitle stating the location, which then cuts to an establishing shot of the building from the outside. The sheer mass of the structure filling the entire frame is daunting, which is then compounded when one considers the purpose of the building to house the homeless, suggesting the magnitude of such social problems in Berlin. The establishing shot cuts to the main figure, Robert Kramer, in the foreground of a crowded room full of others just like him. Over the door in the background is written "Room 22," signaling that this is just one of many such crowded rooms. According to Lamprecht, filming on location in the asylum for the homeless was a challenge at the time due to technical aspects. He describes it as a "photographic problem" because celluloid then required more light; therefore, the film crew had to improvise lighting in the dark space of the asylum.[37] That the natural state of this space was too dismal for filming reveals some technical limitations of photography at the time and shows its limitations in documenting reality.

Photography and Narrative in *Slums of Berlin*

If the boundaries of reality and fiction are blurred with the opening scene of Heinrich Zille in his workshop, it is further complicated by the figure Rottmann the photographer. Rottmann, a petit bourgeois portrait photographer and a fictional stand-in for Heinrich Zille, chooses to live in the slums of Berlin. In the hallway of the tenement building where Robert lives, he notices Rottmann's business. After helping the photographer carry some equipment up to the office, Robert is asked if he is familiar with photography, and he is offered a job assisting with photographing people in Berlin's decadent bars and clubs. Rottmann's photographic occupation naturally functions as a self-reflexive aspect in the film. While his bearded and somewhat disheveled appearance emulates Heinrich Zille, his craft represents the film's photographic task to document the faces, places, and moments in Berlin's slums. The admirably enlightened nature of Rottmann further reinforces the film's homage to Zille, but also reveres the medium of photography and its capacity of representation. Rottmann's self-reflexive function is also supported by the fact that the photographic devices used in the film are those of the cinematographer Kurt Hasselmann.[38]

In one scene in which Rottmann and Robert are taking photographic portraits of customers in a cabaret theater, photography is emphasized as a means to elicit truth. The scene begins with shots of a large hall with tables upon which sit numerous libations. The boisterous patrons are dressed in modern bourgeois-looking fashion and smoking profusely, while a cabaret act begins on stage. In Lamprecht's original screenplay an intertitle was to include the lyrics of the cabaret performer's chanson that would mention Zille: "hats off to the master, Zille."[39] The inclusion of these lyrics would have made the contrast between Zille's milieu and the image of Berlin's roaring twenties even stronger. Things take a serious turn at the cabaret as the two are suddenly called to photograph a married couple at a table that happens to be Robert's former fiancée Gerda and her husband. As Robert stands behind the camera, Rottmann attempts to stage the pose at the table, arranging the couple and items in order to heighten the impression of conviviality. Gerda, however, cannot mask her shame and guilt in front of the camera and Robert, who stands behind it. In this juxtaposition, Gerda's compromised morality and her staged position are no match for Robert's ethical character and photography's perceived ability to find truth.

This faith in the medium of photography echoes August Sander's theory about the new direction of the medium in the Weimar Republic. In 1931 Sander gave a series of lectures about photography on German radio in which he declared his hope that it would expand its capacity to document objective reality and develop its abilities as a truth-telling medium.[40] This is most evident in his portrait photography of the 1920s. In these portraits there is something for the viewer to behold, such as a physical trait or body language, that speaks truths about the subjects and their social reality. Lamprecht employs a similar technique with his use of photographs in *Slums of Berlin*. In the portrait taken by Robert, we see Gerda with an uneasy facial expression, somewhat distanced from her husband. Her remorse for her crime and abandonment of Robert is evident. Her husband, unaware of her past, sits jovially in a relaxed position with one arm stretched out on Gerda's shoulder, smoking a cigarette, and libations on the table in front of him. His clothing and physiognomy clearly mark him as a 1920s bon vivant.

The narrative's inclusion of photography in *Slums of Berlin* posits photography as a source of enlightenment and harbinger of truth. In a subsequent scene, Rottmann, whose keen eye has read into the developed photograph, takes it to Robert to inquire about Gerda's uneasy look. Here, the feeling of guilt that Gerda harbors for betraying Robert is evident in her startled and apprehensive expression. Likewise, the photograph exposes a truth about Robert's past, and he tells the photographer about his shameful fall from a solid bourgeois existence into the lowest depths of society. Robert undergoes a transformation after encountering the photographer Rottmann for the first time in front of the darkroom.

At this point, Robert's secret and his station as an unemployed exconvict have yet to come to light. As Rottmann confronts Robert with the photograph, he turns on a lamp, symbolically inviting Robert to come into the light with his secret and begin to find a way out of the slums. This path also mirrors the dark to light technical process of developing photographic material. Rottmann sees truth in the snapshot of Robert's life and eventually convinces him to work his way back into bourgeois society. In this way, the photographer functions as the intermediary between the lower and middle classes—like Heinrich Zille, whose work both separated him from and united him with the lower classes.[41] The penultimate scene of the film shows Rottmann handing out candies to a group of street urchins as he gazes upon them with compassion.

Critics have taken issue with the deus ex machina at the end of the film that lifts Robert out of the depths to which he has socially fallen, and back into the solid grounding of the bourgeoisie.[42] After becoming successful once again through hard work and perseverance, as well as finding a suitably bourgeois wife, Robert is able to reflect on the living conditions of the fifth estate to which he momentarily belonged. He tells his new wife, "Poverty and misery, vice and alcohol turn people into what is called the fifth estate."[43] The intertitle cuts to an image of Robert and his wife gazing with concern at one another that is superimposed with an image of the destitute masses marching forward, representing their perpetual search for sustenance and a better life. In the final intertitle, Robert pessimistically observes, "People who cannot escape their fate. A world of its own which we attack rather than fix."[44] On this cynical note, the film ends. The final statement suggests the inevitability of these conditions and provides no instructions on how to combat these social ills. The restraint in this final message harbors much of the ambivalence typical of New Objectivity. Like the work of Zille and his contemporaries, *Slums of Berlin* uses a photographic approach to depict the faces and places of the destitute but offers no explicit solution to the problems that plague this milieu. While the final statement may seem to be a curious message for a film that purports to cultivate compassion for these lower classes, it also represents the struggles Rottman, Robert, and even Zille himself experienced. In one sense, these figures used photography as a means to a higher station—a vantage point from which they could critically examine, reflect upon, and share their experience. In a similar fashion, *Slums of Berlin* uses photographic dimensions to represent the lives of these characters and provide the viewer with the opportunity to inhabit and reflect upon the social conditions of Berlin.

Jason Doerre is Visiting Assistant Professor of Language and Culture Studies at Trinity College. His article "Staging the New Reichshauptstadt or Berlin Encounters Modernity in Hermann Sudermann's *Die Ehre* (1889)" was recently published in *German Studies Review*, and his work on Erich Maria Remarque's *All Quiet on the Western Front*, the cinema of Stanley Kubrick, and the historical novel in the age of nationalism is forthcoming. As a former Project Assistant at the DEFA Film Library, he worked with archival film prints and translated and subtitled many DVD productions.

Notes

1. Heinrich Zille, "Die Verrufenen," *Kinematograph: Filmkritische Rundschau* (1925): 19.
2. Before its release, the film was originally titled *Der fünfte Stand* (*The Fifth Estate*), which then became the subtitle. At some point the film censor forbade this title on film posters, ostensibly because of the potential for class agitation. See Aros [Alfred Rosenthal], "'Sein Miljöh!' Bemerkungen zum Zille Film," *Film-Echo: Beilage zur Sonderausgabe des Berliner Lokal-Anzeigers* (1925).

   Der fünfter Stand, or fifth estate, refers to class discourse of the nineteenth and early twentieth centuries. This category, stemming out of the *vierter Stand*, or fourth estate, were those dregs of society cast off because of vagabondage, criminality, etc. For an early conservative take on this social issue, see Karl Friedrich Freiherr von Fechenbach-Laudenbach, *Der "fünfte" Stand und die Regierungen* (Berlin: Puttkamer und Wühlbrecht, 1884). For a twentieth-century assessment that is sympathetic to the plight of this class, see Erich Mühsam, "Der fünfte Stand," *Der Sozialist: Organ des Sozialistischen Bundes* 2, no. 13 (1910): 97–99.
3. Nonetheless, in 1924 Zille was inducted into the Academy of Arts.
4. The subject matter of Zille's life work—daily life of the lower classes—aligns with the literary program of naturalism. It is documented that he was versed in the literature and theory of naturalism. See Winfried Ranke, "Heinrich Zille Photographien," in *Heinrich Zille: Photographien Berlin 1890–1910*, ed. Winfried Ranke (Munich: Schirmer Mosel, 1975), 16–18.
5. The term New Objectivity is somewhat difficult to define since it is not restricted to a particular school or movement. My use of the term, regarding Weimar cinema, denotes a socially critical realism that stands in contrast to Expressionism in content and form. See Richard McCormick, "Private Anxieties/Public Projections: 'New Objectivity,' Male Subjectivity, and Weimar Cinema," *Women in German Yearbook* 10 (1994): 3–4; Sabine Hake, *German National Cinema* (New York: Routledge, 2008), 38.
6. Gero Gandert, "Transcript of interview with Gerhard Lamprecht about *Slums of Berlin*," in *Gerhard Lamprecht Collection* (Berlin), Folder 465.
7. Ibid.
8. W. Theile, "Letzte Nachrichten - Zille Propaganda im Rundfunk," *Der Film*, 16 August 1925.
9. "Der Beifall zum Schluß steigerte sich zur jubelnden Ekstase, zum zwischenrufdurchmengten Beifall der Berliner, die hier gebannt werden, weil sie gebannt wor-

den sind, in einem Film, der typisch Berlin ist, der das Berlin des fünften Standes unkonstruiert konstruiert und echt ist, echt das ganze Stück hindurch – bis auf den Schluß." "Filme der Woche: Die Verrufenen (Der fünfte Stand)," *Deutsche Filmwoche*, 11 September 1925.

10. Andor Kraszna-Krausz, "Die Verrufenen," *Filmtechnik: Organ des Österreichischen Kinotechnischen Vereins* 9 (1925): 209.
11. W. Theile, "Vertreib und Verleih – Lustbarkeitssteuer-Ermäßigung für Zille," *Der Film*, 23 August 1925.
12. "Auf die ersten Ankündigungen des von der National-Film A.G. unter meiner Mitwirkung hergestellten Films 'Die Verrufenen (Der fünfte Stand)' gehen mir aus dem Publikum dauernd soviele Anfragen zu, daß ich außerstande bin, sie einzeln zu beantworten. Ich wäre Ihnen deshalb zu Dank verpflichtet, wenn Sie durch Aufnahme dieser Zeilen in Ihr geschätztes Blatt feststellen wollten, daß das Manuskript des Films nicht von mir herrührt. Wohl aber geht die Handlung des Films auf ein tatsächliches Erlebnis aus meiner ersten Schaffenszeit zurück. Im Übrigen sucht der Film das in meinen Zeichnungen wiedergegebene Milieu des fünften Standes auf der Leinewand lebendig zu machen." Heinrich Zille, "Der Zille-Film," *Lichtbild-Bühne* 165 (1925): 22.
13. "Eigentlich hatte ick's verschworen – nach den 'Verrufenen' nochmals wat mit dem Film zu tun haben zu wollen. Nee, nich det der Film nich jut jewesen wäre! Ich wünschte, ick könnte solche Szenen zeichnen, wie sie der Lamprecht jedreht hat . . . Und det Drehbuch (so heist et ja woll?) war auch jut, war ja'n wahret Erlebnis." Newspaper clipping from unknown source: "Heinrich Zille, 'Ick werda wieda gefilmt,'" in *Gerhard Lamprecht Collection, Die Verrufenen (Slums of Berlin)* (Berlin), Folder 9.
14. One telling example of Zille's compassion for the poor can be found in a letter he wrote to Lamprecht during the film's production. In it he laments the fact that not all of the extras that were taken from the slums would be listed in the film's credits, and asks personally for their names. See "Letter from Heinrich Zille to Gerhard Lamprecht," in *Gerhard Lamprecht Collection, Die Verrufenen (Slums of Berlin)* (Berlin), Folder 9.
15. Ranke, "Heinrich Zille Photographien," 11–12.
16. Heinrich Zille, *Mein Photo-Milljöh: 100 x Alt-Berlin aufgenommen*, ed. Friedrich Luft (Hanover: Fackelträger-Verl. Schmidt-Küster, 1967).
17. Ranke, "Heinrich Zille Photographien," 19.
18. Siegfried Kracauer, *Theory of Film: The Redemption of Reality* (New York: Oxford University Press, 1960), 4.
19. Ibid., 9.
20. For more about the *Zeitfilm* genre, see Hake, *German National Cinema*, 46.
21. For one example, see Lotte Eisner, "Die neue Jugend und der Film," *Film-Kurier* (1928).
22. For more about this critical perspective, see Jonathan Munby, *Public Enemies, Public Heroes: Screening the Gangster from Little Caesar to Touch of Evil* (Chicago: University of Chicago Press, 2014).
23. Marc Silberman, "Whose Revolution? The Subject of *Kuhle Wampe* (1932)," in *Weimar Cinema: An Essential Guide to Classic Films of the Era*, ed. Noah Isenberg (New York: Columbia University Press, 2009), 311–30.
24. Bruce Murray, *Film and the German Left in the Weimar Republic: From Caligari to Kuhle Wampe* (Austin: University of Texas Press, 1990), 82–88.
25. Ibid., 88.

26. Peter Jelavich, *Berlin Alexanderplatz: Radio, Film, and the Death of Weimar Culture* (Berkeley: University of California Press, 2006), 204–5.
27. Hake, *German National Cinema*, 46.
28. In Lamprecht's directorial notebook, he writes "Armseliger Hof" (miserable courtyard) to describe the look of this location. Gerhard Lamprecht, *Regie Filmbuch*, in *Gerhard Lamprecht Collection, Die Verrufenen* (*Slums of Berlin*) (Berlin).
29. "Wir haben ihr nischt jetan. Aber bei uns is et so feuchte in die Wohnung."
30. Jelavich, *Berlin Alexanderplatz*, 204.
31. Rudolf Arnheim, "Der Zille-Film," *Das Stachelschwein* 19 (1925): 45–46.
32. Ibid., 46.
33. "Menschen, die so sehr ihre Klasse, ihren Stand, ihre Kaste repräsentieren, daß das Individuum für die Gruppe genommen werden darf." Cited in Suzanne Lange, "Ein Bekenntnis zur Photographie: Überlegungen zum Leben und Werk von August Sander," in *August Sander 1876–1964*, ed. Manfred Heiting (Cologne: Taschen, 1999), 22.
34. Kurt Hasselmann, "Kurt Hasselmann letter to Gerhard Lamprecht, 25 July 1957," in *Gerhard Lamprecht Collection, Die Verrufenen* (*Slums of Berlin*) (Berlin), Folder 2.
35. "Die Nahrung formt den Menschen die Luft und das Licht, in dem er sich bewegt, die Arbeit, die er verrichtet oder nicht verrichtet, dann die spezielle Ideologie seiner Klasse." Alfred Döblin, "Von Gesichtern, Bildern und ihrer Wahrheit," in *August Sander 1876–1964*, ed. Manfred Heiting (Cologne: Taschen, 1999), 14.
36. "Die Bilder aus dem Asyl der Obdachlosen, der Wäschereikeller, die düsteren Höfe der Armeleutequartiere, all das ist nicht nur mit Regiekunst, sondern mit echter Menschlichkeit filmgemäß umgesetzt." Zille, "Die Verrufenen," 19.
37. Gandert, "Interview with Lamprecht," Folder 465.
38. Lamprecht, *Regie Filmbuch*, Folder 465: scene 68.
39. "Und grüßt mir Meister Zille" (Lamprecht, *Regie Filmbuch*, Folder 465: scene 70).
40. Anne Halley, "August Sander," *The Massachusetts Review* 19, no. 4 (1978): 663.
41. The presentation of this class configuration of the lower classes being separated from the upper classes, until a mediator is able to bridge them, is reminiscent of the resolution in Fritz Lang's *Metropolis*, when the heart becomes the mediator between the head and the hands. In *Slums of Berlin* it is the photographer who stands as a bridge between the classes, not unlike Zille's identification with the bourgeoisie and the lower classes.
42. For a more detailed criticism of the film's narrative, see Siegfried Kracauer, "The Little Shop Girls Go to the Movies," in *Mass Ornament: Weimar Essays*, ed. and trans. Thomas Levin (Cambridge, MA, 1995), 294–95.
43. "Armut und Elend, Laster und Alkohol machen die Leute zu dem, was man den fünften Stand nennt."
44. "Menschen, die ihrem Geschick nicht entgehen können. Eine Welt für sich, die man bekämpft – aber nicht heilt!"

Bibliography

Arnheim, Rudolf. "Der Zille-Film." *Das Stachelschwein* 19 (1925).

Döblin, Alfred. "Von Gesichtern, Bildern und ihrer Wahrheit." In *August Sander 1876–1964*, edited by Manfred Heiting, 14. Cologne: Taschen, 1999.

Eisner, Lotte. "Die neue Jugend und der Film." *Film-Kurier* (1928).
"Filme der Woche: Die Verrufenen (Der fünfte Stand)." *Deutsche Filmwoche* (1925).
Gerhard Lamprecht Collection. Folders 2–465. Berlin: Deutsche Kinemathek.
Hake, Sabine. *German National Cinema*. New York: Routledge, 2008.
Halley, Anne. "August Sander." *The Massachusetts Review* 19, no. 4 (1978): 663.
Jelavich, Peter. *Berlin Alexanderplatz: Radio, Film, and the Death of Weimar Culture*. Berkeley: University of California Press, 2006.
Kalbus, Oskar. *Vom werden deutscher Filmkunst: Der stumme Film 1*. Altona-Bahrenfeld: Cigaretten Bilderdienst Altona, 1935.
Kracauer, Siegfried. "The Little Shop Girls Go to the Movies." In *Mass Ornament: Weimar Essays*, edited and translated by Thomas Levin, 294–95. Cambridge, MA: Harvard University Press, 1995.
———. "Photography." Translated by Thomas Levin, *Critical Inquiry* 19 (1993): 421–36.
———. *Theory of Film: The Redemption of Reality*. New York: Oxford University Press, 1960.
Kraszna-Krausz, Andor. "Die Verrufenen." *Filmtechnik: Organ des Österreichischen Kinotechnischen Vereins* 9 (1925): 209.
Lange, Suzanne. "Ein Bekenntnis zur Photographie: Überlegungen zum Leben und Werk von August Sander." In *August Sander 1876–1964*, edited by Manfred Heiting, 16–27. Cologne: Taschen, 1999.
McCormick, Richard. "Private Anxieties/Public Projections: 'New Objectivity,' Male Subjectivity, and Weimar Cinema." *Women in German Yearbook* 10 (1994): 3–4.
Mühsam, Erich. "Der fünfte Stand." *Der Sozialist: Organ des Sozialistischen Bundes* 2, no. 13 (1910): 97–99.
Munby, Jonathan. *Public Enemies, Public Heroes: Screening the Gangster from Little Caesar to Touch of Evil*. Chicago: University of Chicago Press, 2014.
Murray, Bruce. *Film and the German Left in the Weimar Republic: From Caligari to Kuhle Wampe*. Austin: University of Texas Press, 1990.
Ranke, Winfried, ed. *Heinrich Zille: Photographien Berlin 1890–1910*. Munich: Schirmer Mosel, 1975.
———. "Heinrich Zille Photographien." In *Heinrich Zille: Photographien Berlin 1890–1910*, edited by Winfried Ranke, 7–43. Munich: Schirmer Mosel, 1975.
Rosenthal, Alfred. *Mein Photo-Milljöh: 100 x Alt-Berlin aufgenommen*, edited by Friedrich Luft. Hannover: Fackelträger Verlag, 1967.
———. "'Sein Milljöh!' Bemerkungen zum Zille-Film." *Film-Echo: Beilage zur Sonderausgabe des Berliner Lokal-Anzeigers* (1925).
Silberman, Marc. "Whose Revolution? The Subject of *Kuhle Wampe* (1932)." In *Weimar Cinema: An Essential Guide to Classic Films of the Era*, edited by Noah Isenberg, 311–30. New York: Columbia University Press, 2009.
Theile, W. "Letzte Nachrichten—Zille Propaganda im Rundfunk." *Der Film* (1925).
———. "Vertreib und Verleih—Lustbarkeitssteuer-Ermäßigung für Zille." *Der Film* (1925).
von Fechenbach-Laudenbach, Karl Friedrich Freiherr. *Der "fünfte" Stand und die Regierungen*. Berlin: Puttkamer und Wühlbrecht, 1884.
Zille, Heinrich. "Die Verrufenen." *Kinematograph: Filmkritische Rundschau* (1925).
———. "Der Zille-Film." *Lichtbild-Bühne* 165 (1925): 22.
———. *Mein Photo-Milljöh: 100 x Alt-Berlin aufgenommen*, edited by Friedrich Luft. Hanover: Fackelträger-Verl. Schmidt-Küster, 1967.
"Zille-Première." *National Film Korrespondenz: Mitteilungen der National Film A.G.* (1925).

Filmography

Backstairs (Hintertreppe). Directed by Leopold Jessner. Berlin: Henny-Porten Film, 1921.
Children of No Importance (Die Unehelichen). Directed by Gerhard Lamprecht. Berlin: Gerhard-Lamprecht-Film, 1926.
Joyless Street (Die freudlose Gasse). Directed by G. W. Pabst. Berlin: So-Far-Film, 1925.
Kuhle Wampe oder Wem gehört die Welt? Directed by Slatan Dudow. Berlin: Prometheus Film-Verleih, 1932.
Mother Krause's Journey to Happiness (Mutter Krausens Fahrt ins Glück). Directed by Phil Jutzi. Berlin: Prometheus Film-Verleih, 1929.
People to Each Other (Menschen untereinander). Directed by Gerhard Lamprecht. Berlin: Gerhard-Lamprecht-Film, 1926.
Shattered (Scherben). Directed by Lupu Pick. Berlin: Rex-Film, 1921.
Slums of Berlin (Die Verrufenen). Directed by Gerhard Lamprecht. Berlin: National-Film AG, 1925.
The Street (Die Straße). Directed by Karl Grune. Berlin: Stern-Film, 1923.

Chapter 2

Objecting Objects

Photographs and Subjectivity in *The Blue Angel* (1930)

Martin P. Sheehan

In *Photography: A Middle-brow Art*, Pierre Bourdieu mourns photography's lost potential to disturb. Instead of unsettling and unmooring society's sense of reality, the medium, he laments, too often serves to reinforce concepts foundational to society, such as identity and connection: "far from seeing its specific vocation as the capturing of critical moments in which the reassuring world is knocked off balance, ordinary practice seems determined, contrary to all expectations, to strip photography of its power to disconcert. . . . Only ever capturing moments which have been torn from the temporal flow by virtue of their solemnity, and only capturing people who are fixed, immobile, in the immutability of the plane, [photography] loses its power of corrosion."[1] Photographic images might halt the flow of time in an eerie or uncanny way, yet those who make, view, collect, and share photographs have grown accustomed to—if not enamored of—the halting effect. Although this apparent stopping of time should topple the viewing subject's sense of balance, it instead stabilizes it. Bourdieu's sense of the "ordinary practice" surrounding both the production and consumption of photographs somehow suppresses the object's true, disruptive nature. Unfortunately, Bourdieu alludes to photography's collective ability to disrupt without explaining how or why they do so. Photographic objects might carry at their core the potential to upset, yet this disruptive potential and the ways subjects overcome it remain a mystery.

However, the medium's potential to disrupt subjects' apparent stability is at the center of Josef von Sternberg's 1930 film *The Blue Angel* (*Der blaue Engel*). This masterpiece of early German cinema tells the story of an isolated, bourgeois educator, Immanuel Rath, who falls for the free-spirited cabaret singer Lola Lola. Indeed, a set of mass-produced picture postcards, each featuring a different photograph of Marlene Dietrich's Lola, initially brings Emil Jannings' buttoned-down teacher to Lola's seedy nightclub. Once he confiscates images of her from his mischievous students, Rath becomes entranced and entangled—determined to restore his authority by ferreting out what is making his students more raucous and difficult to control than usual. What Rath finds—in the classroom, in the photo postcards, and in his subsequent marriage to Lola—is reminiscent of Bourdieu's warning about photographs: "The photographic image, that curious invention which could have served to disconcert or unsettle . . . came to fulfill functions that existed before its appearance, namely the solemnization and immortalization of an important area of collective life."[2] Although photographs seem to promise a "collective life"—understood here as a stabile subject identity within the social community, defined through relational power dynamics and "immortaliz[ed]" on film—the photographic postcards in *The Blue Angel* simultaneously undermine this stability because they tantalize male characters with a sense that control, security, and power in relations to others are possible. However, as close readings of Sternberg's film will demonstrate, the desire to control photographic objects is in perpetual conflict with their explosive potential—a struggle repeatedly visualized in the mimesis.

In this manner, *The Blue Angel* does more than just contribute to Marlene Dietrich's rise to iconic stardom,[3] illustrate psychoanalytic motives in its male characters,[4] or illuminate gender politics in the Weimar era.[5] The film offers a means of understanding Bourdieu's intuition that photographs are actually disruptive and corrosive to those who would use them to bolster their superior subject position. At multiple points throughout the film, male characters interact with Lola's postcards in ways that suggest these viewing subjects can exert control over the photographs, thereby strengthening their sense of male identity or power. For Professor Rath, this chaos begins in the classroom and extends into his personal life. In numerous scenes these men gaze at, conceal, or organize the postcards to strengthen their own agency, only to have that sense of agency dashed either in the same scene or in subsequent sequences. By juxtaposing instances of assumed control with assertive chaos, the film visually demonstrates how photographic objects actually represent disorder, instability, or insecurity, despite how male characters use them to provide a sense of order and identity. These male characters become entranced by the postcards either to strengthen their already established subject position (i.e., Rath) or to catalyze their own evolution toward a future subject position (i.e., Rath's students). If Bourdieu's intuition is right, then *The Blue Angel* is not about a conflict between Rath and Lola; rather, the central tension is in fact between the subject Rath and the photographic objects.

To investigate this claim, this chapter begins by exploring how Professor Rath exerts a high level of control over himself before the disruptive images enter his life. His morning routine reinforces and insulates his agency as a subject. When the setting shifts to his classroom, we see how Rath exerts a level of autocratic control over his students, thereby keeping them in an obsequious object position: he barks commands at them, weeds out troublemakers, and humiliates those who do not meet his standards. However, as soon as he encounters the postcards, Rath's subject position begins to collapse; the images destabilize his dynamic with his students before completely eroding the professor's identity as a controlling subject. In other words, Professor Rath experiences the disruptive effects of images in his classroom before he feels the effects in his personal life. With these counterpoints, *The Blue Angel* articulates a central problem of photography and its cultural impact during (and perhaps even since) the Weimar Republic—namely, what could happen to an individual when they encounter the phenomenon of Siegfried Kracauer's *Bilderflut*, the sudden proliferation of photographs and images that began during the Weimar era.[6] When images are everywhere, how does one negotiate their own identity within the dizzying, aesthetic experience caused by the rapid propagation of photographs in society?

A Controlling Subject

Before he encounters the photographs, Rath operates as a self-controlled and domineering subject, which the film's expositional sequences visualize. After a close-up on Rath's nameplate dissolves to the exterior of his apartment, a young girl runs up the stairs into the frame to deliver milk, which his maid receives before bringing the professor his breakfast. His maid next knocks on his bedroom door and announces that Rath's breakfast is ready. After a few beats, the professor emerges. Although he responds to the knock, it is clear that he is operating in his own time. It is not until the maid is leaving the room that Rath emerges into the medium long shot from behind his bedroom door, fastidiously dressed. He does not rush over to the table to consume his breakfast. Instead, we see him pat down his pockets in an effort to locate a small notebook. He will come to his breakfast in his own time, when he is ready and he deems his dressing routine complete. Framed by the horizontal stovepipe above his head, he appears all the more removed from the world around him. Thus, our first glimpse of the protagonist shows him in isolation.

Indeed, so much of his morning regiment insulates and shields him from any direct challenge to his agency. Yet Rath's maid clearly disapproves of her employer's chaotic lifestyle: when she arrives with his breakfast on a tray, she must move multiple books to make a space for the tray. According to the screenplay, she "grumbles as she looks around at the general disorder"[7] as she cleans up cigar butts and ash among the "piles of books and papers all over the study, all covered in dust."[8] She is disgusted with how he lives, but he appears unaware of that. Within his study, crowded with open books and covered with loose papers from the day before, he does what he pleases. If this sequence fairly represents Rath's ever-repeating morning routine, Rath never witnesses the maid's disapprobation and therefore is unaware of her disgust. He is ossified in his routine because he does not have to consider others. As an upper-class male subject in his domestic space, he lives and operates how he likes.

In fact, it is only when his routine is interrupted that Rath seems to reflect on the world around him and his inability to control it. Over his coffee, he whistles different melodies to cajole his pet bird into singing—one assumes as he has done every morning for a long time. When he receives no song in reply, he brings a sugar lump over to the cage as a bribe, showing how resolved he is that his routine follows its regular rhythm. This attempt to share a part of his breakfast—to reach out to another creature—fails, and when it does, Rath seems dazed. Only with this disruption in his habits does he realize that there is instability in the world and his relationship to it. His vain attempts to bribe the bird into singing indicate that he has no real control, and he remembers there is much beyond his control. Though his morning routine makes his life appear stable, this expositional sequence suggests that Rath begins to see that perhaps his subject role is limited or insecure.

Object Lessons in the Classroom

If Rath's domestic space allows him to operate according to an identity-reinforcing routine, then the same might be said of his professional space, his classroom. Here he also enjoys a routine within an environment that flatters his controlling subject role, at least until the photographs of Lola and their effect on his students are revealed. When we first see him enter his classroom, Rath asserts his subject position and its concomitant control over his students in the classroom immediately. His pupils rise to attention at the sight of the opening door, take their seats immediately after Rath commands them to, and avoid eye contact when the teacher discovers graffiti on one of his notebooks. However, once Rath orders them to compose in-class essays and he begins strolling, self-satisfied, up and down the rows, the hidden photographs and their pull on the students are revealed. Although Barbara Kosta argues that Rath is "angered by . . . the impertinent challenge to his authority,"[9] the images unsettle Rath because his students are learning to use the objects. As their interactions with Lola's photographs suggest, Rath's students seem eager to interact with the photographic objects in order to develop their own subject identities, thereby undercutting or diminishing their professor's authority.

When viewing the photographs, the boys violate the restrictive, ruled space of the *Gymnasium* (University Preparatory High School). Before Rath arrives, the schoolboys ferment together in a throng, which disrupts the visual order and spatial hierarchy of the classroom. The desks cannot be seen, as the boys crouch, kneel, and sit on top of desks instead of in chairs, thereby obscuring their surroundings. They are piled impossibly to fill the frame around Lohmann, the boy in the central position. The neatly arranged desks lose their intended purpose. The group seems removed from the previous environment of the ordered, hierarchical classroom, as we watch Lohmann in the center of the frame interacting with something. The blonde boy blows on a card he is holding, yet precisely why he does this remains unclear for the moment. Although Lola's feather skirt photo postcard is revealed to us later, at this point in the film, we are shut out from seeing it. We only see the pleasure of male characters as they share and interact with the photographic object. After he indulges in viewing the card a few times, Lohmann shows off the photograph knowingly to those around him, looking for and receiving reassurance.

This disturbance continues later when the besotted Lohmann interacts with the image instead of completing Rath's assignment. And it is the photograph's disruption—not the many others students who are flagrantly cheating—that draws Rath's attention and ire. Goldstaub, who is seated behind Lohmann when we see Rath's POV shot, is very obviously attempting to look over Lohmann's shoulder to see what he is writing. Rath angrily marches up and confiscates Lohmann's disruptive photograph yet has nothing to say about Goldstaub's wandering eye.

The image's content is not shown, yet the unsettling effect of the photograph is displayed when Rath grabs and views it: "RATH comes up, leans over and snatches the photograph from LOHMANN. He holds it up and looks at it in horror, then looks sternly from one pupil to the other. Suddenly, he turns around, still holding the photograph. Pan after him as he goes to the window, and shuts it with a bang. The sound of the girls' choir is muted. RATH hurries back to his desk."[10] Rath must confiscate the photographs because they are encouraging his students to develop their own subject identities, though the professor constantly attempts to remind them that they must be obedient objects to him. For these reasons, Rath runs to the open window to close it hastily. The chaste voices of the distant girls' choir indeed do conflict with the "lewd nature of the postcard image," as Frank Pilipp notes.[11] However, Rath also fastens the window in order to reassert his control against the photograph's disruptive influence. His classroom is on lock down. Thus, the double function of the photograph comes into view: the images undermine Rath's control while allowing the boys to develop their own subject identity.

The professor understands that by gazing at the photo, the political dynamics of subjectivity have been upset in his classroom. The photo not only prevents his students from focusing on the assignment; it also upsets Rath's own place in the subject/object order. As framed, Rath appears surrounded by the boys (though he is standing while they sit, facing the front of the classroom). For this reason, Rath returns to his desk, the symbolic locus of his authority, in a one shot. Then, a shot reverse shot isolates the professor and the disobedient Lohmann in separate frames, while Rath barks commands at the boy, intending to reinforce the sense of physical control that the teacher has over the boys and their bodies. Rath growls the simple imperatives of "get up!" and "sit down!"[12] because they demonstrate Rath's power, which he feels he must reassert after the disruption caused by the image. Thus, an important pattern comes to light with this scene: the agents of order are constantly struggling with the chaos unleashed by the photo postcards.

The subsequent scene outside the *Gymnasium* demonstrates how the images disrupt both the world of the characters and the visual language of the film. The sequence fades in on a medium shot of Erztum and Lohmann framed in a dark, undefined space. It is unclear where we find ourselves. Erztum stares with intensity at the right of the frame as Lohmann turns his head from left to right. Just as Erztum moves his head slightly to the left, a cut to a long shot reveals that the two students are not standing but crouching outside a door that we assume is their school's main entrance. The low camera placement here contrasts sharply with the higher perspectives from earlier in the film, which provided an overview of Rath's classroom. Next, numerous anonymous torsos and legs pass through frame—some walking and some breaking into a run—until we finally see Rath's cane and self-assured gait. After the professor leaves the frame, we might expect an establishing shot to confirm that it is indeed Rath that we have seen or a shot that follows Rath, given that he seems to be the film's central character. However, just when we might anticipate a cut, a new torso leaves the doorway and enters the frame. Whom the torso belongs to is unclear to us. Erztum acts: he sticks out his right leg to trip the figure before quickly running through the doorway into the school to hide. The resulting crash causes Rath, in a medium shot, to close his eyes reflexively before whipping his head back to the right. In a shot reverse shot, we see Rath's most obedient student, Angst; disheveled and prostrate on a staircase, the boy uneasily lifts his head to regard Rath, as if to stabilize himself. Angst's head is framed where it would be in a traditional medium shot; however, Angst's body is coming from the left of the frame, not the bottom, and with his hands he is grasping the lip of a stone step. Rath reacts with shock and disapproval, and a tracking shot reveals why—Lola's images, once hidden within the pages of a textbook, have burst forth and are now revealed (figure 2.1). Although he appears to be Rath's most ardent agent, even the bespectacled Angst is flirting with the subjectivity that the photographs provide.

It is significant that we get our first full glimpse of the front sides of the postcards as a result of such a disruptive moment. Given their positioning, the images seem to burst forth from the pages of Angst's composition notebooks. Being tripped is a similar disruption/unsettling of the regular order, and a mess is the result. The clatter of the fall causes Rath to turn around, unexpected as it is. The impossible, unnatural composition of the (both literally and metaphorically) fallen Angst resembles the jarring array of the photographs. Angst looks over at Rath, who in a separate shot regards the student before his eyes catch the mess caused by his fall. The diagonals produced by the book and notebooks stress the disorder—and unsurprisingly this is when the images are first shown to us. This reveal occurs only after we witness the disorder that the photos—and that looking at the photos—have caused in the prior sequence, which is juxtaposed with Rath seizing the photo-

Figure 2.1. *The Blue Angel* (*Der blaue Engel*). Directed by Josef von Sternberg. New York: Kino Lorbeer Films, 2013. Screen capture by Martin P. Sheehan.

graphs. More importantly, this disruptive moment reveals that Angst, himself a fledgling agent of order, possesses the photographs too and has been using them to catalyze his own subject position. Although he later suggests that the other boys planted the photos on him, it makes sense that Angst would flirt with the sense of power and agency that he believes the objects could offer him. His attempts to conceal the images, though, are in vain; their disruptive nature must emerge, as this sequence suggests.

Here, we must ask why Rath reacts in such a puzzling way when he interrogates Angst about the postcards' provenance. Once he sequesters Angst in his office, the professor seems so taken aback when Angst mentions the Blue Angel nightclub that Rath must confirm the name. He is confounded for a number of reasons: first, Rath learns that the boys have their own routine. Instead of eating their breakfast alone in the mornings or retiring to an empty home office at night like their teacher does, Lohmann, Erztum, and Goldstaub frequent the Blue Angel every night, where—as Angst confesses—women can be found. The students do not live a cloistered life as Rath does. Unlike their professor, the students visit a third environ (besides their domestic dormitory and the workspace of their classroom) where they have different identities; they are more than just students that Rath rules over, which necessarily challenges Rath's subject position over them. Second, and perhaps most troubling for Rath, the photos have a direct, local connection; photographs can function as indexes—visible traces of a real-world referent. Rath appears floored by the news that the photo postcards have a local referent instead of being some general image of a distant body or object. Though the postcards might be produced in mass quantities, they are reproductions of individual photographs that were printed from light sensitive negatives. And those postcards were made to promote a performer in a local venue, where the boys are developing their sexual and subject identities. It is not moral corruption that concerns Rath. Instead, he worries that his students are using the nightclub and the photographs they buy there to bolster their own agency. They are becoming subjects at the expense of Rath's own subjectivity. Perhaps the Blue Angel, the newly discovered challenge to his subject position, is what inspires him to interact with the cards alone.

Shaken by these realizations, Rath requires a boost, something to reassure him once Angst leaves. With all three photographs neatly fanned out in his hand, Rath has three versions of Lola to look at—a medium-length portrait of Lola looking over her shoulder is on the left, on the right is a full-length portrait of Lola in some kind of a feathered hat, and front and center is a full-length image of Lola that has down feathers physically pasted onto it over her waist (figure 2.2). The feathers obscure her upper thighs, but when Rath, or any subject, blows lightly on the feathers, they rise and expose Lola's legs and undergarments.

The photographs beguile Rath because they seem to reinforce his subject position. They appear to present him with an illusion of control over Lola, the photographed object. Similar to his dynamic with his pupils in the classroom, Rath has an audience with these cards. Instead of obedient students, the three images provide Rath with a harem of women (albeit, the same woman) whom he can regard and whom he forces to regard him. Alone in his office, he can interact with them on his own terms and in his own time. He controls Lola's clothes, blowing on them so that he can leer at what is underneath. The feather photograph allows him to control what he sees and when he sees it.

Though it is important that we see all the cards—especially the one with down feathers that so enthralled Rath's boys—before we meet Lola in person, it is all the more significant that we see Rath interact with the

Figure 2.2. *The Blue Angel* (*Der blaue Engel*). Directed by Josef von Sternberg. New York: Kino Lorbeer Films, 2013. Screen capture by Martin P. Sheehan.

images alone. He must fulfill his role of keeping the order while in the classroom, and he must keep up this appearance when interacting and disciplining Angst. Yet when he is by himself, removed from his social identity, he interacts in a subject-affirming way similar to that of the boys. He can let down his constant offense in keeping the order. By glancing over his shoulder, he is checking that no one else can witness him indulge in the visual pleasure the photographs provide him. By contrast, when he suddenly glances around the classroom after he discovers Lohmann interacting with the image *in flagrante*, he is performing his social role. In discovering the photographs—the objects of disruption—Rath looks around in an overdetermined manner to show the others his shock. Alone, he revels in the control that the photographs seem to provide him. After their discovery, though, the images incite a plot that dismantles Rath's identity completely, thereby fulfilling the function that Bourdieu sees as the true effect of photographs: despite our attempts to master them, images carry within them the ability to destabilize reality and one's collective life within it.[13]

The Subject Objectified

Across *The Blue Angel*'s narrative, the photographs of Lola seem to proliferate invisibly: the single image that Rath confiscates in his classroom soon becomes the jumble that spills from Angst's notebooks outside the school, which eventually becomes a heap that unexpectedly pours from Lola's suitcase in a hotel room at an undetermined location. Upon each appearance, the photographs challenge the prevailing order or assumed reality: Lohmann cares more about the photograph than Rath's assignment while it is revealed that the prim teacher's pet also indulges in the images. Most importantly, as *The Blue Angel* seems to suggest, the photographs are growing in number, unseen until they burst forth when characters grow inattentive. Demanding ever more attention in the private sphere, the photographs seem to push their way from the controlled personal context of an individual out into the larger social world to be seen by others. The images overwhelm and envelop the individuals who encounter them.

Although originally applied to the rapid increase of printed photographs in mass media periodicals in the 1920s, Siegfried Kracauer's *Bilderflut* (flood of images) could also characterize the dizzying, aesthetic experience of photographic postcards and their proliferation seen in *The Blue* Angel and during the larger Weimar period in which it was produced. "Never before," Kracauer writes in his seminal essay "Photography," "has an age been so informed about itself, if being informed means having an image of objects that resembles them in a photographic sense."[14] Comprised as it was by countless photographic "reproductions," the *Bilderflut* (in all its forms) inundated German citizens with vast amounts of visual information of the evolving world. The proliferation of cheaply produced photographs underscores "a sense of lost totality that was pivotal to Weimar intellectual debates from Kracauer to Georg Lukács and beyond."[15] On the one hand, the increasing ubiquity of the photographic image could have helped stave off change. Mass produced photographs had the potential to ossify tradition by capturing, cataloging, and disseminating fixed indexes of the way objects exist (across the world in all manner of manifestations). However, instead of functioning as "an aid to memory," the *Bilderflut* instead "swe[pt] away the dams of memory,"[16] further undermining attempts to control the rapidly changing face of society during the Weimar era. For reactionary figures trying to survive the 1920s in the Weimar Republic (like Professor Rath), so many dimensions of their lives were in flux—political instability, hyperinflation, and the ever-changing role of women in society and politics—and the "flood of images" reified the velocity of this flux. The sheer number of images produced in illustrated magazines and photographic postcards was overwhelming.

Just how overwhelming images could be for German citizens during this age is the core of *The Blue Angel.* The sudden ubiquity of photographs shocks Rath in the film, yet what proves to be more shocking is that the photographs in this new age seem to gain the upper hand by upending his subject identity as photographs seemed to do to many at the time. Writing in 1921, nine years before Sternberg's film, Erich Bürger speaks to the sudden omnipresence and power of images:

> No longer does the photograph have the simple significance of a memento that you carry around with you in your billfold or that you carefully preserve in the most protected corner of a glass case. No, the days are gone when a picture was nothing but a museum attraction, eye candy for holidays, an apt activity for family gatherings, the filling for the gold frames of loving couples. The picture, the photograph, has penetrated our most mundane life, saturated every minute. Each second it races before our eyes in a thousand forms: another one, a new one, again and again. Suddenly the world turns more quickly; each second becomes precious.[17]

Bürger's language here stresses how subjects have lost control over photographic objects due to mass production. Images, he tells us, were once tucked away in a wallet to be taken out and observed whenever the subject preferred. Similarly, photographs were kept on static display in glass cases that subjects could visit whenever the mood struck them. The male characters in *The Blue Angel* seem to subscribe to this older understanding: instead of a wallet, Angst attempts to carry his photographic postcards of Lola packed secretly within his notebooks before they burst forth. Although it is a creature instead of a photograph, Rath is accustomed to visiting his caged songbird and cajoling it to sing whenever he pleases—a move that stresses his subjectivity while foreshadowing the loss of his assumed subject position, which photographs delineate in the film. Indeed, Rath regains some of the subjectivity that he lost in his classroom (thanks to the disobedience inspired by the photographs), by arranging the images in his hand so that he can observe them all simultaneously for as long as he likes. In this manner, the professor attempts to secure his subjective agency against the flood of images as well as the inevitable disruption they produce, which resembles the way he locates, clumsily courts, and finally marries Lola, the images' referent. Each is an attempt to order the uncertainty of life that the proliferation of images denotes.

So much of the film's plot after the photographs first appear is determined by Rath's attempts to secure his subject position. He travels to the club at night to ferret out and punish his students who would dare deviate from the object position that he forces them into. Once there, the subject/object tables are turned on him when, during one of her songs, Lola literally puts Rath in a spotlight, which further upsets his accustomed dynamic. The blinding light prevents him from viewing both Lola and his students, so Rath becomes doubly determined to reassert and secure his agency. Later, Lola seems to yield to Rath. In an echo of the feather photograph, Lola changes her costumes in front of Rath, apparently allowing him to objectify her, though she is actually the more secure subject in control. When his students witness Rath returning to the club on subsequent nights, he finds his authority and subjectivity in his classroom undermined. Consequently, his students draw suggestive cartoons on the blackboard featuring their professor and Lola, which leads the school's principal to question Rath about the path he seems to be taking with the nightclub singer. Unaccustomed to challenges to his subjectivity in his classroom, Rath quits his job. Exiled from his school and the main source of his agential identity, Rath then proposes to Lola in an effort to stabilize his subjectivity over his objectified wife. On their honeymoon, though, Lola's photographs burst forth again as they did previously on the steps of the school, thereby disrupting everything by reminding Rath that all attempts to exploit objects to reinforce one's power are in vain.

As Rath eagerly awaits his first nuptial night with his new wife, he seems unaware that everything he has tried to overcome or hide is about to break out. After the unseen ordering ritual of their wedding, the camera fades in. Rath smiles, smokes, and paces in a well-appointed hotel suite while Lola's shapely shadow moves suggestively upon a silky curtain that separates the two. Numerous times throughout the long, continuous shot, Rath looks to the curtain and the two-dimensional image of his wife's body. Eventually, she pokes her smiling face out from the curtains and requests her smaller suitcase, most likely so that she can retrieve playful lingerie, one supposes. Suddenly, something disrupts the scene: when Rath attempts to pick up the unlatched suitcase for his wife, a torrent of photo cards tumbles onto the floor. The cards and what seem to be Lola's intimate undergarments spill out as Rath kneels down to clean up the clumsy mess he has made—the whole time with his eyes trained on his wife off-screen. Rath's glee turns to concern when he sees the mess: in what the screenplay calls a "high-angle shot,"[18] he slowly crouches down into a kneeling position. As he lowers his eyes to see what has spilled out, he places his cigarette in his mouth. Picking up a pile of photo cards with his right hand and placing them in his left, Rath attempts to bring order to—and to make sense of—the mess that erupted before him. His slow movements suggest an initial uncertainty that gives way to a dawning recognition. Rath cannot escape the postcards and what they represent—his lack of control in his life, his undoing (figure 2.3).

Again, the sudden, messy appearance of the images proves to be significant. After coming from the ordering ritual that is a wedding ceremony, Rath might believe he has tamed Lola just as he believed he had tamed his students. She is, it would seem, as easy to collect as the postcards that advertise her performance. Before the photos spill out, a self-satisfied Rath is reveling in a newly stabilized subject position (or so he thinks). Having lost his songbird early in the film, he has now secured another; she has become the subservient hen to his virile and vocal rooster, as their wedding reception seems to suggest. While it is true that he has lost his public identity as a professor—as well as control over his students—it would seem that the disruptive events set in motion by the photographs have finally led to firm footing. With the loss of his desk as a panoptical pulpit, Rath scrambled to secure a new subject position over Lola. His momentary flirtation with chaos and disorder has paid off, it would appear. He has beaten the images and their disruption; what is more, he has proven himself to be their master with his marriage to Lola. And yet, though he might feel stable and excited when the sequence begins, Rath's reaction when Lola's photos spill onto the floor of their nuptial suite reminds him that his identity is unstable.

The chaos caused by the photographs is overwhelming in the postmatrimonial, precoital scene. To Rath, the postcards spill out at the worst time. Having just married Lola, he is ready to consummate (and celebrate) his stabilized subject position over the object of his affection. In an effort to make sense of the mess, Rath—ever the agent of order—scoops up and shuffles stacks and stacks of photographs, many more than the three that he held earlier in his office. Using the imperious tone usually reserved for his classroom, he barks at Lola, "Why did you bring these postcards?"[19] Simon Richter identifies here in Rath a "moment of 'enlightenment' (or disillusionment)" in which Rath is angry that "he has become part of a sordid industry that trades on the exchange of erotic images for money."[20] However, Rath's anger goes beyond economic and moral concern. Instead, Rath is convinced the images have no purpose in his new life with Lola because they repre-

Figure 2.3. *The Blue Angel* (*Der blaue Engel*). Directed by Josef von Sternberg. New York: Kino Lorbeer Films, 2013. Screen capture by Martin P. Sheehan.

sent numerous challenges to his subject identity. Indeed, after Lola informs Rath in an innocent tone that the photo postcards are sold every performance night, Rath reasserts his subjectivity: he barks, "So long as I have a single penny . . . they will not be sold."[21] His reply stresses his economic agency over the objects, thereby underscoring his control over them. That is, as long as he has money (i.e., his subject position), he will retain power over the postcards.

After a short fade to black, however, it seems Rath has lost his subject position, a loss of identity that the postcards themselves mark. In a medium shot, Rath sits alone at a table under a poster of Lola in an undefined, darkened space. After taking a few final drags from a cigarette, he glances over his left shoulder. He clears coasters off a metal tray before reaching into his breast pocket. We have associated the gesture previously with his professional notebook, where he would record demerits and keep his other class notes of misbehavior. That happened in his classroom, though; here—wherever this undefined space is—we find Rath reaching into his pocket to pull out postcards, but not a collection for his own enjoyment as he did in his office. Instead, he takes out a thick stack of images, carefully arranges them on a platter, and then walks out of frame after a quick cut to Lola on stage finishing her song.

An ironic transformation has taken place. Despite demanding that the postcards never be sold again in the scene directly preceding this sequence, Rath must now sell them himself. As further humiliation, Rath's solicitations are waved away. In a medium long shot, the camera shows Rath roaming through a full room of seated patrons, clustered together and engaged in conversations. There are apparently no lone figures in this crowd—men and women talk, laugh, and drink together, which presents a deep contrast to the prior shot of Rath, where he sat alone, hunched at a table in the dark with his back to Lola performing on stage.

This composition contrasts sharply with Rath's position and posture in his classroom. There, he sat front and center on a raised platform behind a large desk. All eyes were on him as he barked out commands. In the club, though, he enjoys neither the frontality nor the centrality that he once experienced. Outside of his controlled environment (or outside the environments that he controlled), he and his agency are marginalized. Though it will change later when he becomes Kiepert's clown assistant, Rath's identity in this moment is a photo postcard seller. Whereas earlier he was a revered or feared subject, now he is ignored. The solidification that enticed him, the permanent agency that he had assumed would come with courtship and marriage—both promised conditions—are absent here. In this sequence he wades through a sea of tables and chairs. Gone are the ordered rows of desks, where seated students all faced Rath, their professor. Instead, Rath appears flattened and unmoored as he walks through the room. The patrons appear to follow their own order—some sit in the foreground, others in the background. They all face different directions, and—with the exception of the few that wordlessly decline Rath's solicitation—they all ignore the lone figure. Within the flattened framing, it is nearly impossible to discern the furniture and how it is grouped, unlike the many desks at the *Gymnasium*.

The aural channel reinforces the loss of subjectivity while underscoring the contrast between Rath's classroom before the photographs and the venue he sells them in now. Voices are woven together. The cacophony of conversation and diegetic music function as a wall that further isolates Rath and demonstrate his loss of subjectivity. They are all talking whereas Rath is silent. Unlike his classroom where he issues commands that are immediately obeyed, he now plaintively proffers the postcards with only body language. Thanks to the disruptive nature of the postcards he once tried to suppress and now must sell, the professor has been stripped of his subjectivity and agency.

Conclusion

Rath's long journey from domineering subject to undistinguished object is not yet complete, as the rest of the film's plot shows. Following Rath's postcard selling sequence, he launches a final protest against his loss of status and subjectivity before giving up completely. Once he does finally resign himself to his nonsubject status, the film quickly jumps to four years in the future, where we find Rath sitting in front of a mirror, applying clown makeup "with a disillusioned air."[22] It would seem he abandoned hope of regaining his subject position, yet he is not fully content assuming the identity of assistant to the director/conjurer Kiepert. Rath exists in this later stage of the film as an object that mourns the loss of subjectivity. The former professor still clings to a memory of once having agency and authority, which is why he resists Kiepert's "good news" that the troupe will be performing at the Blue Angel club in Rath's hometown. For Rath, the return reminds him of his transformation into an object, a long journey of disruption, chaos, and loss that the photographs instigated. His subsequent performance is an ultimate humiliation for Rath because it marks his total loss of agency: he is heckled by his former pupils and bullied by Kiepert while watching the strongman Mazeppa kiss Lola offstage. Rath thus experiences the loss of his professional, personal, and sexual subjectivity, which leads to a violent nervous breakdown. Desperate to reclaim a sense of agency, Rath runs backstage, rams through a locked door, and chokes Lola until she is able to escape and the male performers are able to restrain Rath fully in a straitjacket. Restricted in this manner, Rath is forced to submit to an existence as an inert nonsubject.

We can see that although Bourdieu does not fully explain *why* he believes photographs should unsettle and corrode, *The Blue Angel* offers a means of understanding how they destabilize. In the Weimar Republic, the ever-increasing quantities of photographs are disturbing because the images turn subjects into objects, thereby problematizing how subjects perceive reality and their place within it. Numerous male characters in Sternberg's film use photographs to reinforce or provide a sense of agency, superiority, and stability in their community by convincing themselves that their relations to others are defined through photographs—objects that appear to support subject superiority because the images immortalize others as objects. When viewed in this way, photographs are not easy means to an end, as the characters in the film understand them; photographs cannot be used to solidify social identity or relationships. Photographs are objects that object; they challenge the control of the would-be subjects.

Martin P. Sheehan is Interim Chair of the Department of Foreign Languages and Associate Professor of German at Tennessee Tech University. His research on dramatic form, performance, and photography has been featured in *Seminar, Archiv, Colloquia Germanica, Interdisciplinary Humanities,* and *Studia Neophilogica.* A member of the digital humanities research collective at Vanderbilt University since 2016, his current projects explore visual culture, disability in German dramatic comedy, and social network analysis.

Notes

1. Pierre Bourdieu, *Photography: A Middle-brow Art,* trans. Luc Boltanski (Stanford: Stanford University Press, 2005), 76.
2. Ibid.
3. Elisabeth Bronfen, "Seductive Departures of Marlene Dietrich: Exile and Stardom in *The Blue Angel," New German Critique* 89 (2003): 9–31.
4. Frank Pilipp, "Desire, Deviation, Double Entendre: The Aesthetics of Sexuality in *Der blaue Engel* Revisited," *The Journal of Popular Film and Television* 42, no. 2 (2014): 91–104.
5. Jennifer Williams, "Gazes in Conflict: Lola Lola, Spectatorship, and Cabaret in *The Blue Angel," Women in German Yearbook: Feminist Studies in German Literature & Culture* 26, no. 1 (2010): 54–72.
6. Siegfried Kracauer, "Photography," in *The Mass Ornament: Weimar Essays,* trans. Thomas Y. Levin (Cambridge, MA: Harvard University Press, 1995), 58. For more on the variety of styles and schools that defined the *Bilderflut* in the Weimar Republic, see Andrés Mario Zervigón, *Photography and Germany* (London: Reaktion Books, 2017), esp. 96–113.
7. Robert Liebmann, Josef von Sternberg, and Heinrich Mann, *The Blue Angel: A Film; An Authorized Translation of the German Continuity* (New York: Simon and Schuster, 1968), 20.
8. Ibid.
9. Barbara Kosta, *Willing Seduction:* The Blue Angel, *Marlene Dietrich, and Mass Culture* (New York: Berghahn Books, 2012), 58.
10. Liebmann, von Sternberg, and Mann, *The Blue Angel,* 30.
11. Pilipp, "Desire," 93.
12. Liebmann, von Sternberg, and Mann, *The Blue Angel,* 30–31.

13. Bourdieu, *Photography*, 76.
14. Kracauer, "Photography," 58.
15. Michael Cowan, "Cutting through the Archive: 'Querschnitt' Montage and Images of the World in Weimar Visual Culture," *New German Critique* 120, vol. 40, no. 3 (2013): 18.
16. Kracauer, "Photography," 58.
17. Erich Burger, "Pictures-Pictures," in *The Promise of Cinema: German Film Theory, 1907–1933*, ed. Anton Kaes, Nicholas Baer, and Michael Cowan (Oakland: University of California Press, 2016), 64.
18. Liebmann, von Sternberg, and Mann, *The Blue Angel*, 91.
19. Ibid.
20. Simon Richter, "The Return of the Queen of the Night: Joseph von Sternberg's *Der blaue Engel* and *Die Zauberflöte*," *German Life & Letters* 61, no. 1 (2008): 181.
21. Liebmann, von Sternberg, and Mann, *The Blue Angel*, 91.
22. Ibid., 94.

Bibliography

Bourdieu, Pierre. *Photography: A Middle-brow Art*. Translated by Luc Boltanski. Stanford: Stanford University Press, 2005.

Bronfen, Elisabeth. "Seductive Departures of Marlene Dietrich: Exile and Stardom in *The Blue Angel*." *New German Critique* 89 (2003): 9–31.

Burger, Erich. "Pictures-Pictures." In *The Promise of Cinema: German Film Theory, 1907–1933*, edited by Anton Kaes, Nicholas Baer, and Michael Cowan, 64. Oakland: University of California Press, 2016.

Cowan, Michael. "Cutting through the Archive: 'Querschnitt' Montage and Images of the World in Weimar Visual Culture." *New German Critique* 120, vol. 40, no. 3 (2013): 1–40.

Kosta, Barbara. *Willing Seduction*: The Blue Angel, *Marlene Dietrich, and Mass Culture*. New York: Berghahn Books, 2012.

Kracauer, Siegfried. "Photography." In *The Mass Ornament: Weimar Essays*. Translated by Thomas Y. Levin, 47–63. Cambridge, MA: Harvard University Press, 1995.

Liebmann, Robert, Josef von Sternberg, and Heinrich Mann. *The Blue Angel: A Film; An Authorized Translation of the German Continuity*. New York: Simon and Schuster, 1968.

Pilipp, Frank. "Desire, Deviation, Double Entendre: The Aesthetics of Sexuality in *Der blaue Engel* Revisited." *The Journal of Popular Film and Television* 42, no. 2 (2014): 91–104.

Richter, Simon. "The Return of the Queen of the Night: Joseph von Sternberg's *Der blaue Engel* and *Die Zauberflöte*." *German Life & Letters* 61, no. 1 (2008): 171–85.

Williams, Jennifer. "Gazes in Conflict: Lola Lola, Spectatorship, and Cabaret in *The Blue Angel*." *Women in German Yearbook: Feminist Studies in German Literature & Culture* 26, no. 1 (2010): 54–72.

Zervigón, Andrés Mario. *Photography and Germany*. London: Reaktion Books, 2017.

Filmography

The Blue Angel (*Der blaue Engel*). Directed by Josef von Sternberg. New York: Kino Lorber Films, 2013.

Chapter 3

BEFORE- AND AFTERLIVES

On the Stillness of Photographs at the Outset of Adenauer Cinema

John E. Davidson

Photographs and Talking Pictures

Like postwar cinema in Germany, this chapter begins with Wolfgang Staudte's *The Murderers Are Among Us* (*Die Mörder sind unter uns*, 1946). Since the examples in what follows may not be familiar to most readers, it seems useful to set the stage with one that probably is. So, I risk retracing familiar ground in order to point out a little-discussed incident in Staudte's film, one that introduces photography as a conceptual connection to lives that went before and to afterlives as cinema moved into the Adenauer era. As the reader might know, Staudte made *The Murderers Are Among Us* in 1946 with the support of the newly grounded East-German film studios, the Deutsche Film-Aktiengesellschaft (DEFA) in the Soviet Zone of Occupation. The film centers on two figures: a traumatized surgeon, Hans Mertens, who has returned from the field in the East; and a distinctly untraumatized woman, Susanne Wallner, who has just returned from the camps. The film's ultimate investment is in the redemption of a sovereign (German) masculinity verified by work as the path to normality, coupled with a call to bear witness to and to demand an accounting from those who are responsible, like Mertens' former captain, Ferdinand Brückner.

The film contains a brief attribution of value to the photographic as potential witness and to the role it might play in navigating the post-National-Socialist world. True, *The Murderers Are Among Us* itself "witnesses" very little, restricting the impulse to do so to two flashbacks. The first comprises only the sounds of bombs and battle as the screen fills with a close-up focusing on Mertens' eyes highlighted amid his shell-shocked expression. The second gives a stylized audiovisual reconstruction of the massacre that he blames on Brückner. A photographic camera plays no role there; nevertheless, when we see Mertens for the first time in the apartment in which he is squatting, he rifles through cabinets and drawers and comes across a Leica camera. He inspects it briefly, looking directly into the lens to see if it is whole (an action that cannot but remind the contemporary viewer of taking a selfie), then pockets it. Wallner, the apartment's rightful occupant, returns home for the first time at that moment, and Mertens spars with her obnoxiously, insisting that she has no claim on the place. He eventually helps her bring in her suitcase and then, unable to face the idea of either truly sharing the apartment or moving on, simply turns to go out to drink. After a moment's reflection, he leaves the apartment, but the closing door reveals that he removed the camera from his pocket and left it on the dresser in the entryway. In the subsequent scene the viewer learns that he had promised the camera to someone who works at the bar he frequents—so, we surmise that he must have either found it in the apartment previously or hidden it himself. The dancer, who has already found someone willing to trade schnapps and cigarettes for it, pouts that she thinks it "*mehr als gemein*" (more than mean/common) of him not to have brought it.[1] Mertens tells her that it would have been "*noch gemeiner*" (even meaner/even more common) to have done so. The camera incident, it seems, is meant to plant a seed for the audience that he is good underneath—neither mean nor common at all. Despite his rough interactions with Wallner, which continue for a good while, the unique quality she sees in him has been prefigured.

Mertens' gesture with the camera imputes a value to it that is, on the one hand, unquestioned and, on the other hand, never allowed to manifest itself. Self-evidently a rare possession, the camera has potential value on the black market or as an item of barter for sexual favors, but it never enters into those economies. In the rest of the film the camera neither is used nor even appears, so it is not a smoking gun, and it foreshadows no cache of pictures to be discovered. One might say that the camera in *The Murderers Are Among Us* is a kind of MacGuffin, that is, an element important not in itself but for what it does to show character and animate action—in this case to show that the good heart beneath Mertens' gruff and drunken exterior makes him act nobly. Yet,

Mertens' Leica (the first commercially available personal camera to use 35mm film stock) is more than a MacGuffin for two reasons.

First, one understanding of the photo apparatus is that it provides evidence of the profilmic (literally the "world before the film") and so it has the potential to witness what it encounters. In the context of *The Murderers Are Among Us*, its value might stem from the images that it has already taken (and holds undeveloped within) or that it might take in the future. It has the power to capture a moment that undeniably has been. Staudte's film recognizes this because each time photographs appear, they are tied to documenting the past; however, they do not spark memories themselves. In the backstage scene mentioned above, small, framed photographs decorate the dressing room, and the attentive viewer can just make out that they are of these entertainers in previous moments and roles. Later, in a key scene in which Mertens decides he must kill Brückner, two photographs frame the Christmas tree that reminds him of the holiday-time slaughter he witnessed in Poland in 1942.

These photographic images all show what has been, but their placement in the mise-en-scène renders their historical traces unrecognizable; they hint at what photography can be but bear no witness themselves. Instead, their mere presence on the wall signals the return to normality for which Wallner strives in reclaiming the apartment (a return to normality that she explicitly associates with forgetting in an earlier conversation with Mondschein). The reader will remember that Staudte focuses on the printed word to witness past atrocities, using newspaper headlines and field reports to augment and verify Mertens' filmed memories; individual photographs are not allowed to show us anything in this film. Viewers come closest to being aware—taking cognizance—of a photo when the X-ray images used to replace broken windows make them see through people while Mertens speaks about the "miracle" of his first surgery and then the "miracle" of the war. Without ever providing us a still photograph to see, *The Murderers Are Among Us* proceeds from the vignette of the camera through the X-rays to the enlivening of superimposed images of the dead. At the end it sets a kind of cinematic equivalent of X-rays in motion as Brückner screams that he is innocent, rather than letting us "recognize" a photo and, beyond that, take cognizance through what Roland Barthes describes as photography's untimeliness in regard to the viewer.[2]

For all its efforts to provide striking visuals of the rubble matched with soundscapes that enhance emotional impact, Staudte's story of Mertens' redemption—with its call for future, earthly retribution—

indicates that the history of media's inexorable convergence is filled with lags, setbacks, contradictions, and even resistance. Indeed, in cases like *The Murderers Are Among Us*, some forms of media (print, music) meld with the filmic medium effortlessly, whereas the photographic medium seems to hold the potential to give it pause at this particular historical moment.[3] Here the intermedial incorporation specifically neutralizes the power of the photographic, removing the possibility that it could be explored "as a wound."[4]

According to Barthes, the photograph confronts the viewing subject with duplicitous evidence: the "that-has-been" of the image and the inevitability of death. He reads in this asynchronous relationship the appearance of a "flat death," which gives mortality a place in modern society without the metaphysical framework of religion or ritual:

> For Death must be somewhere in a society; if it is no longer (or less intensely) in religion, it must be elsewhere; perhaps in [the photograph], which produces Death while trying to preserve life. Contemporary with the withdrawal of rites, Photography may correspond to the intrusion, in our modern society, of an asymbolic Death, outside of religion, outside of ritual, a kind of abrupt dive into literal Death. Life/Death: the paradigm is reduced to a simple click, the one separating the initial pose to the final print.[5]

For Barthes, the relationship of the viewer to the photograph is at heart a connection that runs through death. It actualizes an awareness of a common fate between the viewing subject and the photographed object in a (meaningless) death. The moving picture does not offer time to take cognizance of that relationship, whereas the photograph insists on a temporal and psychological pause that affords that opportunity. No pause occurs in Staudte's film until the superimpositions of the dead are replaced by a field of crosses, and the cinema camera disappears into the heart of a cross and darkness fills the screen.

The camera-as-MacGuffin faces a second complication arising from the serialization of individual images to make moving pictures to which sound can be added. Staudte's metonymic substitution of the camera for the still image points to an intermedial dilemma for sound film, one that I suggest has particular weight following the founding of the two German states. Dwelling on a photograph presents an actual *Problemstellung* in film.[6] It forces an awkward embrace of what Campany calls the photograph's "stillness" in terms of both motion and sound, and neither kind of stillness can exist easily within the "belief systems" of feature-film cinema.[7] The formal *Problemstellung* at the site of a photograph must be recouped within that system. *The Murderers Are Among Us* marginalizes the problematic stillness of photos in its mise-en-scène and leaves the potential of confronting its memorializing of "flat deaths" literally undeveloped. It is worth remembering that Mertens regains his masculine sovereignty when he saves a life, a moment concretized by his issuing commands that cause things in the frame, and then the camera itself, to move. *The Murderers Are Among Us* first gestures to "flat death" as "common" (*gemein*) but then denies the photograph the opportunity to give it a form; however, in doing so it points to a tension that many films of post-World War II and the Adenauer period must confront directly. Where Staudte's use of religious symbols throughout his film renders ambiguous the cross that finally overwhelms the screen, no such indecision haunts these examples from the Adenauer era, which smooth over the tensions posed by the photograph to facilitate an unambiguous presentation of the markers of Christianity.

In what follows, my reading of how such tensions are resolved concentrates on films that see in the photograph evidence of a common, meaningless death—evidence that these films seek to eradicate by reestablishing meaning through religious habitus. They do this by transposing the formal challenge of the photograph to the narrative level through dialogue and sound. This analysis gives specific historical context to Christian Metz's claim that "film is less a succession of photographs than, to a large extent, a destruction of the photograph, or more exactly [of] the photograph's power."[8] This chapter focuses on three examples from the outset of the Adenauer era: *Nachtwache* (Braun, *Keepers of the Night*, 1949); *Der Kaplan von San Lorenzo* (Ucicky, 1953); and *Die seltsame Geschichte des Brandner Kaspar* (von Báky, 1949).[9] Photographs play a role in these works, but they are "talked" for the viewer in a variety of ways that encase and then defuse their stillness in narrative. Each of these examples brings a reflexivity about film and the flat death of the photograph to the surface in order to banish it preemptively and propose in its place a mode of redemption rooted in Christianity. This echoes the contemporary religious institutions' attempts to reestablish themselves as moral arbiters of the social and political worlds at the outset of the Adenauer era, but it is not necessarily steered by them.[10] Photographs confront us with the "that-has-been" of life once before the camera, and these films' denial of it serves to posit an afterlife. The end of this chapter turns briefly to the dilemma posed by the histories of these directors; as Tim Bergfelder points out, Braun and von Báky are two of the directors with deep roots in the Nazi-era industry who nonetheless help Erich Pommer in his attempts to revitalize West German cinema.[11] Ucicky has a similar portfolio. In that context, what can be made of their promotion of an afterlife through a denial of previous deaths at the outset of the Adenauer era?

Talking (the) Pictures

The feature films that are central to the visual media of the Adenauer age are generally skittish of reflexivity, and of silence, and thus they tend to "talk" photographs in order to mask their formal disruptions. When photographs appear, the objects provide evidence of an already-exercised power, quite often amorphously waved to simply as the past, or at best named as the war. What becomes interesting for the following analysis are the ways that the viewing of photographs is handled within these narratives and mediated for the cinema audience. A prototypical moment is offered by Harald Braun's *Nachtwache*, one of the most popular and critically well-received films of the late 1940s. Like so much of the cinema of the day, *Nachtwache* takes place in a religious context and seeks to brush against questions of faith—in this case, about suffering, perseverance, doubt, and hope.[12] The setting is a diocese hospital where, according to a review in the primary evangelical film journal, "four typical figures of our time" are brought together.[13] The first two are modern: a skeptical doctor, Cornelie Badenhausen, and a nihilistic actor, Stefan Gorgas, former lovers who are both captive to the past. Their respective attitudes can be traced to the death of their daughter, although Gorgas had already separated from his lover to become a pilot by that time.[14] Badenhausen carries a photo of their lost child in a locket around her neck. Early in the film she shows it to a patient who also struggles with the loss of a child, and then looks at it herself; the film audience, however, does not get a glimpse. As she closes the locket, tucks it back into her smock, and turns back to her work, the doctor comments soberly, "I don't have her anymore, either. She is dead."[15] Throughout the rest of the film, the photo never appears, and the locket fails to reappear, so, once again, something holding an unseen photograph serves as a means of indicating deep character motivation. In this case it serves to root the doctor's skepticism in her experience rather than her science.

The film "talks" the picture rather than showing it, with the doctor's words exposing the viewers to its Barthesian function as a personal documentation explicitly insisting on the finality of death: "that-has-been" and "will-be." The refusal to grant the audience direct access to the image keeps its privacy seemingly intact, even as the doctor's words make its content public. It is useful to remember here that Metz, perhaps expanding on comments made by Barthes, draws a distinction between film and photography based on the association of the former with collectivity and the latter with privacy.[16] While pointing out (quite rightly) that this distinction is a social myth, he nonetheless recognizes its power. In *Nachtwache,* as in other Adenauer-era movies, we see that the dynamic of the unseen-yet-narrated presentation of photos underscores that myth. Braun avoids subjecting the privacy of the photo to a common, public scrutiny, and thus keeps its fetish character intact. This also maintains the flat death that Barthes senses in the photograph: its object has a before- but not an afterlife, for it has no future and always will-be dead. The photograph's fetish character is profane rather than sacred.

The other two so-called typical figures in *Nachtwache* are directly involved in the administration of the sacred in the face of an increasingly profane world: a Catholic chaplain, steady and solid in the rituals of his sect, and a Protestant pastor, a beacon of hope whose faith is sorely tested late in the film. An accident leaves the daughter of Pastor Heger severely injured, and a complicated procedure performed by Badenhausen fails to save her. The struggle for faith takes place during the night vigil by her bedside as her life slips away. Yet instead of giving into despair, Pastor Heger's strength in suffering is steadfast. He forgives Gorgas, who caused the accident, and convinces him not to take his own life. Standing by his daughter's bed—whose life has expired in a soft-focus shot of her head on the pillow complete with halo lighting—the pastor murmurs, "in the darkness God awaits us."[17] His strong belief begins to move Doctor Badenhausen away from her skepticism, although to say that it saved her would be going too far—something for which the two primary religiously based film journals are thankful.[18] Cinematically aligned with the doctor, the audience sees the photo-ready but filmed portrait of the departed Lotte Heger, which counterbalances the photo of Badenhausen's own daughter that remained unseen, pictured while alive and yet loved as dead, as trapped in a meaningless, flat death. The systems designed to reencase death in meaning grow undeniably stronger at the end of *Nachtwache*. As the Pastor sings "Jesus, my Joy" ("Jesu meine Freude"), the doctor recognizes the power of his faith to bestow meaning: "He doesn't need me,"[19] she says, as a type of bookend to her previous statement "I don't have her."[20]

The Chaplain von Imhoff in *Nachtwache*, embodied by actor Dieter Borsche as calm and constant, is touched but not challenged in his faith by empathy for his counterpart's pain. Already practicing the stiff, slightly distant bemusement that will mark the characters he becomes famous for portraying in later "doctor films," Borsche played a string of spiritual figures at the outset of the Adenauer era (for example, Braun's next film, *Der fallende Stern* [1950]). In *Der Kaplan von San Lorenzo* (Ucicky, 1953), Borsche again appears as a man of the cloth but this time one at the center of the spiritual struggle. A film that bears remarkable similarities to Hitchcock's *I Confess* (which was released a month later in February 1953), *Der Kaplan von San Lorenzo* revolves around a holy man who claims responsibility for a murder that he did not commit in order to maintain the seal of confession. He is driven to this extreme by his unconsummated, yet amorous relationship with Gilda, the young woman who stands to be convicted by overwhelming, if circumstantial, evidence. Photographs, both unseen and seen, play a vital role in the chaplain's trials, but not as evidence in the juridical sense. The key sequence in which he reveals his feelings for Gilda to his brother in faith, Quirino, is conveyed initially through a voiced-over flashback, in which the private viewing of photos (i.e., photos seen by characters but not by the film audience) rewards close examination.

Don Stefano reports that he first saw Gilda when she appeared at his service in Verona and fainted from weakness caused by hunger. She became his charge, and feelings grew between them over time. Their adventures together even included a play-acting scene at the "Romeo and Juliet Balcony," which the audience sees superimposed as the chaplain speaks to Quirino. In a key moment for their relationship, Gilda shows him her most treasured belongings, photos from the life that the war had taken away. The screenplay describes the way that Gilda:

> *shows him photos from a big envelope one after the other. / Original sound from the [interior] scene*
> GILDA. That was our factory in Orvieto—Naturally it's all destroyed now—and here is my father hunting . . . he often took me with him—I was eight there—that was in the second year of the war—just before my father fell—and here (*she smiles in slight embarrassment*) my first boyfriend, Giovanni—we played a lot of tennis together—then he fell, too.[21]

As in *Nachtwache*, these photographs from the war years are shown privately. The superimposition quite clearly shows Gilda exhibiting the pictures to Don Stefano but keeping them masked from the film audience; however, their content and meaning are "talked" into the story.[22] They serve to document the life before, what has-been, but now has no meaning except to be accepted as dead, as having no afterlife: "I don't have her." In the diegetic conversations about these photographs between characters who can see them, those qualities are then described for the audience in order to reinforce loss; it also controls the potentially palpable connection to an undesirable past that might be animated for many viewers. That intermedial *Gemeinheit* (meanness/commonality) is instead transposed into the level of narrative. As Gilda finishes, Don Stefano gives the photo back and stands up saying, "Nice young man" (*Netter Bursche*), which indicates his sense of rivalry with and yet connection to the younger "friend" (strengthened by being nearly a pun on Borsche's name). Then he launches into a conversation explicitly highlighting the similarities in background between himself and his much younger charge, similarities that are far from "common": both came from money, played tennis, drove cars very fast, and, "naturally," lost everything because of the war. Connection to and distance from the past are attributed to the photograph by "talking" the pictures rather than showing them.

The film's form enacts this doubling and diffusing of "pastness," as the screenplay illustrates. Don Stefano first narrates the beginnings of his relationship with Gilda accompanied by images of their early time together that the audience sees in superimposition; however, in the scene with the photos, the presentation switches to original soundtrack and the superimposition drops away, as does the present scene between Quirino and Don Stefano. Gilda "talks" the pictures of her distant past in the war directly from the more recent past in Verona. The photograph of Giovanni, returned by the pensive Don Stefano to the slightly embarrassed Gilda, goes back into the envelope with the others—like Dr. Badenhausen's photo of her daughter, it is kept as an unseen, private talisman.

The fate of the other photo that features prominently in *Der Kaplan von San Lorenzo* is quite different. The Friar Quirino visits the prison after Don Stefano refuses to retract his confession in order to free himself. He berates the chaplain for the sin of lying, which, he points out, does not honor the true meaning of the seal of confession. But then he changes his mode. Since the police are planning to search Don Stefano's quarters for damning evidence, Quirino feels it better that they not find "this": he produces a photo of Gilda, which he holds out for the captive (and the audience) to see. A slightly high-angle shot approximating Don Stefano's POV excludes everything except the photo and a portion of Quirino's hand. The photo is a portrait shot of Gilda in the same dress that she wore in the two flashback moments already discussed. Ucicky shows this photo to the audience in a manner that corresponds to Metz's description of the photographic *voici*: "an actualizing and demonstrative 'there is,' . . . inherent and proper to [photographic] images rather than film."[23] In inserting this formal difference, the photograph and its referent become overtly communal and present. The intermedial stillness of the photograph, occupying nearly the entire screen but clearly remaining within the frame, issues a formal challenge that must be addressed. The film answers this challenge narratively. Don Stefano does not take the snapshot; instead, he says, "destroy it" (*vernichte es*), upon which his friend tears the photo into pieces, returns them to his wallet, and tucks it away. In terms of narrative motivation, Don Stefano refuses to hold onto—or even to hold—the picture because he is trying to free himself from a love that he knows is wrong according to the vows of his order. However, it is also a refusal of what the image entails according to Barthes, Metz, and others—namely, that *that* Gilda is dead, and he must learn to love her as dead. Had Don Stefano taken the photo and secreted it away he, in essence, would have echoed Dr. Badenhausen: "I don't have her anymore. She is dead." That gesture would have negated his sacrifice to let her live.

Remarkably, this sequence as filmed differs from the description in the screenplay. In the script, Quirino shows the image to the prisoner and then simply puts it away, keeping it to himself (presumably for Don Stefano). In the film's final version, the one released in 1953, the death of the photo's object is countered by the destruction of the photo itself, and, since the image is proffered formally to the audience along with Don Stefano through the POV shot, this makes public the private, fetish character of the photo. The destruction of the portrait eradicates the temptation to fetishize for Don Stefano (and the play on that fetishization through the film *à* la Metz);[24] its aftermath gives the audience back the woman herself. She appears for the viewer near the film's end, moving to a new country and life, while the chaplain (cleared of the charges by a dogged detective and the death of the real murderer) "never sees Gilda again" (*sieht Gilda niemals wieder*).[25] He is exiled to service in the remote and destitute village of Cavallo, where he is to reestablish his relationship with God. By intervening at the narrative level to destroy Gilda's photograph in front of the audience and to point Don Stefano back toward God, the final version of *Der Kaplan von San Lorenzo* solves the intermedial dilemma posed by the photograph within it.

One last example serves to establish the lengths films go to in order to combat the dangerousness of photography's temporal disturbance, private presence, and secular stillness at the outset of Adenauer-era cinema. *Die seltsame Geschichte des Brandner Kaspar* (von Báky, 1949) stands out among late 1940s productions for being a mainstream film almost entirely in Bavarian dialect.[26] It exhibits a regional pride that perhaps sprang from the same source that six months earlier led the Bavarian Parliament to make a show of rejecting the new Basic Law for its insufficient federalism. Still, it is also full of loving jibes at the locality's foibles that help the plot's initial two strands roll into one. It starts as young Mena is courted and walked home from a village fair by two characters: the impish poacher, Gidi, and the much older hunting guide (or *Brandner*), Kaspar. Unlike so many post-World War II films, this story avoids age-inappropriate love motivations, because Kaspar realizes on their way into the mountains that Mena is smitten with Gidi and so resigns himself to a more properly paternal relationship with her.[27] Leaving the two lovers, he walks back to his cabin, where he looks at a photo of his deceased wife, Nannerl. As if in response to a silent rebuke, he remarks that he was only interested because Mena has "eyes like yours" (*deine Augen*). The photo, framed on the mantelpiece, serves as the fetish object showing that Kaspar has come to love Nannerl *as* dead; however, this presentation lacks the visual intimacy and immediacy that the audience senses in the *voici* moment with Gilda's photo in *Der Kaplan von San Lorenzo*. Kaspar's private moment is shared visually with the audience in a shot reverse shot sequence—the standard formal means of putting the viewer within a dialogue. A comic tension is generated between the formal presentation and the dialogue itself because it consists only of Kaspar's voice. Following this introduction, the consistent presence of Nannerl's framed image in the mise-en-scène normalizes the *Brandner*'s private world as a communal space that includes the film audience.

The second, and actually primary, strand of the film begins with this address to Nannerl's photograph, which manifests the permanence of her death. Later that same night, Death himself visits Kaspar because it is his time; the *Brandner*, however, has other ideas and initiates a wild drinking bout during which he swindles death out of twenty extra years of life. The seventy-year-old literally feels that he has a renewed youth, while Death gets in humorously hot water with his superiors, who are checking names in front of the pearly gates. In order to correct the heavenly ledgers, they send Death back down to get Kaspar, but, having given his word, Death now has to convince him to come to the great beyond voluntarily. Needless to say, Kaspar is having none of it—at least not until the other plot strain intervenes.

Figure 3.1. *Seltsame Geschichte.* Directed by Josef von Báky. Munich: Bavaria Filmkunst, 1949. Source: Deutsche Kinemathek archive, Berlin, Germany, used with permission.

The local game warden, Kreitmeier, who seems equally hot to win Mena and nab Gidi, lays a trap for the poacher. After helping her lover sneak out the back, Mena dons his clothes and goes out in the twilight to lead the warden away but is shot and killed in the process. The sadness Kaspar feels at this makes him susceptible to Death, who explains that although it *seems* unfair that Mena is gone, she is going to be happier, and that Brandner could convince himself of that if he would just come along for a visit. Here is the second key moment in the film when Kaspar talks to Nannerl's photograph. He asks rhetorically what she thinks of Death's proposal; but instead of remaining silent, the photo suddenly comes to life inside its frame and speaks. Her saucy response is that he should give it a try, since she has now seen that younger girl, and she does have "my eyes!" (*meine Augen!*). The prospect of reuniting with his heart's companion (Nannerl) in a world that looks just like the one he loves so much is enough to send Kaspar on his way with Death.

The photo of Nannerl not only becomes the point of conjunction between the two plot strands, subsuming the tragic one into the comic one; it also becomes animated to defeat—or at least ban from this farce—the photograph's multifaceted connection to death. In this film, the audience initially sees the image as a token of meaningless death that opens Kaspar's private world to the audience. This "opening" was withheld at key moments of private sharing about loss in *Nachtwache* and *Der Kaplan von San Lorenzo*. However, once the picture comes to life in von Báky's film it denies the existence of any such private world in two ways. Formally, the animated image moves all images into the common world of cinematic belief by destroying the photograph as a possible repository of the private. In doing so, the animated image thematically removes any distinction between the social world's private and shared arenas in favor of an all-encompassing Christian community under the eyes of a God who permits no privacy. If the still photograph maintains a trace of the myth of the private, it cannot be left to stand in the *Brandner*'s "unusual story." It is forced to give way through animation to a timeless eternal life posited by the film's playful dogma precisely as an absence of stillness. The quiet pause entailed in the photographic *voici* becomes the frenetic annunciation of an imaginary *voila*![28]

Coda: Animation and Adventure

The three examples mentioned above narrativize how cinema destroys the photograph in the service of a faith that denies reflexive constructions. That destruction is deemed necessary as a matter of belief both cinematic and religious. Campany points out that the stillness of photography does not partake of the "voyeuristic unfolding" of cinema, which suspends disbelief, because photography itself "can suspend the world but not . . . disbelief."[29] *Nachtwache* puts disbelief in abeyance by enclosing it in a locket with a photo-portrait near the film's outset and then countering it with a filmed sequence of a girl's portrait-ready passage to the afterlife near the end. *Der Kaplan von San Lorenzo* brings the private, profane fetish of a portrait into public view within the narrative, but then uses the photograph's destruction to reopen a path to faith. Von Báky's *Die seltsame Geschichte des Brandner Kaspar* takes the furthest step by animating Kaspar's dead wife's photograph—that is, eradicating its dual stillness by infusing it with movement and speech—which formally embeds a willful suspension of disbelief in the service of a faith that insists on the nonexistence of death. These films deny the lives that-had-been before the photographic camera and thus defuse the photograph's potential to witness and to spark. Notably, they do this from within a range of genres and tones: Braun's film, a somber melodrama; Ucicky's, equal parts coy love story, crime procedural, and spiritual journey; and von Báky's, a farcical comedy that nonetheless believes.[30] What they share is the goal of keeping control over the animation of the viewer. Barthes gives us a hint when he says that out of the "glum desert" of images "a photograph reaches me; it animates me, and I animate it. . . . The photograph itself is in no way animated (I do not believe in 'lifelike' photographs), but it animates me; this is what creates every adventure."[31]

This chapter concludes with perhaps a more familiar example of animation and adventure. Another von Báky product, *Münchhausen* (1943), is a filmic farce that denies death's purchase on German existence, although the pan-German presence of Hans Albers' timeless Münchhausen differs a good deal from the regional specificity of Carl Wery's Kaspar. The filmmakers use all manner of cinematic sleight-of-hand to present the roguish Baron's exploits, but the key moment comes at the conclusion, in one of the three instances when a painting is animated on screen. Judging by the clothes, the viewer assumes that the 1943 film ends roughly in the present, although no sign of the war troubles the screen. After his bawdy, earthly, and extraterrestrial adventures from a span of some two hundred years have entertained the viewer for over two hours, Münchhausen decides that he desires nothing more than to grow old and pass on with his beloved Baroness. As he looks up at the portrait above the mantelpiece showing his younger self from the 1700s, he renounces the spell that has made him immortal and turns back to join his Baroness as an aged man. The old couple retires from the drawing room, symbolically "going to bed"; however, when the attendant dims the electric lights to retire using candlelight, the portrait of the adventurer as a young man comes to life three times to blow out the flames, wreathing itself in smoke that then morphs into the closing script, "Ende."

This final painting-come-to-life gag is arresting because it functions in a way opposed to what we saw in von Báky's later film. *Münchhausen* uses the formal trick to make the acceptance of death the real means to mythic immortality. The portrait's steady presence in the mise-en-scène enunciates a life from "before" that never was, and its coming to life at the film's end animates the viewer in the continuation of the adventurer's myth.[32] As Barthes notes, "painting can feign reality without having seen it," but "no painted portrait, supposing that it seemed 'true' to me, could compel me to believe its referent had really existed."[33] The German hero who never existed cannot escape the world of the National Socialists, his death and its impending destruction notwithstanding, because that death is the essence of its existence.

The audience members in 1943 *were* to be animated through that trick. Alternately, giving life to Nannerl's photo in *Die seltsame Geschichte des Brandner Kasper* dispels formal tensions by raising them to the level of narrative and defusing them, which inaugurates the denial of death and the embrace of the religious afterlife. It *prevents* the animation of which Barthes speaks.

Surely, it can be surmised that von Báky is playing on audience's memories of the trick from his earlier, immensely popular film when he erases the stillness of Nannerl's photo on the mantelpiece, denying its connection to a death that-has-been and will-remain. Yet, that gesture back to his work from just six years earlier counteracts the redemption that *Die seltsame Geschichte des Brandner Kaspar* works so hard to introduce into the world. As Sabine Hake notes regarding *Münchhausen*, it had a dual project of erasing the lines between fact and fiction combined with those of the "distinctions evoked under the heading of 'film and the other arts.' [In turn they] demonstrate the power of film to appropriate, incorporate, and reconfigure existing art forms."[34] *Die seltsame Geschichte des Brandner Kaspar* turns on a similar attempt to reanimate a still image, but in doing so it risks showing what is more than common about the photograph in Adenauer-era cinema. The photographic medium, its ritualized colocation through cultural communication, holds the potential to expose the moving-image industry's roots in the myth-making of the National Socialist era, roots inseparable from the eradication of lives in its project of recreating an eternal afterlife for those in the present. Ultimately, the films discussed here proceed as they do in order to keep the photograph within the film from animating the adventure of probing the wounds of before- and afterlives in the early Adenauer era.

John E. Davidson is Professor of Germanic Languages and Literatures at Ohio State University. He is the author of *Deterritorializing the New German Cinema* (1999). His articles on German Cinema spanning from early film to films of the Third Reich to TV documentaries have appeared in journals like the *Alexander Kluge-Jahrbuch, Colloquia Germanica, German Studies Review, New German Critique*, and *PMLA* and edited volumes like *A Companion to Werner Herzog* (2012), *German Cinema since 2000* (2011), *The Collapse of the Conventional: German Film and its Politics at the Turn of the New Century* (2010) and *Light Motives* (2003) among others. His current projects include manuscripts on "Damaged Life and the Cinema: Art, Media, and Cultural Politics in the Long Adenauer Era."

Notes

1. I prefer *mean* to *mean-spirited* because it carries the same ambiguity as the German *gemein* through its Old English root. It carries the sense of both "low-quality" as well as "common, public . . . shared by all." *Mean-spirited* evacuates that resonance.
2. Cf. Roland Barthes, *Camera Lucida: Reflections on Photography*, trans. Richard Howard (New York: Hill and Wang, 1981), 62ff. David Campany notes that this out-of-sync mediation in Barthes constitutes a "pause," and that pause allows for a pensiveness that moving pictures do not admit. See David Campany, *Photography and Cinema* (London: Reaktion Books, 2008), 96. Both Barthes and Siegfried Kracauer approach terms like *cognizance* and *recognition* in a manner that seems more in line with a Benjaminian innervation than more recent cognitive approaches to film. See Siegfried Kracauer, *Theory of Film: The Redemption of Physical Reality* (Princeton: Princeton University Press, 1997), 15; for Walter Benjamin's sense that there is "no imagination without innervation," see Walter Benjamin, "One-Way Street" and, for a more utopian formulation, Walter Benjamin, "Surrealism," in *One-Way Street and Other Writings*, trans. Edmund Jephcott and Kingsley Shorter (London: Verso, 1985).
3. On the idea of media convergence in German film of the 1940s, see Sabine Hake, "The Münchhausen Complex: From Adaptation to Intermediality," *ILCEA Online* 23 (July 2015): 1–13. My use of the "filmic medium" follows from Lisa Gitelman's understanding that "media [are] socially realized structures of communication, where structures include both technological forms and their associated protocols, and where communication is a cultural practice, a ritualized collocation of different people on the same mental map, sharing or engaged with popular ontologies of representation." Lisa Gitelman, *Always Already New: Media, History, and the Data of Culture* (Cambridge, MA: MIT Press, 2006), 7.
4. Barthes, *Camera Lucida*, 21. Eric Rentschler points out that the Staudte's transformation of the rubble into a nighttime set through lighting was itself turned into a surreal photograph of postwar Berlin by Henry Ries, carrying over the acts of remediation from the Weimar era that Andreas Huyssen has identified. Eric Rentschler, "The Management of Shattered Identity," in *The Use and Abuse of Cinema: German Legacies from the Weimar Era to the Present* (New York: Columbia University Press, 2015), 145.
5. Barthes, *Camera Lucida*, 92.
6. *Problemstellung*, the posing of a problem, contains a sense of placement that is important for my argument but can be lost in the English phrase. The photograph within film inhabits a site that itself is a formal problem.
7. Campany, *Photography and Cinema*, 139.
8. Christian Metz, "Photography and Fetish," in *Photography and Cinema: 50 Years of Chris Marker's* La Jetée, ed. Margarida Medeiros, Teresa Mendes Flores, and Joana Cunha Leal, (Newcastle upon Tyne: Cambridge Scholars Publishing, 2015), 19.
9. The films in this chapter will be referred to with their German titles.
10. While scholars have established the clear investment of Christian institutions in post-World War II cinema as an arena to reassert their claims of moral and social authority, relatively little has been written on the role of the religious in structuring cinematic works themselves. See Heide Fehrenbach, *Cinema in Democratizing Germany: Reconstructing National Identity after Hitler* (Chapel Hill: University of North Carolina Press, 1995); Robert G. Moeller, "Winning the Peace at the Movies: Suffering, Loss, and Redemption in Postwar German Cinema," in *Histories of the Aftermath: The Lega-*

cies of the Second World War in Europe, ed. Frank Biess and Robert G. Moeller (New York: Berghahn Books, 2010); Ute G. Poiger, *Jazz, Rock, and Rebels: Cold War Politics and American Culture in a Divided Germany* (Berkeley: University of California Press, 2000). Olaf Möller is leading the way in investigating the centrality of (Christian) religious forms in the films of this period. I am especially indebted to the work that he put into mounting the *Seelennot* (*Spiritual Distress*) series at the Zeughaus Kino of the Deutsches Historisches Museum in Berlin in summer 2017.

11. Tim Bergfelder, "From Rubble to Prosperity: Reconstruction of a National Film Industry," in *International Adventures: German Popular Cinema and European Co-Productions in the 1960s* (New York: Berghahn Books, 2005), 27.
12. The accepted English translation of *Nachtwache* as *Keepers of the Night* misses the religious notion of the vigil that is embedded in the original.
13. "Vier typische Menschen unserer Tage." HS, "Nachtwache," *Evangelischer Film-Beobachter* 21, (1949): 93.
14. The film and screenplay name no cause of death, but some of the reviews point to an aerial bombing.
15. "Ich hab' sie auch nicht mehr. Sie ist tot."
16. Metz, "Photography and Fetish," 15. Barthes confesses that "I am uncomfortable during the private projection of a film (not enough of a public, not enough anonymity), but I need to be alone with the photographs I am looking at." Barthes, *Camera Lucida*, 97. The *Problemstellung* of the photograph within the film could shake the comfortable anonymity of the public film audience.
17. "In der Dunkelheit wartet Gott auf uns."
18. "The beauty of this film is the fact that nobody is converted" (*Das Schöne an diesem Film ist die Tatsache, dass keiner bekehrt wird*). Werner Hess, "Zur Uraufführung von *Nachtwache*," *Kirche und Film* 21 (1949): 2. Variations of this sentiment appear throughout the first "Echo" from the daily and trade-press about *Nachtwache*, which is glossed in the same publication. Ibid., 3–7. It includes nonreligious publications such as the *Hannoversche Allgemeine Zeitung*: "It is the strength of the film, that it doesn't try to convert" (*Es ist die Stärke des Filmes, dass er nicht zu bekehren versucht*). Ibid., 6. This response continues to shape the public perception of the film as reported by organs of the *Evangelisches Pressverband für Deutschland*: "The intention of the film is neither to preach nor convert, but rather the elucidation of the emotional/spiritual situation of our time" (*Die Absicht des Filmes sei nicht zu predigen oder zu bekehren, sondern die Aufhellung der seelischen Situation unserer Gegenwart*). NA, "Frank Thiess spricht in Bremen zur *Nachtwache*," *Kirche und Film* 3 (1950): 5. Werner Hess' article contains numerous references that explicitly state that the film's strength is that it did not try to convert anyone, a sentiment echoed by Frank Thiess as well. See Hess, "Zur Uraufführung," 2, 3–7, 6; see also NA, "Frank Thiess," 5.
19. "Der braucht mich nicht."
20. "Ich habe sie nicht."
21. "*Ziegt ihm aus einem grossen Briefumschlag nacheinander einige Fotos. / Originalton der Szene/ GILDA*: 'Das war unsere Fabrik in Orvieto—Jetzt ist natürlich alles kaput—und hier ist mein Vater auf der Jagd . . . er hat mich oft mitgenommen—da war ich acht—das war im zweiten Kriegsjahr—kurz bevor mein Vater fiel—und hier—[*sie lächelt ein bisschen verlegen*]—mein erster Freund Giovanni—wir haben viel miteinander Tennis gespielt—er ist dann auch gefallen." Kurt E. Walter, "Der Kaplan von San Lorenzo" (unpublished screenplay), (Berlin: Schriftgutarchiv, Stiftung Deutsche Kinemathek, 1952), 122.
22. While the film itself does not reveal the front side of the photos, the publicity and production images all do. See, for example, the image in *Film-Dienst*, the organ of the

Catholic film commission in CK Film Dienst 3. The autonomy of the "Filmstandbild" that Winfried Pauleit discusses puts them at odds with the meaning of the film as I elucidate it below.

23. Christian Metz, "The Impersonal Enunciation, or the Site of Film (In the Margin of Recent works on Enunciation in Cinema)," trans. Béatrice Durand-Sendrail and Kristen Brookes, *New Literary History* 22, no. 3 (1991): 756.
24. Metz concludes: "After this long digression, I turn back to my topic and purpose, only to state that they could be summed up in one sentence: film is more capable of playing on fetishism, photography more capable of itself becoming a fetish." Metz, "Photography and Fetish," 24.
25. Walter, "Der Kaplan von San Lorenzo" (unpublished screenplay), 160.
26. In this, at least, it follows the story that served as the source, first published in the year that the German Empire was grounded (Franz von Kobell, "Der Brandner Kaspar," *Der fliegenden Blätter* [1871]). It is perhaps worth noting that firms in and around Munich (co-) produced all the Adenauer-era films that I discuss in this chapter (*Nachtwache* was coproduced with the Filmaufbau in Göttingen).
27. See Jaimey Fisher's work for a discussion of age-appropriateness in post-World War II cinema. Jaimey Fisher, *Disciplining Germany: Youth, Reeducation, and Reconstruction after the Second World War* (Detroit: Wayne State University Press, 2007). While Carl Wery's character removes himself from that embarrassing scenario, it should be noted that Viktor Staal is perhaps a bit mature for the role he plays here as scamp and lover.
28. A review in a Catholic film-research publication bemoans the occasional moments when the film fails to keep its various internal tones consistent but finds that, even though the movie transgresses good taste occasionally, it does so in keeping with its folksy temperament. It does not really disrespect the holy at any point. In fact, precisely because of the film's indexical quality, von Báky's over-the-top presentation may be the only mode of cinema that can safely approach representing the heavenly sphere. VF, "Der Brandner Kaspar," *Kirche und Film* 24 (1949): 7–8.
29. Campany, *Photography and Cinema*, 139.
30. The directors discussed here are difficult to bring under a single rubric, and definitive cultural–political tendencies are difficult to discern even within their individual oeuvre. Braun and Ucicky made what the times told them would sell, which took them across a range of genres and attitudes, as did von Báky. Although the *Münchhausen / Der seltsame Geschichte des Brandner Kaspar* connection that I point out below indicates a parallelism between the mythmaking of the NS and of the forces for Christianity in the Adenauer age, von Báky is in many ways the most multifaceted and nuanced of these three directors. Johannes von Moltke points to his *Via Mala* (1944) as belonging to the tradition that challenges *Heimat* as dark and sinister, something to be left behind rather than extolled and restored. Johannes von Moltke, *No Place like Home: Locations of Heimat in German Cinema* (Berkeley: University of California Press, 2005), 112–13. Similarly, von Bàky's *Der Ruf* (1949, filmed and premiered before the signing of the Basic Law) looks squarely at vestiges of the Nazi era that survive into the postwar occupation.
31. Barthes, *Camera Lucida*, 20.
32. This in some ways rehearses the historical role of the oil painting following its introduction as the cultural vehicle of the new class that had not had a previous existence but was to rise to near mythical dominance over life. John Berger, *Ways of Seeing* (London: BBC and Penguin Books, 1972).
33. Barthes, *Camera Lucida*, 76.
34. Hake, "The Münchhausen Complex," 8.

Bibliography

Barthes, Roland. *Camera Lucida: Reflections on Photography*. Translated by Richard Howard. New York: Hill and Wang, 1981.

Benjamin, Walter. *One-Way Street and Other Writings*. Translated by Edmund Jephcott and Kingsley Shorter. London: Verso, 1985.

Berger, John. *Ways of Seeing*. London: BBC and Penguin Books, 1972.

Bergfelder, Tim. "From Rubble to Prosperity: Reconstruction of a National Film Industry." In *International Adventures: German Popular Cinema and European Co-Productions in the 1960s*, 19–52. New York: Berghahn Books, 2005.

Campany, David. *Photography and Cinema*. London: Reaktion Books, 2008.

CK. "Der Kaplan von San Lorenzo." *Film Dienst* (1953): 3.

Fehrenbach, Heide. *Cinema in Democratizing Germany: Reconstructing National Identity after Hitler*. Chapel Hill: University of North Carolina Press, 1995.

Fisher, Jaimey. *Disciplining Germany: Youth, Reeducation, and Reconstruction after the Second World War*. Detroit: Wayne State University Press, 2007.

Gitelman, Lisa. *Always Already New: Media, History, and the Data of Culture*. Cambridge, MA: MIT Press, 2006.

Hake, Sabine. "The Münchhausen Complex: From Adaptation to Intermediality." *ILCEA Online* 23 (July 2015): 1–13. https://journals.openedition.org/ilcea/3310.

Hess, Werner. "Zur Uraufführung von *Nachtwache*." *Kirche und Film* 21 (1949): 1–7.

HS. "Nachtwache." *Evangelischer Film-Beobachter* 21 (1949): 93–94.

Huyssen, Andreas. *Miniature Metropolis: Literature in an Age of Photography and Film*. Cambridge, MA: Harvard University Press, 2015.

Kracauer, Siegfried. *Theory of Film: The Redemption of Physical Reality*. Princeton: Princeton University Press, 1997.

Metz, Christian. "The Impersonal Enunciation, or the Site of Film (In the Margin of Recent works on Enunciation in Cinema)." Translated by Béatrice Durand-Sendrail and Kristen Brookes. *New Literary History* 22, no. 3 (1991): 747–72.

———. "Photography and Fetish." In *Photography and Cinema: 50 Years of Chris Marker's* La Jetée, edited by Margarida Medeiros, Teresa Mendes Flores, and Joana Cunha Leal, 14–24. Newcastle upon Tyne: Cambridge Scholars Publishing, 2015.

Moeller, Robert G. "Winning the Peace at the Movies: Suffering, Loss, and Redemption in Postwar German Cinema." In *Histories of the Aftermath: The Legacies of the Second World War in Europe*, edited by Frank Biess and Robert G. Moeller, 139–55. New York: Berghahn Books, 2010.

NA. "Erste Echo aus der Tages- und Fachpresse zur *Nachtwache*, Das." *Kirche und Film* 21 (1949): 3–7.

———. "Frank Thiess spricht in Bremen zur *Nachtwache*." *Kirche und Film* 3 (1950): 4–5.

Pauleit, Winfried. *Filmstandbilder: Passangen zwischen Kunst und Kino*. Frankfurt: Stroemfeld, 2004.

Poiger, Ute G. *Jazz, Rock, and Rebels: Cold War Politics and American Culture in a Divided Germany*. Berkeley: University of California Press, 2000.

Rentschler, Eric. "The Management of Shattered Identity." In *The Use and Abuse of Cinema: German Legacies from the Weimar Era to the Present*, 133–58. New York: Columbia University Press, 2015.

von Kobell, Franz. "Der Brandner Kaspar." *Der fliegenden Blätter* (1871).

von Moltke, Johannes. *No Place like Home: Locations of Heimat in German Cinema*. Berkeley: University of California Press, 2005.

VF. "Der Brandner Kaspar." *Kirche und Film* 24 (1949): 7–8.
Walter, Kurt E. "Der Kaplan von San Lorenzo" (unpublished screenplay). Berlin: Schriftgutarchiv, Stiftung Deutsche Kinemathek, 1952.

Filmography

Listed with the German title first for this chapter only, except Hitchcock.

Der fallende Stern. Directed by Harald Braun. Munich: NDF, 1950.
Der Kaplan von San Lorenzo. Directed by Gustav Ucicky. Munich: Willi Zeyn Film, 1953.
Der Ruf. Directed by Josef von Báky. Munich: Objektiv-Film, 1949.
Die Mörder sind unter uns (The Murderers Are Among Us). Directed by Wolfgang Staudte. Berlin: Deutsche Film AG, 1946.
Die seltsame Geschichte des Brandner Kaspar. Directed by Josef von Báky. Munich: Bavaria Filmkunst, 1949.
I Confess. Directed by Alfred Hitchcock. Burbank: Warner Brothers, 1953.
Münchhausen. Directed by Josef von Báky. Berlin: UFA, 1943.
Nachtwache (*Keepers of the Night*). Directed by Harald Braun. Munich: NDF, 1949.
Via Mala. Directed by Josef von Báky. Berlin: UFA, 1944.

Chapter 4

Filming after Walker Evans

Wim Wenders' "American Photographs" in *Kings of the Road* (1976)

Stefanie Harris

> Two of the things photography does best:
> clarify as though on a dare; and celebrate things as they are.
>
> —Walker Evans, "Photography," 198

In the late 1980s, Wim Wenders was asked to serve as guest editor of the four hundredth issue of *Cahiers du cinéma*. The general theme of the issue was "*cinéma en germe*," and the issue included an extended article in which Wenders elaborated on the "seeds" or origins of the thirteen full-length features he had produced to date.[1] Throughout the article, Wenders highlights especially the roles of music and of specific images (photographs, album covers, and paintings) as his catalysts, and the article is interspersed with film stills and numerous photographs taken by Wenders both during and outside of film production. As Alain Bergala and Serge Toubiana note in their introduction to the issue, Wenders was well-known, at the time, for his photographs and for the ways in which those images often served as "latent fictions" that became touchpoints for his films.[2] The section of the article on Wenders' film *Alice in the Cities* (*Alice in den Städten*, 1974), for example, includes a two-page photo spread with photographs Wenders took on location in Rockaway Beach, Queens; various street scenes around New York City; and images broadcast on the television. With these photographs, Wenders is both scouting possible locations for filming and exploring themes that would

Figure 4.1. Walker Evans, *Savoy Barber Shops, Vicksburg, Mississippi*, 1936, gelatin silver print, New York, The Metropolitan Museum of Art. Photo: © Walker Evans Archive (The Metropolitan Museum of Art), used with permission.

go on to be developed in the film. Similarly, the section of the article on his road film *Kings of the Road* (*Im Lauf der Zeit*, 1976) includes five photographs of the exteriors of movie theaters that Wenders shot while scouting locations along the border of West and East Germany and which serve as settings for a series of episodes in the film. Immediately following these images of movie houses, however, Wenders provides another "seed" for his film when he reprints two photographs taken by the prominent twentieth-century American photographer Walker Evans (1903–75). A third Evans photograph appears later in the issue within a sequence of Wenders' own photographs from a solo exhibition at the Centre Georges Pompidou in 1980 titled, "Written in the West." Evans' reprinted photographs all date from 1936 during his work for the Farm Security Administration (FSA), and they depict the exteriors of a warehouse, a barber shop (figure 4.1), and a gas station, all in the American South.

Figure 4.2. *Kings of the Road (Im Lauf der Zeit*). Directed by Wim Wenders. Munich: Wim Wenders Produktion, 1976. Screen capture by Stefanie Harris.

In longhand, Wenders draws the reader's attention to three specific elements of Evans' photographs: the framing, the light, and the texture of the building façades. All three of these characteristics are duplicated and are on display in the cinematic images of *Kings of the Road*, and the image (figure 4.2) of two of the film's characters at a train station is explicitly juxtaposed with Evans' photos in Wenders' article. This is more than just a visual reference. *Kings of the Road* incorporates both the material and aesthetic structures of Evans' photographs and photobooks, including the seriality of their organization, the composition of the shots, and the statements they make about the social and media landscapes of their respective countries.

If *Kings of the Road* is about "the consciousness of cinema in Germany" (as its director purports), then it can be understood as a visual catalog of the everyday, registering the industry's decline and change—generational and technological—while tenderly documenting the unheralded components of the West German postwar social condition.[3] Walker Evans' photography and his photobook *American Photographs* (1938) serve as touchstones for Wenders in *Kings of the Road*, not only for its depiction of the material landscape of the seemingly abandoned border of a divided Germany but also for the film's presentation of the state of West German cinema in the 1970s.[4] Many of the images in *Kings of the Road* are a way of seeing and preserving the last vestiges of a cinematic history whose social and economic value is in rapid decline. No single image communicates this comprehensive statement, however. Nor does the film build linearly to a climax and resolution. Instead, the juxtaposition of multiple scenes and images that repeat, contradict, refer forward and back, and link associatively have the cumulative effect of presenting an alternative cinema through a series of images that depicts its decline. Although scholars have frequently addressed Wenders' love–hate relationship to American film, music, and popular culture, the specific relationship of Wenders' films to Walker Evans' photographs and photobooks permits us to explore the American influence of a certain photographic practice.[5]

If the photobook has often been compared to cinema, I reverse the analogy here and consider film through the medium of the photobook.[6] Both as a unique art form (such as Evans' *American Photographs*) and as an artistic method more broadly, the photobook has much to offer the filmmaker. In particular, by offering a model that is sequential but not linear, the serial nature of the photobook allows for active consumption practices and fosters a mode of seeing that relies on a slow accumulation of visual information freed from conventional narrative form. And in emulating Evans' documentary aesthetic, specifically, Wenders produces series of images that allow the viewer to apprehend physical reality in a different light. For the power of Evans' photographic images is not, as Joel Snyder has argued, that they show what any spectator might have seen if she were standing next to the photographer at the time the photograph was taken; but rather, the photographs are best "characterized as an act of the imagination" in which Evans "gave expression to his rules of attending, and in so doing he taught his audience to attend in the same manner."[7] Ultimately, Wenders' use of Evans' *documentary style* reveals how photography, especially photographs in a series, can function as a metaphor for critical inquiry and a model for criticism. In denaturalizing the viewer's relationship to the photographic image, Wenders rebuilds a spectatorial platform that reclaims a tradition of realist cinema and engages a critical mode of seeing so crucial to New German Cinema.

Evans' *Documentary Style*: Realism with a Difference

Wenders writes that the appeal of Evans' photographs lies in their ability to "go right to the heart of the Depression."[8] Evans' photographs do not just show us places and people, but communicate a broader series of circumstances, emotions, and thoughts in their straightforward approach to material reality and in their deliberate sequencing in the photobooks in which the images publicly circulated.[9] Wenders links the subject matter of Evans' project to his own when he goes on to state: "The part of Germany we drove through, the no-man's land by the East German frontier, struck me as depressed too—everyone was leaving, it was an area without hope. We felt we were producing a kind of report, a little in the manner of Walker Evans."[10] A visual examination of Wenders' film shows the pictorial influence apparent in his selection of locations (gas stations, commercial buildings, abandoned buildings), the composition of the images (inclusion of advertising and signage, prominence of objects in enclosed spaces, contrast of organic forms and the built landscape), and the way in which shots are framed (frontal views with a minimum of shadow). Like Evans, Wenders spent weeks on the road, though Wenders brought along actors and film crew, creating *Kings of the Road* with only a loosely episodic structure. The result is a road-movie that follows two men traveling in a caravan along the former West German border with East Germany, from Lüneburg to Hof. Bruno Winter is a traveling repairman, visiting small movie theaters along the route and repairing film projectors; Robert Lander, a linguist who has left his wife, joins Bruno after surviving a suicide attempt. The small towns the two men visit resemble the content of Evans' photographs, and the desolate highways where they make camp bring intense visual focus on peripheral spaces and the detritus of a region far from the power centers of postwar West Germany, culminating in the climactic scene and confrontation staged in an abandoned US Army guard post on the East German border. Describing his film, Wenders wrote:

> You can detect the presence of Walker Evans, for instance in the scene where Bruno and Robert find these barracks; partly also, I suppose, because they were built by American GIs and have American graffiti on them. We found that little bit of America in no-man's-land in Germany; it's as if our muse and the physical reality coincided there. Often what we saw was determined by Evans' photographs. We would sometimes pull up on the road to shoot scenes because something in the landscape or the building happened to grab us. Once, we passed an old caravan that was being used as a mobile caff . . . and we spent the rest of the day filming in and around that caff. We'd never have noticed it, if it hadn't been for Walker Evans' photographs.[11]

Like Evans, Wenders creates a visual catalog of the everyday and the mundane in his attempt at a visual essay of the German postwar social condition (or, more limited, the male social condition). Wenders' framing technique, like Evans', appears art-less—what Lincoln Kirstein called "straight" photography "in the rigorous directness of its way of looking."[12] Both eschew dramatic camera angles or lighting as markers that draw attention to the photographer. And yet, the images are not wholly spontaneous. Wenders, like Evans, does not create snapshots;

Figure 4.3. Walker Evans, *Roadside View, Alabama Coal Area Company Town*, 1936, gelatin silver print, printed c. 1969 by Charles Rodemeyer, New York, The Metropolitan Museum of Art. Photo: © Walker Evans Archive (The Metropolitan Museum of Art), used with permission.

both the framing and presentation of the image are deliberate, even as the immediate photographic subject appears unplanned. Wenders' link to Evans is significant, however, not only in terms of a certain iconic identification with what Evans' photographs show, but also, and perhaps more importantly, in how the pictures show it, which is to say how the images are arranged in series. The film follows a series of repetitions, with similar scenes acted out in ten different movie theaters. In this catalog, or inventory of places, Wenders' camera documents film projection equipment that is either barely functioning or that no one appears to know how to use properly anymore, and the images capture the incidentals and material accumulations of the lived space of projection rooms that appear to be slowly disintegrating. Each space is unique and tells its own story of decline and generational and technological change, even as the cumulative effect of these images is

Figure 4.4. *Kings of the Road* (*Im Lauf der Zeit*). Directed by Wim Wenders. Munich: Wim Wenders Produktion, 1976. Screen capture by Stefanie Harris.

to present the viewer with the underlying reality of social dissolution, societal malaise, and the declining role of culture. The boom years of the German economic miracle have become the bust years of the seventies.

Wenders' photographic practice is informed by Evans' self-described program of a "documentary style,"[13] which was Evans' way of asserting that his camera only records what is in front of it but the resulting images are, nevertheless, always a subjective recording from a specific point of view and therefore ambiguous and open in their meaning. By *documentary style*, Evans sought to distinguish his photography from other forms of documentary images: "Documentary? That's a very sophisticated and misleading word. And not really clear. You have to have a sophisticated ear to receive that word. The term should be *documentary style*. An example of a literal document would be a police photograph of a murder scene. You see, a document has use, whereas art is really useless. Therefore art is never a document, though it certainly can adopt that style."[14] Wenders describes a similar paradox in his "dedication" both to the subject to be photographed and "the [technical] form that counterbalances" it.[15] The image both reproduces physical reality and itself functions as a singular moment that is unique and therefore not entirely coincident with the lived moment. This "coexistence" in Wenders' terms or *documentary style* for Evans is an assertion of the possibility of documenting at least some portion of reality and of communicating that reality to others through the image—which is another way of framing the contradiction of a photographic approach that, as Evans wrote in 1969, both "clarifies" and "celebrates" things as they are.[16]

For Wenders this other way of seeing is necessary in a period when social realities are masked by the numbing effects of commercial media, including television. When Bruno Winter's character edits together a highlight reel on infinite loop that repeats scenes of "Brutality! Action! Sex!," he is only creating a generic film trailer for most of the product in cinematic distribution. By contrast, the photographic work of Walker Evans speaks to the double nature of photography, an attribute specific to the medium that is fundamental to Wenders' own work: its ability to both record reality and to reveal reality, to have both a mimetic relationship to reality and to produce a distancing effect whereby social realities are laid bare. This media-specific definition is critical to what I call Wenders' "realism with a difference," an aesthetics of materiality that links Wenders not only to a history of photography, but also to the film theory of Siegfried Kracauer, especially as elaborated in Kracauer's *Theory of Film* (1960).[17] Wenders explicitly referenced *Theory of Film* in his film review of Sergio Leone's *Once Upon a Time in the West* (1968), stating: "Kracauer spoke of film as the 'redemption of physical reality,' meaning the tenderness that cinema can show towards reality."[18] In the preface to *Theory of Film*, Kracauer had immediately sought to set his theory of film apart: "My book differs from most writings in the field in that it is a *material* aesthetics, not a formal one. It is concerned with content. It rests upon the assumption that film is essentially an extension of photography and therefore shares with this medium a marked affinity for the visible world around us. Films come into their own when they record and reveal physical reality."[19]

In his broader categorization of films as either "realistic" or "formative," Kracauer claims that only films of the "realistic tendency" are properly speaking "cinematic," or what he elsewhere calls "photographic films."[20] Kracauer insists that if filmmakers are "true to the medium, they will certainly not move from a preconceived idea down to the material world in order to implement that idea; conversely, they set out to explore physical data and taking their cue from them, work their way up to some problem or belief. The cinema is materialistically minded; it proceeds from 'below' to 'above.' The importance of its natural bent for moving in this direction can hardly be overestimated."[21] Photography creates a different way of seeing, defamiliarizing that which is pictured even as it reproduces it; therefore, as Miriam Hansen has argued, "if Kracauer seeks to ground his film aesthetics in the medium of photography, it is because photographic representation has the perplexing ability not only to resemble the world it depicts but also to render it strange, to destroy habitual fictions of self-identity and familiarity."[22] Kracauer emphatically situates photography in the technological conditions of its production, and the photographic film that Kracauer privileges "explores," rather than "exploits," material phenomena.[23] Photography's affinities are thus with unstaged reality, the fortuitous, the endless, and the indeterminate. These are all hallmarks of what Wenders has referred to in a personal taxonomy as his "A" films (including, *Kings of the Road*), namely films that are more or less unscripted and episodically organized with an open-ended structure in which the film's themes "were identified only during shooting."[24] *Kings of the Road* is about "people who encounter unfamiliar situations on the road; all of them are to do with seeing and perception, about people who suddenly have to take a different view of things."[25] This open-ended method of working from the image out to the narrative (as opposed to from the narrative back to the image) corresponds with Kracauer's insistence on the photographic nature of film.

Although critics have sometimes assailed Kracauer's *Theory of Film* for his so-called naïve realism, recent studies have provided a more nuanced reading that shows a continuity with Kracauer's emphasis on the relationship of media forms to social and political realities.[26] Kracauer makes a telling acknowledgment at the start of his book to Beaumont Newhall, first curator of the Museum of Modern Art's (MoMA) photography department and later director of the George Eastman Museum, and to Edward Steichen, Newhall's successor as curator of photography. And Kracauer begins his *Theory of Film* with a concentrated chapter on photography, which establishes the primary terms of cinematic realism that go on to inform the rest of the book. Kracauer's *Theory of Film* and, specifically, his concept of "photographic film" permits us to broaden the conversation surrounding the relationship of photography and film, especially a discourse that has frequently been based on the construction of dualities: photo/film, static/moving, permanence/flow, past/present, absent/present, death/life, silence/sound, and the like.[27] We might consider Kracauer's statement self-evident. The individual film images that, when projected at speed, create the illusion of movement, are, of course, just so many photographs. But for Kracauer, and as we will see for Wenders too, not all photographs are photographic, in the sense of an openness to the concrete, material world through which the viewer can reclaim an authentic subjective position and individual human experience.

Kracauer wrote *Theory of Film* within the context of a new universalism and a growing discourse of the photograph as a medium for universal communication, epitomized by Edward Steichen's *The Family of Man*, the photographic exhibition that Steichen organized for MoMA in 1955, which was exported to ninety-one venues in thirty-eight countries by 1961. The exhibition included 503 photographs, selected from 273 different photographers, and organized under various section headings including "Lovers," "Marriage," "Revolt," "Man's Judgment," and more. The exhibition was both a spectacular success (in terms of number of visitors, and later inclusion on UNESCO's Memory of the World Register) and the target of withering criticism for its seeming sentimentality and advocacy of a universal humanism that was almost exclusively presented from a European–American point of view.[28] Indeed, *The Family of Man* is often proffered as primary evidence of a strain of Cold War humanist discourse featuring a postideological notion of common humanity. As a result, it is hard to square Kracauer's seeming enthusiasm for the exhibition, even titling the last section of his work "The Family of Man." Blake Stimson's book, *The Pivot of the World*, calls our attention, however, to this neglected period (of the 1950s through the 1970s) between modernism and so-called postmodernism, in which the relations between the individual and the collective, the subject and society are being reworked and an "alternative role is allotted to culture" as a system of social organization that is "neither strictly civic-minded nor strictly consumerist."[29] Following Stimson, we might consider Kracauer's notion of the photographic (as opposed to an ontology of photography) and his privileging of "everyday life" and "our given material environment" in "photographic" films as a way of mapping out these structural and systematic relationships: "All this does not imply that camera-realism and art exclude each other. But if films which really show what they picture are art, they are art with a difference."[30] And it is this art that potentially creates the space for a critical spectator.

The relationship between photographs and film is therefore more complex, and through it Kracauer and Wenders address a problem of image-making itself. Wenders, following Kracauer, advocates for a specific kind of photographic filmmaking, within the context of discourses of photographic realism that were, by the 1970s, increasingly waning as photography moved definitively into the academy, the art museum, and the international art market. The photograph, which pairs realism with a latent resistance to significance, is a way in which Wenders (borrowing from Evans) studies how images work and how we read them. Wenders draws specifically on Evans' examples of photographic practice as a way to elide critiques of naïve realism. This includes both the visual construction of the image as well as a metacritique of the image and photographic/cinematic practices. In this regard, the relationship of photography and film is constituted by the film's general posture to the image. In Wenders' films, the photograph functions as a reminder of the *potential* of the cinematographic effect itself. In an interview with Alain Bergala, Wenders describes this technique through a play on the French word *regarder*: "Behind the photos is a wish to look at something (*regarder*) and to preserve it (*garder*). The French word gets it nicely: *re-garder*. The photos Walker Evans took during the Depression were just that: preserving something that was going to disappear in three- or four-years' time, in your eye and in our memory."[31] Several images in *Kings of the Road* offer a means of capturing and cataloging the relics of cinema's history before they lose all social, cultural, and economic value. This could not be communicated by a single image alone, nor through a linear film narrative with a clear climax and resolution, but only in the juxtaposition of multiple scenes and images that recur, contradict, connect via an associative link, and allude to each other. Unlike the vein of photographic theory that maintains that every photograph asserts the transferal of the reality of the object pictured onto its representation, Kracauer, Evans, and Wenders all present the photographic image as an "encounter" or a "compromise" (to borrow from Rudolf Arnheim) between physical reality and the creative mind of the photographer and/or filmmaker.[32] This is what constitutes the "difference" in Kracauer's idea of art with a difference or Wenders' realism with a difference. Within this creative opening and through this perceptual experience, the viewer gains a new understanding of social and material realities and the possibility of other iterations. By foregrounding the cinematic experience itself in *Kings of the Road*, Wenders' film is consonant with that of broader critiques of narrative cliché and worn-out images, and the attempts by the filmmakers of the New German Cinema to interrogate the preconditions and potential of art in the commercial sphere.

Film as Photographic Essay

The original German title of *Kings of the Road* translates as *In the Course of Time* (*Im Lauf der Zeit*) and echoes Kracauer's privileging of films that are, as he wrote, "permeable to the flow of time," wherein the film's "cinematic quality varies in direct ratio to the degree of its permeability, any increase of the latter being tantamount to an increasing influx of camera-reality."[33] The loose composition of what Kracauer calls the "episode film" accords with the serial-structure of the photobook and is paradigmatic of the so-called photographic film in that "units form part and parcel of an open-ended narrative—open-ended in the sense that it relates in its entirety to the flow of life . . . which only the camera is capable of revealing."[34] As a result, Kracauer privileges films that are organized around patterns of seriality, as opposed to narrative development, and that are open-ended. The story of the episode film is inherent in the succession of images and is communicated through the images of which it is constructed, a process that Kracauer calls "drifting."[35] And drifting might be the best way to describe *Kings of the Road,* which in a series of repetitive episodes shows Bruno and Lander on the road, at gas stations, in abandoned industrial and military buildings, and in a variety of old movie houses that seem destined for oblivion.

Kings of the Road is structured episodically around visits to ten movie theaters, through which the film catalogs the vernacular architecture of these desolate towns along the border between East and West Germany. Movie history is told from an unconventional perspective, namely that of distribution and exhibition (as opposed to production), and the film opens as Bruno speaks with the elderly long-time owner of a small-town movie theater that serves as a bridge between multiple cinematic eras: silent film of the Weimar period, the cinema of the Third Reich, and the gradual collapse of the German film industry by the 1970s into B movies and soft porn. The opening scene gives us almost a brief history of cinema, as Bruno speaks with the proprietor who had been a musician in the pre-talkie era, performing live musical accompaniment to films, and who only recovered ownership of his theater in 1951 because of his former membership in the National Socialist party. The old man notes that the theater survived the transition to sound and the collapse of the industry after the war but appears to be in its last gasps as the changing media landscape (the increasing dominance of television) and the terrible films in distribution may finally spell its end. In addition to the movie theaters, the film restages a slapstick shadow play, highlights movie posters and illustrated magazines, prominently features images of renowned German film director Fritz Lang, and even includes a short disquisition on the importance of the Maltese cross gear mechanism: "Without this little thing, there'd be no film industry." To say with Kracauer that Wenders' movie "drifts," however, is not to assert that it is entirely aimless. For even as *Kings of the Road* documents the decline of the film industry, it models a way forward and a possibility of filmmaking that acknowledges and builds on Germany's cinematic history while depicting the realities of its own time.

In their three-volume history of the photobook, Martin Parr and Gerry Badger identify the photobook as an art form "between the novel and the film."[36] A photobook is distinguished from a catalog of photographic images (such as an exhibition catalog) or a published collection of photographic images (such as a monograph or anthology) foremost by the deliberate placement and relationship of individual photographs to others in the series: "In the photobook, the sum, by definition, is greater than the parts, and the greater the parts, the greater the potential of the sum."[37] The photobook thus demonstrates intention and coherence in design in the construction of a sequenced totality with a particular subject or theme. Parr and Badger argue, a photobook "should be an extended essay in photographs."[38] Photobooks by definition demonstrate, therefore, a deliberate self-consciousness of the image. These images in series emphasize sequence, rhythm, and flow. They transmit an experience that arises from direct interaction with the images themselves. As a consequence, the photobook may have more in common with film than with books, particularly with nonnarrative, open-ended cinema. Especially in the half-century between the 1920s and the 1970s, the photobook functioned as a hybrid that demonstrates the potential of the photograph as simultaneously mass medium and art medium, images published in mass-circulation magazines and images exhibited in museums or galleries, populist and formalist. And if the history of photography has largely been told as either a history of the mass medium or a history of art, the photobook "resides at a vital interstice between the art and the mass medium, between the journeyman and the artist, between the aesthetic and the contextual."[39] These tensions are precisely those that Wenders is working out in *Kings of the Road*, which uses the template of a photobook to function as an explicit meditation on photographic and film-making practices, the commercialization of images, and the unique nature of the surface realism of photography.

Likewise, Evans' photobook, *American Photographs*, is dominated by references to image-making, starting with its first photograph, *License Photo Studio, New York, 1934*, an image dominated by signs with the word "Photos" appearing six times. Evans' photobook thus announces a work that is not just a collection of photographic images but, more significantly, an explicit presentation of photographic practices. In similar fashion, *Kings of the Road* begins in the projection room of an old movie theater. The photobook and Wenders' film both stage and reflect on the possibility of the photographic presentation of reality in a society overwhelmed with a flood of commercial and industrial, public and private depictions of social reality. Evans' first image is immediately followed by the photograph *Penny Picture Display*, showing over two hundred studio headshots of men, women, and children, all neatly and often formally dressed, smiling head-on at the camera. All the photographs that follow present a stark contrast to these stylized projections. Multiple sequences of images throughout the photobook contrast the commercialized and idealized depictions of politicians, military leaders, couples, and movie stars, with the real men and women that Evans photographs. Evans' book and Wenders' film are filled with faded and torn posters, painted images, cartoon drawings, mirrors, portraits, photo-illustrated magazines, signs, show bills, billboards, graffiti. As Alan Trachtenberg has argued, *American Photographs* "offers by enactment an alternative to the commercial and instrumental methods of seeing which they oppose. In the form of the book they provide an alternative way of seeing and realizing America, making the nation real as one's experience."[40] Wenders' critique of the state of filmmaking in the 1970s is likewise enacted through the alternative method and vision he offers in *Kings of the Road*, transferring this experience to late postwar West Germany.

Evans' photographs of the 1930s are almost exclusively framed in a stark, head-on view. As Lincoln Kirstein wrote in his afterword to *American Photographs*: "The most characteristic single feature of Evans' work is its purity, or even its puritanism. It is 'straight' photography not only in technique but in the rigorous directness of its way of looking. . . . The facts pile up with the prints."[41] Evans' photographs rigorously scrutinize what we might call everyday life: frontal portraits and cluttered interiors, street-scenes and architecture, advertising and other signage, all in black-and-white contrast. They are notable for a fullness of detail that rewards the viewer with repeated viewing. To quote Kirstein again: "There is no need for Evans to dramatize his material with photographic tricks, because the material is already, in itself, intensely dramatic. . . . The power of Evans' work lies in the fact that he so details the effect of circumstances on familiar specimens that the single face, the single house, the single street, strikes with the strength of overwhelming numbers, the terrible cumulative force of thousands of faces, houses and streets."[42] Select prints from Evans' body of work have become cultural icons—seemingly singular representative statements of the human condition. As the publication of *American Photographs* demonstrates, however, Evans considered the photographs as elements in a series in which meaning is derived from the ways in which the photographs relate to each other.

If the individual photograph has been raised to the level of an autonomous art object, the series presents "the whole aspect of our society, the sober portrait of its stratifications, their backgrounds and embattled contrasts."[43] In order to achieve this, the photobook employs two standard editing principles: an associative sequence linked by theme or subject, and an inventory sequence. Evans spends a lot of time showing us how individual images superimpose a particular narrative. By distinction, in the cumulative effect of the series there is the potential that social realities might be revealed. Viewed in sequence, the images eschew fixed meaning and remain indeterminate despite the frames in which generations of critics might try to fix them.[44] Likewise, *Kings of the Road* involves a significant amount of associative drifting and repetition of an inventory of images—movie theaters, gas stations, abandoned industrial spaces—and of isolated individuals in these abandoned landscapes. In effect, Evans and Wenders seek to solve the problem of how to critique image-making practices within the form of the medium itself, without duplicating them. Both "celebrate" reality in their straightforward pragmatism and "clarify" it through their cumulative effect.[45] To say that photographs both "celebrate" and "clarify" reality, as Evans' wrote in the epigraph that frames this chapter, is to take seriously the idea that these mechanical images do not just make automatic and faithful recordings of the material world but reveal something specific of the nature of that reality, not least of all through the photographer's decisions about framing, lighting, and contrast—the specific elements in Evans' images that were the seeds for Wenders' own imagination.

In *American Photographs* Evans emphatically rejected the fashionable *Life* magazine photo-essays that were popular during the period with their linear narrative structure. *American Photographs* instead presents single images on the right-hand folio, faced by a blank page. In this structure, every image is important individually *and* by virtue of its relationship to the sequence of images in which it appears. This duality creates the space in which the images do not simply record but might reveal a facet of reality through the altered way of seeing that is brought about by the placement of the images in series. In *Kings of the Road,* Wenders likewise shuns the art of the commercially dramatized narrative and gestures to the compromised status of photography and filmmaking in a culture saturated with advertising and the soundtrack of popular music. The rundown movie houses that Bruno visits are either run by inexperienced hacks who know nothing about film and the technologies of film projection, or elderly people a generation removed. In this generational divide, Wenders makes clear the stakes for West

German culture and society in the 1970s, giving the viewer glimpses of a Germany the filmmaker critiques: the candle shaped like Hitler that is a carnival prize, the slip of a tongue between SPD (Social Democrats) and NSDAP (National Socialists), the proliferation of stereotypical and low budget films (in film posters for *Zwei Bayern im Urwald* [1957]; *Auf der Alm da gibt's koa Sünd* [1976]; and *Magdalena—vom Teufel besessen* [1976]).

Instead, Wenders reminds us that the photographic film is precisely the medium that has the potential to connect us to genuine experience, that offers a plenitude rather than an exhaustion of the image, and that gestures to a way of reclaiming the image or of redeeming reality in the over-saturated media landscape. If, as Wenders writes, "The camera set-ups are predetermined so that millions will take the pictures which will confirm the picture that already exists,"[46] then how is a filmmaker or photographer to avoid duplicating and thereby affirming that image? It is here that the serial construction of the photobook—or the episodic structure of Wenders' film—attempts to offer an alternative, precisely in the way in which images are ordered and reordered outside of the dominant social logic so as to depict visually previously undefined forces at work in the world. For example, Wenders does not show us the stylized action sequence of a fatal car accident, but only the solitary grief of its aftermath.

Kings of the Road ends, as it must, with the two protagonists parting ways, Lander on a train and Winter steering his caravan in the opposite direction. Their destinations remain unknown to us. Each man's final scene alone, however, brings us back to the question of filmmaking, and more specifically what I have been calling, after Kracauer, a photographic approach to film. In what will turn out to be Bruno's final job repairing projection equipment, he visits a movie theater whose owner refuses to show any films—or at least to show the films currently produced in, imported for, and distributed in the West German film market and embraced by the public. This is how Wenders described the film industry in the 1970s: "the future belongs to the very worst Z-movies, to the pictures that block off your vision and to the sounds that clout you across the ear. What other films are there left to go to, a few exceptions apart? Seeing becomes an act of missing."[47] Wenders bemoans the loss of "those faces that are never forced into anything; those landscapes that aren't just backgrounds; those stories which, even if they're funny, are never foolish."[48] In other words, the cinematic landscape of the mid-1970s impedes vision and offers only visual loss, in no small part because the images that it presents are over-determined in advance (or what in *Alice in the Cities* Peter Winter had called "commercials for the status quo"). The notable absence of film stills in the window cases as Winter exits the last movie theater is a devastating visual statement. Only empty frames appear under "Now Playing" and "Coming Attractions," where decades of film stills once hung. Wenders' film, of course, attempts to offer an alternative. An ongoing joke in the film involves a play on the German idiom "*in der Tinte stecken*," or what an English-speaker might call "being in hot water" (to be in trouble or to have problems). But the idiom is literalized when Lander dreams of a new "ink" (*Tinte*) that would allow him to write and see and think differently. In a different context, Wenders will claim that this new ink is the domain of his "favorite photographers . . . . Craftsmen who use light."[49]

Kracauer's description of photographic films urges us to consider how photography might function as a metaphor for critical inquiry or as a model for criticism itself, by establishing photography as an epistemological paradigm: "Cinematic films evoke a reality more inclusive than the one they actually picture."[50] In effect, he reclaims individual experience (of the image, for example) as a critical component that cannot be wholly plotted and determined in advance. In "Der Essay als Form," Theodor Adorno underscores the antisystematic truth of the essay in order to present the essay as the singularly adequate form of social criticism.[51] This essayistic form is likewise the hallmark of the photobook. As Carolin Duttlinger has argued regarding Walter Benjamin's and Theodor Adorno's writing on photography, "Photography encapsulates a critical stance characterized by a mixture of distance and involvement, objectivity and distortion, intellectual detachment and personal involvement."[52] In Kracauer's theory, a properly "photographic" photograph can permit access to the heterogeneous world of experience that exceeds the hierarchical laws and categories of intellectual reason. Thus, by delineating what constitutes a photographic film from others, Kracauer puts the idea of photography into play as a critical term, albeit one that is not necessarily tied to every instance of photography. In other words, photographs may be material objects categorized by the technological specificity of their production, but that is not a sufficient criterion for defining every photograph (or film) as photographic. By adopting the serial logic of the photobook, *Kings of the Road* breaks with the overdetermined film narratives and camera setups that play in the very movie theaters that Bruno and Lander visit. This juxtaposition of representational practices emulates the deliberate contrast of image production that Evans had employed and that functions as one of the through lines of *American Photographs*. The result is a reorientation of the filmgoer's experience to a self-consciousness of the image itself and an engagement of the spectator in processes of critical reflection. Although the generation of independent German filmmakers associated with the *Filmverlag der Autoren* (some of whom are featured in Wenders' guest edition issue of *Cahiers du cinéma*) did not share a common aesthetic style, they were all deeply invested in offering an alternative cinema to the mainstream film industry and the growing dominance of television.

Redemption of Physical Reality

In one of the last scenes in *Kings of the Road*, an unnamed young boy is left to voice the way for the filmmaker to redeem physical reality through the image. Lander walks onto a train platform, empty except for a young boy writing in a notebook. In Wenders' most concise statement on the way he makes/takes pictures, the boy almost seems to construct a photobook or to write the screenplay of the very film that is drawing to a close:

> LANDER. What are you writing?
> BOY. I'm describing a train station. Everything I see.
> LANDER. And what do you see?
> BOY. The tracks, the gravel, the timetable, the sky, the clouds. A man with a suitcase. An empty suitcase! A grin! A black eye. A fist . . . throwing a stone.
> LANDER. It's as easy as that?
> BOY. That easy!

By placing this scene near the end of his film, Wenders seems to imply that this artistic approach will be adopted moving forward. However, its meaning can also be applied retroactively to the film in that it describes the serial process of representing what is seen that is highlighted throughout.

Kings of the Road is, in some sense, a film about the end of filmmaking; but with it, Wenders seeks to offer an alternative to the bankruptcy of the commercial image and its role in a calculated narrative in which there is no "harmony left between 'reality'—such that the human mind could seize and pass it on—and the product there on the screen."[53] Wenders does not proceed from an *a priori* discursive structure to which images are then subordinated, or look for images to confirm a narrative. Instead, like Evans' *American Photographs*, the film is both highly ordered *and* open and spontaneous, endlessly associative *and* generative. The series of images of abandoned movie houses, gas stations, and industrial structures drift at an uneven pace—long takes and traveling shots, brief action sequences and long periods of stasis—that break with cinematic conventions of storytelling and tempo and create a mode of subjective experience that is tied to concrete reality. The stark black-and-white tones of the film reinforce the framing of space, place, and time—"celebrating" material reality even as it "clarifies" the social realities that commercial media obscure. The photographer Robert Frank claimed that the *documentary style* of Walker Evans' photographs could "transform destiny into awareness" because of Evans' ability to depict visually previously undefined forces at work in the world.[54] These *American Photographs* are, for that reason, the travel guide for Wenders and his film crew in their road movie on the past, present, and future of the movies. In *Kings of the Road,* the protagonists' road trip and fumbled attempts at self-understanding merge with questions over the identity of German cinema itself and the role of a new generation of filmmakers in contributing to a viable commercial cinema.

Stefanie Harris is Associate Professor of German at Texas A&M University and Head of the Department of International Studies. Her research on interdisciplinary approaches to literature and media, the relationship of aesthetics and politics, "photographic" texts, and film has been featured in *Germanic Review, The German Quarterly,* and *New German Critique,* and her media studies scholarship can be found in volumes such as *A Companion to Werner Herzog* (2012), *Handbuch Literatur & Visuelle Kultur* (2016), and *German Television: Historical and Theoretical Perspectives* (2016). She is the author of *Mediating Modernity: German Literature and the "New" Media, 1895–1930* (2010).

Notes

1. Wim Wenders, "Le souffle de l'Ange," *Cahiers du cinéma* 400 (Oct. 1987): 54–91.
2. *Cahiers du cinéma* 400 (Oct. 1987): n. pag.
3. Wim Wenders, "Death Is No Solution: The German Film Director Fritz Lang," in *Emotion Pictures: Reflections on the Cinema,* trans. Sean Whiteside (London: Faber and Faber, 1989), 107.
4. Walker Evans, *American Photographs* (New York: Museum of Modern Art, 1938). *American Photographs* was remaindered when it was first published in 1938 but was reviewed widely and received positively when it was reissued in 1962. The 1960s and 1970s saw a resurgence of interest in Walker Evans' work, and his FSA photographs of the 1930s were ubiquitous by the mid 1970s. In 1971, John Szarkowski curated

a large retrospective of Evans' work at the Museum of Modern Art in New York in which over two hundred prints were exhibited. The show traveled to seven other venues and led a new generation of photographers, who had been too young when *American Photographs* was published, to discover Evans' work. In 1971, Evans also taped a lengthy interview with Leslie Katz that was edited and published in *Art in America* and provided his most complete reflections on his artistic work and thought. In a curious connection to Wenders, Evans began photographing exclusively with a color Polaroid camera in the early 1970s, including architectural views, signs, detritus, and the faces of friends and students. One project dating from 1974 included over two thousand color Polaroids. Wenders' film *Alice in the Cities* (1974) prominently features a Polaroid camera and photographs. The actor who plays the photographer in *Alice in the Cities*, Rüdiger Vogler, is the co-lead in *Kings of the Road*. See Leslie Katz, "Interview with Walker Evans," *Art in America* (1971): 82–89; James R. Mellow, *Walker Evans* (New York: Basic Books, 1999), 569–75; John Raeburn, *A Staggering Revolution: A Cultural History of Thirties Photography* (Urbana: University of Illinois Press, 2006).

5. George Kouvaros' article on Wim Wenders' work in both film and photography stresses the particular temporal relationship of the photographic and cinematic images and the ways in which these media simultaneously evoke different registers of time: the past as present and the present as past. Photography allows for "a form of temporal experience in which we confront the ending and the surviving of things." In this context, Kouvaros discusses Wenders' debt to Walker Evans and his acknowledgment of "the figures and influences that have brought us to where we are." Taking a different approach, my work examines the ways in which photographs in series, and Walker Evans' photographs and photobooks in particular, stage a particular metacritique of the image. See George Kouvaros, "As If It Were for the Last Time: Wim Wenders—Film and Photography," *New German Critique* 42, no. 2 (2015): 82, 93.
6. In his afterword to *American Photographs*, Lincoln Kirstein wrote: "Physically the pictures in this book exist as separate prints. They lack the surface, obvious continuity of the moving picture, which by its physical nature compels the observer to perceive a series of images as parts of a whole. But these photographs, of necessity seen singly, are not conceived as isolated pictures made by the camera turned indiscriminately here or there. In intention and in effect they exist as a collection of statements deriving from and presenting a consistent attitude." See Lincoln Kirstein, "Photographs of America: Walker Evans," in *American Photographs*, ed. Walker Evans (New York: Museum of Modern Art, 1938), 192–93. Similarly, Alan Trachtenberg has argued that Walter Evans' appreciation of cinematic devices "holds a key to the book's form." See Alan Trachtenberg, *Reading American Photographs: Images as History, Matthew Brady to Walker Evans* (New York: Hill and Wang, 1989), 258.
7. Joel Snyder, "Picturing Vision," *Critical Inquiry* 6, no. 3 (Spring 1980): 510.
8. Wim Wenders, "Le Souffle de L'Ange," in *The Logic of Images: Essays and Conversations*, trans. Michael Hofmann (London: Faber and Faber, 1991), 96.
9. Some of Evans' photographs of this period are also published in his coauthored work with James Agee, *Let Us Now Praise Famous Men* (Boston: Houghton Mifflin, 1941); 2nd ed. (Boston: Houghton Mifflin, 1960).
10. Wenders, "Le Souffle," *Logic*, 96–97.
11. Ibid., 97.
12. Kirstein, "Photographs," 197.
13. Katz, "Interview," 85.
14. Ibid.

15. Wim Wenders, *Written in the West, Revisited* (New York: Distributed Art Publishers, 2015), 13.
16. Wenders, *Written in the West, Revisited,* 13; Walker Evans, "Photography," in *Quality: Its Image in the Arts,* ed. Louis Kronenberger (New York: Atheneum, 1969), 198.
17. Siegfried Kracauer, *Theory of Film: The Redemption of Physical Reality* (Princeton: Princeton University Press, 1997). Wenders has written brief introductions to several books of photography: cf. Sylvia Plachy, *Signs & Relics* (New York: Monacelli, 1999); Ode Pälmke, *Facades* (Berlin: Jovis, 2013); and Janet Sternburg, *Overspilling World: The Photographs of Janet Sternburg* (Berlin: Distanz, 2016). In addition to exhibition catalogs of his photographs and companion volumes to his films, Wenders has also published numerous photobooks and photo essays, including most recently, *Sofort Bilder* (Munich: Schirmer Mosel, 2017), and *Places, Strange and Quiet* (Ostfildern: Hatje Cantz, 2013). Wenders published the expanded *Written in the West: Photographien aus dem amerikanischen Westen* (Munich: Schirmer/Mosel, 1987), his collection of photographs taken in the western United States during preproduction for his film *Paris, Texas* (1984). A second edition includes additional photographs of the town of Paris, Texas: *Written in the West, Revisited* (2015). In an interview with Alain Bergala printed in the second edition of the photobook, Wenders names both Walker Evans and Robert Frank as reference points for his own photographs (*Revisited,* 9, 12, 13). In his documentary, *The Salt of the Earth* (2014), Wenders collaborated with the son of the celebrated Brazilian photographer Sebastião Salgado in depicting Salgado's large-scale project of photographing global landscapes.
18. Wim Wenders, "From Dream to Nightmare: The Terrifying Western *Once Upon a Time in the West,*" in *Emotion Pictures: Reflections,* 24.
19. Kracauer, *Theory of Film,* xlix.
20. Ibid., 37.
21. Ibid., 309. Kracauer's contrast of proceeding from "below" or "above" will later be echoed in the German author and film and television director Alexander Kluge's own idiosyncratic realistic method that establishes a critical relationship to the normalizing effects of media. Kluge's so-called strategy from below seeks to arouse the senses and the imagination, rather than reflecting and reinstating preprogrammed logical facilities and learned behaviors and ideologies that would only serve to duplicate the strategy from above. See Stefanie Harris, "Kluge's *Auswege,*" *The Germanic Review* 85, no. 4 (2010): 294–317.
22. Miriam Bratu Hansen, "Introduction," in *Theory of Film: The Redemption of Physical Reality,* ed. Siegfried Kracauer (Princeton: Priceton University Press, 1997), xxv.
23. Kracauer, *Theory of Film,* 301.
24. Wim Wenders, "Impossible stories. Talk given at a colloquium on narrative technique," in *The Logic of Images: Essays and Conversations,* trans. Michael Hofmann (London: Faber and Faber, 1991), 55.
25. Ibid., 56.
26. See Johannes von Moltke, *The Curious Humanist: Siegfried Kracauer in America* (Berkeley: University of California Press, 2016).
27. Kracauer, *Theory of Film,* xlvii.
28. See Roland Barthes, "La grande famille des hommes," in *Mythologies* (Paris: Éditions du Seuil, 1957), 173–76; Allan Sekula, "The Traffic in Photographs," *Art Journal* 41 (1981): 15–25.
29. Blake Stimson, *The Pivot of the World: Photography and Its Nation* (Cambridge, MA: MIT Press, 2006), 4.
30. Kracauer, *Theory of Film,* 304, 302.

31. Wenders, *Written in the West, Revisited*, 9.
32. Rudolf Arnheim, "On the Nature of Photography," *Critical Inquiry* 1 no. 1 (Sep. 1974): 157, 159.
33. Kracauer, *Theory of Film*, 254.
34. Ibid.
35. Ibid., 256.
36. Martin Parr and Gerry Badger, *The Photobook: A History* (London: Phaidon, 2004), vol. 1: 6.
37. Ibid., 7.
38. Ibid., 8.
39. Ibid., 11.
40. Trachtenberg, *Reading American Photographs*, 285.
41. Kirstein, "Photographs," 197.
42. Ibid.
43. Ibid., 192.
44. Trachtenberg has analyzed the way in which individual photographs by Evans have appeared in different sequences in different publications in order to talk about photographic sequencing and the dominance of the FSA (Farm Security Administration) narrative of "hardship and heroism"; however, as Trachtenberg goes on to state, "the very openness of *American Photographs* implies skepticism toward closed forms and fixed meanings." Trachtenberg, *Reading American Photographs*, 257–58.
45. Evans, "Photography," 198.
46. Wenders, "The American Dream," in *Emotion Pictures: Reflections*, 121.
47. Wenders, "Emotion Pictures: Slowly rockin' on," in *Emotion Pictures: Reflections*, 49.
48. Ibid.
49. Wenders, *Written in the West, Revisited*, 13.
50. Kracauer, *Theory of Film*, 71.
51. Theodor Adorno, "Der Essay als Form," in *Noten zur Literatur: Gesammelte Schriften* (Frankfurt: Suhrkamp, 1974), vol. 11: 9–33.
52. Carolin Duttlinger, "Snapshots from the Hereafter: Benjamin, Adorno, and the Critic as Photographer," in *In(ter)discipline: New Languages for Criticism*, ed. Gillian Beer, Malcolm Bowie, and Beate Perrey (Cambridge, UK: Legenda, 2007), 163.
53. Wenders, *Emotion Pictures: Reflections*, 128.
54. Jonathan Day, *Robert Frank's* The Americans*: The Art of Documentary Photography* (Bristol: Intellect, 2011), 161.

Bibliography

Adorno, Theodor. "Der Essay als Form." In *Noten zur Literatur: Gesammelte Schriften*, 9–33. Frankfurt: Suhrkamp, 1974.

Agee, James, and Walker Evans. *Let Us Now Praise Famous Men*. Boston: Houghton Mifflin, 1941.

———. *Let Us Now Praise Famous Men*, 2nd ed. Boston: Houghton Mifflin, 1960.

Arnheim, Rudolf. "On the Nature of Photography." *Critical Inquiry* 1, no. 1 (Sep. 1974): 149–61.

Barthes, Roland. "La grande famille des hommes." In *Mythologies*, 173–76. Paris: Éditions du Seuil, 1957.

Cahiers du cinéma 400 (Oct. 1987).

Day, Jonathan. *Robert Frank's* The Americans*: The Art of Documentary Photography*. Bristol: Intellect, 2011.

Duttlinger, Carolin. "Snapshots from the Hereafter: Benjamin, Adorno, and the Critic as Photographer." In *In(ter)discipline: New Languages for Criticism*, edited by Gillian Beer, Malcolm Bowie, and Beate Perrey, 162–73. Cambridge, UK: Legenda, 2007.

Evans, Walker. *American Photographs*. New York: Museum of Modern Art, 1938.

———. "Photography." In *Quality: Its Image in the Arts*, edited by Louis Kronenberger, 169–211. New York: Atheneum, 1969.

Hansen, Miriam Bratu. "Introduction." In *Theory of Film: The Redemption of Physical Reality*, edited by Siegfried Kracauer, vii–xlv. Princeton: Princeton University Press, 1997.

Harris, Stefanie. "Kluge's *Auswege*." *The Germanic Review* 85, no. 4 (2010): 294–317.

Honnef, Klaus, Rolf Sachsse, and Karin Thomas, eds. *German Photography 1870–1970: Power of a Medium*. Köln: DuMont, 1997.

Katz, Leslie. "Interview with Walker Evans." *Art in America* (1971): 82–89.

Kirstein, Lincoln. "Photographs of America: Walker Evans." In *American Photographs*, edited by Walker Evans, 189–98. New York: Museum of Modern Art, 1938.

Kouvaros, George. "As If It Were for the Last Time: Wim Wenders—Film and Photography." *New German Critique* 42, no. 2 (2015): 81–95.

Kracauer, Siegfried. *Theory of Film: The Redemption of Physical Reality*. Princeton: Princeton University Press, 1997.

Mellow, James R. *Walker Evans*. New York: Basic Books, 1999.

Pälmke, Oda. *Facades*. Berlin: Jovis, 2013.

Parr, Martin, and Gerry Badger. *The Photobook: A History*. London: Phaidon, 2004.

Plachy, Sylvia. *Signs & Relics*. New York: Monacelli, 1999.

Raeburn, John. *A Staggering Revolution: A Cultural History of Thirties Photograph*. Urbana: University of Illinois Press, 2006.

Sekula, Allan. "The Traffic in Photographs." *Art Journal* 41 (1981): 15–25.

Snyder, Joel. "Picturing Vision." *Critical Inquiry* 6, no. 3 (Spring 1980): 499–526.

Sternburg, Janet. *Overspilling World: The Photographs of Janet Sternburg*. Berlin: Distanz, 2016.

Stimson, Blake. *The Pivot of the World: Photography and Its Nation*. Cambridge, MA: MIT Press, 2006.

Trachtenberg, Alan. *Reading American Photographs: Images as History, Matthew Brady to Walker Evans*. New York: Hill and Wang, 1989.

von Moltke, Johannes. *The Curious Humanist: Siegfried Kracauer in America*. Berkeley: University of California Press, 2016.

Wenders, Wim. *Emotion Pictures: Essays und Filmkritiken 1968–1984*. Frankfurt am Main: Verlag der Autoren, 1986.

———. *Emotion Pictures: Reflections on the Cinema*. Translated by Sean Whiteside. London: Faber and Faber, 1989.

———. "Le souffle de l'Ange." *Cahiers du cinéma* 400 (Oct. 1987): 54–91.

———. "Le Souffle de L'Ange." In *The Logic of Images: Essays and Conversations*, trans. Michael Hofmann, 89–113. London: Faber and Faber, 1991.

———. *The Logic of Images: Essays and Conversations*. Translated by Michael Hofmann. London: Faber and Faber, 1991.

———. *Places, Strange and Quiet*. Ostfieldern: Hatje Cantz, 2013.

———. *Sofort Bilder*. Munich: Schirmer Mosel, 2017.

———. *Written in the West: Photographien aus dem amerikanischen Westen*. Munich: Schirmer/Mosel, 1987.

———. *Written in the West, Revisited*. New York: Distributed Art Publishers, 2015.

Filmography

Alice in the Cities (*Alice in den Städten*). Directed by Wim Wenders. Munich: Filmverlag der Autoren, 1974.

Kings of the Road (*Im Lauf der Zeit*). Directed by Wim Wenders. Munich: Wim Wenders Produktion, 1976.

Once Upon a Time in the West. Directed by Sergio Leone. Hollywood: Paramount Pictures, 1968.

Paris, Texas. Directed by Wim Wenders. Neuilly: Argos Films, 1984.

The Salt of the Earth. Directed by Wim Wenders and Juliano Ribeiro. Paris: Decia Films, 2014.

Figure 5.1. *Potter's Bull* (*Potters Stier*). 1981. Directed by Jürgen Böttcher. Potsdam: DEFA Studio für Dokumentarfilme, 1981. Screen capture by Matthew Bauman.

Chapter 5

The Transgression of Overpainting

Jürgen Böttcher's Radical Experiments with Intermediality in *Transformations* (1981)

Matthew Bauman

The focus in East German film studies to this point has largely been on narrative films; yet increasingly attention is being paid to the contributions of nonfiction filmmakers in East Germany's state-run film industry DEFA (*Deutsche Film-Aktiengesellschaft*). Jürgen Böttcher is a unique figure among the film directors sanctioned by DEFA; his willingness to push back (often successfully) against the programmatic strictures placed on the arts in the German Democratic Republic (GDR) earned him a place in that country's "true avant-garde."[1] In addition to his career as a filmmaker, for which he has received international acclaim, he has also cultivated a career as a painter under the pseudonym Strawalde, earning him a reputation as one of Germany's most well-known contemporary artists despite decades of official GDR skepticism toward the value of his work. Böttcher's strongest cinematic rebellion against these strictures is his trilogy of short films entitled *Transformations* (*Verwandlungen*, 1981), also referred to as his "Overpaintings" (*Übermalungen*) trilogy. Scholarship has shown that East German feature films far transcended the "propaganda" stereotypes applied to them by the West, and Böttcher's trilogy is a radical intervention that demonstrates how complex the narratives surrounding all iterations of East German film can be. What follows is a step toward a more complete examination of an influential but understudied piece of East German documentary and experimental film history.[2]

The three nonnarrative films comprising Böttcher's trilogy were the only experimental films ever released by the DEFA Studio for Documentary Films (*DEFA-Studio für Wochenschau und Dokumentarfilme*). In *Potter's Bull (Potters Stier)*, *Venus According to Giorgione (Venus nach Giorgione)*, and *Woman at the Clavichord (Frau am Klavichord)*, Böttcher (as the director of the film) documents his alter ego, Strawalde (the artist), at various stages of creating "overpaintings." Overpainting is Böttcher's term for postcards featuring photomechanical prints of canonical fine art paintings that Böttcher (i.e., Strawalde) embellishes by drawing various combinations of doodles, patterns, and abstract shapes directly onto the postcard. Some of these overpaintings are also projected onto unusual surfaces using diapositive slides. In this way, Böttcher combines his painterly and cinematic talents to explore the interactions of various forms of media including painting, still photography, film, and television—what Seán Allan calls a "constant process of dialogue with existing artistic traditions."[3] In particular, Böttcher's use of still photography in the film can be understood as a meditation on intermedial forms and an important, unencumbered, outside perspective on issues that are also raised by Western theories of film and image. Drawing on ideas put forth by André Bazin and Walter Benjamin, this chapter analyzes how Böttcher uses photographs in *Transformations* as a bridge between his painter and film-maker personalities—a vantage point from which he radically engages with and challenges Western conceptions of visual media, provides thoughtful responses to foundational texts of the field, challenges the orthodoxies imposed on the East German artistic community, and uses his personal commitment to his vision to reinsert humanity into the equation.

Strawalde's Art on Film: The Results of Process

Although Böttcher works primarily in the media of film and painting, it is a third medium—photography, in the forms of postcard reproductions[4] and diapositive slides[5]—that plays the most important role in Böttcher's project. Photographic images link painting and film by simultaneously connecting and dismantling their formal confines so that Böttcher's two personae can radically experiment with the conventions of these artistic media. In the process of layering and exploding these established forms, they can simultaneously critique different cultural, artistic, and political economies.

The presentation of Strawalde's overpaintings in the *Transformations* films takes four main forms. The simplest form is a sequence of full-frame shots of each overpainting held for several seconds (usually between five and ten) with a two second fade-out and fade-in separating the images. There is also a variation on this form after the opening credits of *Potter's Bull* and *Venus According to Giorgione*. Here, Böttcher stands in front of the camera holding a stack of postcards, which he displays in quick succession. The first postcard is unmodified, an "original," as it were. This is followed by a handful of overpainted postcards of the same image before a new "original" is displayed and the process repeats. The third form is more active and process-focused. It also begins with a full-frame shot, this time of an unmodified postcard; but instead of cutting to a new image, Strawalde's hand, gripping an artistic implement, appears in the frame and begins to paint or draw on the postcard. The shot stays with this process to varying stages of completion and ends with a jump cut to another shot. Lastly, the fourth form is a radical departure from the first three. Here, instead of the overpaintings themselves, diapositive slides of the overpaintings are projected onto various objects and surfaces in and around Böttcher's East Berlin apartment.

In terms of Strawalde's production process, the postcards on which he paints serve as the conveyance of a mechanically captured image from life. Böttcher's films strip these images of their signifiers as postcards altogether: each small, full-color reproduction is uncaptioned and is never written on, addressed, stamped, mailed, or postmarked in the films; the postcards are used solely for their image content. This, combined with the fidelity of the photomechanical reproduction process, presents the viewer with a pure image. The idea that postcards can function as pure images akin to photographs finds support in French critic Serge Daney's preference for postcards that, as Christa Blümlinger describes, "did not feature any inscriptions, signatures, prints, or postal marks, representing instead—in a purely Bazinian logic—'the imaginary sampling of a piece of landscape,[6] which becomes an image in the process.'"[7] Indeed, the opening titles of the three *Transformations* films refer to the objects interchangeably as "art postcards" (*Kunstpostkarten*) or "art prints" (*Kunstdrucke*), acknowledging their format but emphasizing that their primary purpose is to faithfully depict works of art.

By taking a reproduction of an artwork as his starting point, Strawalde is liberated from the confines of a blank canvas. He is therefore able to layer on his painterly vision and manipulate the grand illusion of art history and the reverence associated with the canon. The use of diapositive slides functions in a similar way. Projecting a two-dimensional image onto anything other than a flat white screen distorts the image's proportions and its colors as well as the colors of the surface or object onto which the image is projected. This distortion simultaneously dismantles the notion of exhibition and allows Strawalde to reclaim his power as an artist through the mutability of images and space. Highlighting the photographic in *Transformations* adds a new layer to previous readings of Böttcher in the context of Socialist Realism. But first, a deeper exploration of *Transformations* within the context of the director's dual personalities and background will anchor the new theoretical reading.

Transformations and a Split Personality

While Böttcher often receives praise from critics for using his painterly vision to inform his cinematography, the *Transformations* trilogy is a rare instance where he has explicitly incorporated himself as an artist into his films. The distinction between his personalities is made explicit in the hand printed opening credits: Jürgen Böttcher receives the directorial credit, but the title cards inform that all the painting in the films is carried out by Strawalde. Wearing an artist's smock (a filmic signifier of a painter according to Roland Barthes),[8] Strawalde appears after the opening credits of both *Potter's Bull* and *Venus According to Giorgione* holding a series of "painted over" postcards, which he flips through with a grin, showing off for the camera. Here, viewers become explicitly aware of the distinct personalities established in the opening credits—they witness the painter Strawalde in front of the camera creating his artworks while knowing that Böttcher is meant to be behind it directing the film. From the beginning of the films, we see a rupture of personal identity with Böttcher using his two personae to establish a strict formal dichotomy between visual art and film.[9]

Indeed, the photomechanically reproduced postcard provides the surface where painting and filmmaking are combined, while the photographic image itself serves as a location where Böttcher and Strawalde relieve the tension created by the immediate split of one person into two personalities. Böttcher demonstrates that the medium bridges the two sides of himself, painter and filmmaker, on opposite sides of the camera—allowing them to best practice their craft simultaneously. For example, shortly after a jump cut to a postcard reproduction of a painting of a sleeping nude in two films of the trilogy,[10] Strawalde's hand gripping a paint brush is interposed between the camera and the postcard as he begins to paint over the artwork represented. This surface then functions as the space where Böttcher's commentary can take place. This commentary is further underscored by the diapositive slides used to project Strawalde's overpaintings not onto a blank screen but into the "real world" (i.e., his apartment, the street outside, etc.), thus emphasizing the accessibility of photographs. Their use of the postcards shows how the films not only document the action of painting but also function as theoretical texts that engage with painting, photography, and film in the broader context of thought and scholarship on the intersection of the three.

Specifically, the films can be understood as an illustration of ideas presented by Western film theorists André Bazin and Walter Benjamin in several ways. First, the postcards in the films play with Benjamin's concept of the aura as described in "The Work of Art in the Age of Mechanical Reproduction."[11] Secondly, and more directly, the films offer a cinematic counterpart to Bazin's written attempts to triangulate the relationship that painting, photography, and cinema have to each other as well as the historical progression that evolved all three of them.[12] After laying out Böttcher's development as an artist in the context of the GDR, the next section analyzes relevant portions of Benjamin's and Bazin's theories, explores their intersections with the *Transformations* trilogy, and contextualizes their standing in East Germany at the time as well as their relationship to "mainstream" East German media theory of the period.

Böttcher's Background

Born in 1931, Böttcher showed an interest in art from a young age and studied painting at the prestigious *Hochschule für Bildende Künste* in Dresden from 1949 to 1953. When he struggled to exhibit his deeply personal, stylized paintings in an East German art scene dedicated to Socialist Realism by decree of the ruling Socialist Unity Party (*Sozialistische Einheitspartei*, SED), he changed careers and enrolled in the newly founded *Deutsche Hochschule für Filmkunst* in Potsdam in 1955. There, he intended to become a director and make films in the style of the Italian Neorealists and early Soviet filmmakers such as Sergei Eisenstein.

After graduating film school, Böttcher was employed at the East German state-run *DEFA-Studio für Wochenschau und Dokumentarfilme* in

1960 and immediately courted the same controversy that dogged his painting career. Of the nine films he made there between 1961 and 1965 (all documentary shorts), two were banned for portraying East German youth "unfavorably."[13] Then in 1966, *Born in '45* (*Jahrgang 45*), Böttcher's first attempt at a feature film, aesthetically indebted to Italian Neorealism and the French New Wave, did not survive the cull that arose out of the infamous Eleventh Plenum, and it, too, was consigned to the archives.[14] This failure to placate the censors restricted him to directing documentary films.[15] Nevertheless, Böttcher gained a reputation for developing trusting relationships with his often working-class subjects who allowed him to tell their stories as human beings and not merely as exponents of government-mandated economic production plans in the GDR, as was common in East German documentaries at the time.[16] As Richard Kilbourn states: "Bottcher's documentary œuvre, the series of documentaries for which he is best remembered, is in many ways a realization of . . . an emotional and intellectual commitment to revealing important truths about the lives of unsung heroes in factories or elsewhere in the workplace. In this respect, his work represents a kind of homage to working people."[17] This ability to humanize and individualize the working class through his films also served to counteract the disapproval of his formalist tendencies from the party functionaries in the film industry.

Even so, those two facets remained inseparable in Böttcher, and the formalist conceptions of visual composition that he had honed during his first career as a painter are readily identifiable throughout his career. Britta Hartmann writes of Böttcher's filmography: "the influence of the filmmaker's background in painting is clear . . . he attempts to mimic the compositional methods and attributes of visual art in his films. He constructs precise and atmospheric settings, mostly in black and white, shot on 35mm film."[18] These latter talents are most distinctly on display in Böttcher's work in the 1980s. Working together with cameraman Thomas Plenert, Böttcher turned his attention almost exclusively to images. His documentaries during this decade do away almost entirely with the voiceover, commentary, and interviews typical of the genre, instead trusting the visual aspects of the films to speak for themselves. This heavy reliance on images and camerawork and the concomitant lack of a clear, verbal articulation of the films' intentions pushed back even more against the authorities' mistrust of Formalism and Western cinema. Nevertheless, Böttcher was able to avoid censorship by continuing to focus on the working class, as in films such as *Shunters* (*Rangierer*, 1984) and *The Kitchen* (*Die Küche*, 1986). *Transformations* also works in this direction: by inserting his own painterly persona as the main character and prominently featuring his hand at work in the painting sequences, Böttcher positions the painter as someone who engages in literal "manual" labor and thus an appropriate subject for a film produced by the self-proclaimed "Workers' and Peasants' State."

Despite this shift toward an almost exclusively image-centric focus, nearly all of Böttcher's films from this period still fit well into his established style. In the *Transformations* trilogy Böttcher creates spaces in which he and his viewers can explore, examine, and even play with the tensions between moving and still images as well as those between images made by a camera and by hand. Their lack of an overt, sequential narrative thread or unified subject matter and the openness to interpretation renders them decided outliers in both Böttcher's filmography and the DEFA film catalog. These three films comprise Böttcher's most direct and radical engagement with film and with the nature of images. Moreover, given his position as the most overtly experimental DEFA filmmaker, *Transformations* is the most radical cinematic engagement with film and image theory ever officially produced in the GDR.

As stated above, the trilogy does not find its parallels in criticism from the Warsaw Pact, but rather in the writings of the Western critics André Bazin and Walter Benjamin. Government fiat dictated that the arts in East Germany, as well as the scholarship surrounding it, be dominated by the anti-Formalist tenets of Socialist Realism. Thus, the typical way that East German visual studies scholars could publicly engage with the works of Western theorists was to reaffirm the foregone conclusion that these ideas were ultimately inferior to Socialist Realism.[19] Böttcher, however, does not participate in this reaffirmation. Instead, his trilogy invites strong comparisons to Western experimental film. Though each author was either not known (in Benjamin's case) or disapproved of (in Bazin's) in the GDR, both can be applied to interpret the use of photographs in Böttcher's trilogy and their relationship to objectivity, framing, duration, and aura.

The Benjaminian in Böttcher

Until the late 1980s, Walter Benjamin remained largely an insider tip in GDR criticism circles, as there was no readily accessible published edition of his works.[20] Despite efforts by figures such as Bertolt Brecht and Ernst Bloch to proselytize on his behalf in the early years of the GDR, "Benjamin's writings played no role in the theoretical foundations of the Marxist literary criticism that was establishing itself in the GDR."[21] Given this marginal status, it is unclear how much of Benjamin's work Böttcher himself was actively aware of; but regardless, by featuring mechanical reproductions of paintings in the *Transformations* films, Böttcher engages with the concept of the aura, which Benjamin proposes in his seminal 1936 essay, "The Work of Art in the Age of Mechanical Reproduction."[22]

According to Benjamin, the aura of an artwork is created by the work's unique position in space and time and "its being imbedded in the fabric of tradition," something neither a technical nor a manual reproduction can replicate.[23] An object with an aura is always some distance away, however small, either temporally or spatially from the spectator, and the spectator is obliged to reduce that distance. However, because there is no limit to the number of prints one can make from a photographic negative, lens-based art does not possess this aura in the way a painting or a sculpture does.[24] As Benjamin states, "to ask for the 'authentic' print makes no sense," and without authenticity, there can be no aura.[25] For Benjamin the rise of mechanical reproduction is concomitant with the decay of the aura, as both the quality and quantity of the reproductions obviate the need to experience the original, unique object—the attraction of which, previously, had been its aura. According to Miriam Hansen, Benjamin was profoundly ambivalent about this decay.[26] On the one hand, the authority of the object is endangered, so the loss of the aura is to be lamented; yet it is only through the absence of the aura that it is possible to recognize that it ever existed.[27] Moreover, the decline of the aura indicates that new relationships between art and spectator are being formed, which may prove more advantageous and applicable to the circumstances in modern society—a thread later taken up by Bazin. Indeed, Böttcher's resonances with Bazin hinge partly on Bazin's assessment of these new relationships.

Böttcher's *Transformation* films interact with the concept of aura in two ways inextricably linked to their conceit, which, when combined, serve as a twofold dismissal of Benjamin's regard for the aura. First, the open use of multiple postcard reproductions of the featured paintings reminds the viewer that the paintings have already been stripped of their aura. This is not just incidental; it is precisely because the postcards lack the authenticity possessed by the original that Böttcher's whole project can come to fruition. Strawalde, of course, would never be allowed to add his own embellishments to the original artworks, nor would it be possible—even if he could conceivably have done it once—to repeat the process dozens of times. With mass-produced photographic postcards, however, Strawalde can create as many unique artworks as he pleases and only the concept of the original painting's aura is disturbed. Despite the fact that the films ignore the reverse side of the postcards, the use of postcards is also telling, as they are designed explicitly to be sturdy and portable enough to traverse the spatial and temporal distances that are so integral to the concept of aura. Böttcher is inviting his viewers to close that distance with him.

The second way in which *Transformations* interacts with Benjamin is precisely through Strawalde's creation of these new works of art. Each of Strawalde's overpaintings is a unique and authentic object in possession of its own aura, as Strawalde shows us when he flips through previous examples of his work on camera. However, even these auras of objects created by Strawalde himself are not considered important. The works are used in service of creating the films, which suggests, in the first place, that the desired effect is in the serial exhibition of the works, none of which individually appears on screen for more than a few moments at most before it is replaced. The value of each individual creation is subordinate to their combined presentation on film. However, there is also a critique inherent in this process. In the process of creating a new exhibition space for Strawalde's overpaintings, the film camera's mechanical reproduction of the images entails a simultaneous creation and destruction of their aura. The viewer is still never able to see the original of any of the overpaintings created throughout any of the three films.

The concept of the aura is by no means a new idea today, nor was it in 1981. Why then does Böttcher's disregard for the auras of the original paintings factor into his film? By disregarding the auras of the artworks on the postcards as well as the new paintings Strawalde creates in overpainting them, Böttcher is able to unite his two personae on a physical object. The surface of the postcard allows for an added dimension to this unification that would not result from simply filming Strawalde painting a blank canvas. When Strawalde paints on the reproduced photographs of paintings, he is engaging with and placing himself within the tradition of painting while still creating a new space where he can present his own voice. Dismantling the aura of the paintings allows Böttcher to set all three media—painting, photography, and film—on an equal footing. Filming this action and including the photographic postcard in the frame allows Böttcher to insert his persona into the tradition of lens-based art (photography being the necessary forerunner of film). Now, to more fully understand the relationships Böttcher sets up among these three media, we must turn to the work of André Bazin.

The Bazinian in Böttcher

In contrast to Benjamin, André Bazin was well-known in the GDR, at least in film circles; but his role in shaping East German film scholarship was nevertheless limited. From the official point of view, Bazin, like all Formalist film theorists, was useful only to the extent that he could serve as a foil for more orthodox Socialist Realist film theory. Still, Bazin did have an indirect impact on East German cinema, in that many East German filmmakers who came of age in the 1950s and 1960s were strongly influenced by Italian Neorealism, a movement that Bazin championed in his criticism. Because of this influence, many East German films, especially before 1965, the year of the Eleventh Plenum, lend themselves quite well to Bazinian readings.[28] Böttcher, who finished film school in 1960, was one such young filmmaker influenced by the Neorealists. To be sure, he does not appear to have stated a position on record regarding Bazin. Yet, it seems likely that Böttcher would have been at least tangentially aware of Bazin's work—he wanted to make Neorealist-style films, he was active in East German film discourse (which featured discussions of Bazin), and he attended international film festivals, where Western filmmakers could have discussed Bazin with him.

Three essays by Bazin stand out as most relevant to *Transformations*: "The Ontology of the Photographic Image" (1945), "Painting and Cinema,"[29] and a 1959 review of Henri-Georges Clouzot's *The Picasso Mystery* (1956). Taken together, these three essays lay out a framework for relating painting, photography, and cinema to each other in a unified way that neatly meshes with Böttcher's project in *Transformations*. "The Ontology of the Photographic Image" provides Bazin's interpretation of the evolution of the plastic (i.e., visual) arts as the sublimation of humanity's continued attempts to triumph over death. Bazin marks the invention of photography as a key inflection point in this evolution, because the superior representational ability of photography frees its predecessor (painting) from the burden of attempting to provide an objective view of reality.[30] "Painting and Cinema" sets up a dialectic between the titular modes of representation and posits films about art, such as Alain Resnais' *Van Gogh*,[31] as the synthesis of the two, its revolutionary act being a radical reorientation of the concept of the frame.[32] Lastly, in his review of *The Picasso Mystery*, Bazin posits that Clouzot's film demonstrates "that duration may be an integral part of the work itself, an additional dimension, which is foolishly ignored once a painting has been completed."[33] Each of the themes mentioned from these three essays applies to an aspect of *Transformations*, leading the trilogy to serve as a succinct encapsulation of several of Bazin's ideas about the combination of painting, photography, and film.

Painting and Photography: Representing Reality

The primary act that Böttcher has Strawalde engage in on film—painting over reproductions of paintings—is a playful physical manifestation of what Bazin proposes as a reconciliation of painting and photography. According to Bazin, all attempts at representation prior to photography would be doomed to dissatisfying results because "no matter how skillful the painter, his work was always in fee to an inescapable subjectivity. The fact that a human hand intervened cast a shadow of doubt over the image."[34] Photography removes this burden from painting by "completely satisfying our appetite for illusion by a mechanical reproduction in the making of which man plays no part."[35] Bazin views this as a positive because painting, having satisfied our "obsession with realism," need no longer strive for photo-realism and can now recover its "aesthetic autonomy."[36] For Bazin, this means that "the photograph allows us on the one hand to admire in reproduction something that our eyes alone could not have taught us to love, and on the other, to admire the painting as a thing in itself whose relation to something in nature has ceased to be the justification for its existence."[37] In *Transformations*, Böttcher reinserts humanity into the equation. This means that a photographic postcard does the work of representing something from the real world (here, ironically, a painting), while Strawalde the painter is free to make any additions he wants to the picture. The reproduction of the painting is satisfying what Bazin believes is the audience's desire to see something representational while Böttcher documents Strawalde exercising the freedom that painting now enjoys thanks to photography.

Böttcher's juxtaposition here further reinforces the link between painting and film. Bazin sees film as the natural extension of photography, with photography being a crucial bridge between painting and film, much as photographs of paintings serve as the focal point for Böttcher the filmmaker and Strawalde the painter. Bazin refers to film as "objectivity in time. The film is no longer content to preserve the object, enshrouded as it were in an instant."[38] Through the use of multiple reproductions of the same photograph, *Transformations* preserves multiple interactions and creative processes, with functionally the same image. Strawalde produces several different overpaintings based on the same image, and the film can toggle among these as it wishes.

Painting in Another Dimension

Transformations demonstrates to its audience what Clouzot's *Picasso Mystery* demonstrated to Bazin; specifically, how the intermediate stages of the creative process of painting "are not subordinate and inferior realities, parts of a process that will result in a final product: they are already the work itself, but a work that is destined to devour itself, or rather to metamorphose, until the painter wants to stop."[39] The key for Bazin in Clouzot's film is how the director understands that time is also a key element of painting and that in film that translates to twenty-four individual paintings per second. That is, with every additional brush stroke, the artist sacrifices one painting to create another. Duration is also the key to *Transformations*. As director, Böttcher could have simply presented an interminable slideshow of already painted over postcards; but instead, he integrated the creative process into the film, showing the audience Strawalde's hand (which Clouzot does not do with Picasso's) as he applies paint to the various photos of paintings. Moreover, he overlaps and combines creative processes, showing part of one and then quickly cutting to another—in this way Böttcher even goes beyond Bazin's conception of what film makes possible for painting.

A second important parallel between the two films is the element of suspense. Speaking of Clouzot's motivations for making the film, Bazin says, "the artistic creation is the only authentically spectacular element, the only cinematic one, because it is essentially temporal. Creation is pure waiting and uncertainty; it is 'suspense,' in that absence or incompleteness of subject creates anticipation in the viewer."[40] Viewing Strawalde's creative process is similarly suspenseful, but the lack of overarching narrative in the *Transformations* trilogy also creates anticipation in the viewer, especially in *Woman at the Clavichord*, which features much darker and more enigmatic drawings than the other two films.

In *The Picasso Mystery* Bazin sees the concept of suspense distilled down to an extreme case:

> "Suspense" in this film could, in fact, no longer be confused with a form of dramatic progression, with a certain ordering of the action, or with its explosion in violence. Literally nothing happens here, nothing but the carrying out over time of the artistic process; what gets emphasized is the performance of the painter's work itself more than the fulfillment of his subject. The action, if there is indeed any, has nothing to do with stock dramatic situations. This is a pure and free metamorphosis that is at root the direct apprehension of the freedom of the mind, made visible through art.[41]

Here again, *Transformations* parallels *The Picasso Mystery* with its focus on Strawalde's overpainting process, allowing viewers to experience the duration of the process as well as the final result.

Out of Frame: Postcards and Diapositive Slides

Though Bazin has anticipated much of Böttcher's experimental cycle, there is a key area where Böttcher moves beyond Bazin's examinations of painting, photography, and film. In addition to recontextualizing the canonical paintings that he features as reproductions on postcards, Böttcher also employs another type of photographic reproduction to explore the tangibility of paintings and bring them into a new context—namely, the diapositive slide. After showing the overpainting process in action and cycling through completed overpaintings for the first several minutes of each film, Böttcher then turns to projecting diapositive images of the original paintings as well as of his overpaintings onto a wide assortment of surfaces, objects, animals, and people.

According to Bazin, a painting's frame is a border between the internal world of the painting and the external reality of the viewer: "This explains the baroque complexity of the traditional frame whose job it is to establish something that cannot be geometrically established—namely the discontinuity between the painting and the wall, that is to say between the painting and reality."[42] When Bazin concludes from this that "space, as it applies to a painting, is radically destroyed by the screen,"[43] he means that the film camera can rob the painting of its orientation by only showing a portion of it on screen and as such the painting "is presented to the imagination as without any boundaries."[44] On the one hand, this is true for any object, but when the object being spatially deconstructed is a work of art meant to be seen as a whole, it becomes an even more radical act. Moving a painting, as opposed to other visual art objects, into the paradigm of lens-based art completely reconceptualizes that painting's relationship to the frame.

In film, the frame is the opposite of what it represents in painting: in cinema the frame comprises "the edges of a piece of masking that shows only a portion of reality."[45] The reality of a painting ends where the painter stops painting, and the picture frame represents those boundaries. The reality of a film or a photograph, on the other hand, is just as large as the one the viewer inhabits. Thus, rather than delimit the reality on screen, the frame instead signifies the point at which the filmed reality is hidden from the viewer. When a painting is seen in person, the frame indicates that there is nothing more to see beyond its borders. When a painting is shown in a film, the frame of the film can conceal parts of the painting and leave viewers with no control over which parts of the painting they can see. This leaves viewers with the knowledge that the film frame is hiding something and creates a potentially unresolved desire to conduct one's own viewing of the painting.

For this reason, the use of postcard reproductions brings an even more radical transformation of the spatial relationships involved. In addition to resizing the works, the photographs on the postcards do not reproduce the paintings' frames, leaving them, following Bazin, already lacking the boundary of the reality they inhabit, even before being filmed. Absent the constraint of the frames, the spatial reality of the authentic painting has, in essence, been transposed and intermingled with the spatial reality of Böttcher's apartment, where the filming takes place.

By incorporating diapositive slides into the films, Böttcher again radically alters the spatial orientation of the paintings by not only removing the frame but also removing the flat, two-dimensional surface of the canvas. Instead of projecting the slides onto a flat screen or wall, Böttcher overlays the images onto the everyday reality around him. He projects the slides onto a bed sheet—given depth and motion by a wafting breeze—as well as actor and fellow artist Erika Dobslaff, a cat, engine parts, a car, and even television programs. Taking Bazin's assertion one step further, that the filmed painting "takes on the spatial properties of cinema and becomes part of that 'picturable' world that lies beyond it on all sides,"[46] Böttcher literally inserts these paintings into the world, where they take on the three-dimensional depth of the objects they happen to fall upon. This depth is ever changing, as well, since Böttcher is constantly panning the projector across the surfaces, and the people he projects onto are almost always in motion.

One of the most interesting juxtapositions is the one that Böttcher leaves the audience with at the end of *Venus According to Giorgione*, when he projects an overpainting of *Sleeping Venus* onto a camera. He also returns to this briefly in the penultimate shot of *Woman at the Clavichord*, this time with *Interior with a Woman at the Virginal* overlaid on the camera. By turning the projections back onto the camera, Böttcher seems to be signaling a reminder that the world the projections inhabit will also be a reproduction, by virtue of its being filmed. Much as the postcards transmit to Böttcher the experience of the original paintings he works with, so the film transmits the creations Böttcher and Strawalde produce.

Conclusion

Even after German reunification, Böttcher has always presented himself as apolitical; he has never described himself as explicitly rebelling against the East German state, as such. Rather, his heterodoxy comes about through his intense artistic commitment to a Formalist vision that stood in contrast to the government's ossified hardline insistence on Socialist Realism.[47] In attempting to do through film what he had not been permitted to do in his visual art exhibitions, Böttcher seems primarily driven by a personal commitment to his own vision. Nevertheless, Böttcher and the *Transformations* trilogy became important to the burgeoning East German experimental, underground art scene that had emerged at the end of the 1970s and was much less circumspect about its opinions of not only GDR artistic policy, but the entire state apparatus. While Böttcher's trilogy remained the only experimental films to come out of the DEFA studios, the films, according to Christoph Tannert, "triggered a whole spectrum of 'alternative filmmaking' in the GDR."[48]

Transformations was profoundly influential to the underground experimental film scene that emerged in East Germany in the late 1970s and early 1980s.[49] Many experimental filmmakers in the GDR were inspired by Böttcher's bold cinematic experiments—what Edward Small calls "direct theory"[50]—and began to explore their own ideas about the effects of combining visual media on film. Independent filmmaker-painters, such as Cornelia Schleime, Helge Leiberg, Christine Schlegel, and Andreas Dress, incorporated the practice of painting over photographs into their own works, which led photographs to become important objects in the late East German underground film movement. Some, such as Schlegel, elided the photographic intermediary entirely and painted directly onto the Super-8 print itself.[51] These and other artists produced their films on Super-8 home movie stock outside of the state filmmaking structure and developed the film themselves in improvised vats of chemicals so as not to draw the attention of the authorities. These filmmakers, some of whom went on to become leading figures in the international art world, have provided documentation of a GDR reality very different from the one presented through official art channels.[52] Böttcher's *Transformations* also resonates within the discourse of international film studies. Speaking of Böttcher's work in these films, Claus Löser remarks that "the film-maker and painter connects up with traditions of the film avant-garde from Stan Brakhage to Jan Svankmajer."[53] The continued success of the artists inspired by Böttcher's films is a testament to the significance of his work. This chapter and, hopefully, others expanding on it will properly situate the trilogy not only within the context of GDR DEFA film, but also in the larger context of global experimental cinema.

Present-day viewers of the trilogy can see *Transformations* not just as a curiosity—a one-time slackening in the ideological strictures of a Marxist–Leninist, state-run film studio, but as a serious engagement with the structures and implications of various forms of visual media. By expanding on Bazinian ideas of what cinema is capable of when it turns its lens to photographs and paintings and adding an additional layer of meaning through the use of photographic reproductions and diapositive slides, Böttcher's implicit discourse with Bazin and Benjamin opens up multiple avenues for thinking about film, representational painting, and photography. Far from being a hodgepodge of jumbled images and recorded moments, the trilogy is a cogent exploration of intermedial forms and an attempt to expand on established visual media criticism and filmmaking techniques. These films further refute the reductive clichés that have historically been applied to East German cinema. By using photography as a bridge between his painter and filmmaker personalities, Böttcher also engaged with and challenged Western conceptions of visual media and provided thoughtful responses to foundational texts of the field that also challenged the orthodoxies imposed on the East German artistic community.

Matthew Bauman is Instructor of German at Transylvania University and a Ph.D. candidate at the University of Cincinnati where he is finishing his dissertation on DEFA and New German Cinema documentaries between 1961 and 1989. His further research interests include Weimar period film and literature as well as adaptation theory.

Notes

1. Wilhelm Roth, quoted in Britta Hartmann, "Böttcher, Jürgen," in *The Concise Routledge Encyclopedia of Documentary Film*, ed. Ian Aitken (London: Routledge, 2013), 104.
2. For previous publications on the *Transformations* films, see Seán Allan, *Screening Art: Modernist Aesthetics and the Socialist Imaginary in East German Cinema* (New York: Berghahn Books, 2019), 191–95; Seth Howes, *Moving Images on the Margins: Experimental Film in Late Socialist East Germany* (Rochester, NY: Camden House, 2019), 25–26; Claus Löser, *Strategien der Verweigerung: Untersuchungen zum politisch-ästhetischen Gestus unangepasster filmischer Artikulationen in der Spätphase der DDR* (Berlin: DEFA Stiftung, 2011), 105–6; and Christoph Tannert, "Von Vortönern und Erdferkeln: Die Filme der Bildermacher," in *Gegenbilder: filmische Subversion in der DDR, 1976–1989:*

Texte, Bilder, Daten, eds. Karin Fritzsche and Claus Löser (Berlin: Janus Press, 1996), 28–29.

3. Seán Allan, "Jürgen Böttcher: A Brief Visit," in accompanying booklet, *ART | WORK Six Shorts*, directed by Jürgen Böttcher (Amherst: DEFA Film Library, 2011), DVD, 7.
4. The image on each postcard featured in the films (as well as the images on nearly all mass-produced postcards made from the 1930s until the advent of digital printing) began as a photographic negative, which was then photomechanically reproduced as an ink print onto card stock. Photomechanical prints can be indistinguishable from photographic prints without close inspection, and numerous websites offer instructions for collectors on how to differentiate the two.
5. Diapositive slides are produced by taking a photograph on reversal film. Developing reversal film produces a transparent positive image or diapositive. Unlike the typical photographic negative, which must be transferred onto paper to be further developed into a positive print, the diapositive can be mounted directly in a frame to produce a slide that can be displayed with a slide projector or other suitable apparatus.
6. Or of a painting, as in the present case.
7. Christa Blümlinger, "Postcards in Agnès Varda's Cinema," in *Between Still and Moving Images*, ed. Laurent Guido and Olivier Lugon (New Barnet: John Libbey, 2012), 278.
8. Cf. Roland Barthes, "The Problem of Signification in Cinema," in *Signs and Images: Writings on Art, Cinema and Photography*, ed. and trans. Chris Turner (London: Seagull Books, 2016), 21–34.
9. Establishing distinct filmmaker and painter identities had practical advantages alongside the aesthetic implications. Jürgen Böttcher the filmmaker was able to exploit his position within DEFA to give Strawalde the painter a forum for his art that was otherwise regularly denied to him by the East German government. This secured a space for both personae to comment on the relationship between mechanical reproduction and artistic expression.
10. In *Potter's Bull* the painting is French Romantic painter Théodore Chassériau's *Sleeping Nymph* (1850), and in *Venus According to Giorgione*, it is the titular *Sleeping Venus*.
11. Walter Benjamin, "The Work of Art in the Age of Mechanical Reproduction," in *Illuminations*, ed. Hannah Arendt, trans. Harry Zohn (New York: Schocken Books, 1969), 217–51.
12. See essays by André Bazin: "*The Picasso Mystery*," in "A Bergsonian Film: *The Picasso Mystery*," trans. Bert Cardullo, *The Journal of Aesthetic Education* 35, no. 2 (2001): 1–9; "The Ontology of the Photographic Image," and "Painting and Cinema," in *What Is Cinema?*, vol. 1, trans. Hugh Gray (Berkeley: University of California Press, 1967), 9–16 and 164–69.
13. Böttcher also contributed a brief segment to the eleven-minute 1962 short *Three of Us—A Film for the Sixth Party Conference of the SED* (*Drei von uns—Ein Film zum VI. Parteitag der SED*) alongside Heinz Fischer and Heinz Müller, but it "cannot be considered as an authentic Böttcher piece." Cf. Claus Löser, "Jürgen Böttcher: Filmography/ Filmographie," in *Jürgen Böttcher: Films/Filme 1957–2001*, ed. Kraft Wetzel (Berlin: Nirwana Edition, 2002), 37.
14. The eleventh meeting of the Central Committee of the Socialist Unity Party (16–18 December 1965) resulted in the official position that East German cultural production should rededicate itself to a stricter adherence to Socialist Realism. As a consequence of this decision, numerous pieces of culture were halted midproduction or, if already complete, banned from release. In addition to *Born in '45*, other prominent examples include Heiner Müller's play *Construction Site* (*Der Bau*, 1965), Frank Beyer's film

Trace of Stones (*Spur der Steine*, 1966), and Kurt Maetzig's film *The Rabbit Is Me* (*Das Kaninchen bin ich*, 1965). Böttcher, like other directors, was able to retrieve his raw footage after German reunification and produce a final cut of *Born in '45* that received a cinematic release in 1990, but the ban had profound effects on him personally and professionally in the intervening three decades. The most prominent of these being that he was not given the chance to make another feature film until the 1980s, at which point he claims to no longer have had the desire. Despite his stated loss of interest in making feature films, Böttcher laments that he has never had the experience of a proper premiere for any of his films. See Jürgen Böttcher, "Jürgen Böttcher: Der Moment, der ist," in *Dokumentarisch Arbeiten*, interview by Christoph Hübner, ed. Gabrielle Voss (Berlin: Vorwerk 8, 1996), 11–13.
15. Documentary was seen as a less prestigious genre given its usual presentation as educational fare or as preshow material for feature films. Böttcher could, however, take some consolation in the fact that "East German documentarists . . . enjoyed certain advantages over their West German counterparts which should not be underestimated." See Richard Kilbourn, "The Documentary Work of Jürgen Böttcher: A Retrospective," in *DEFA: East German Cinema 1946–1992*, ed. Seán Allan and John Sandford (New York: Berghahn Books, 2003), 267.
16. Cf. Nick Hodgin, "Alternative Realities and Authenticity in DEFA's Documentary Films," in *DEFA at the Crossroads of East German and International Film Culture: A Companion*, ed. Marc Silberman and Henning Wrage (Berlin: de Gruyter, 2014), 294.
17. Kilbourn, "Documentary Work," 271.
18. Hartmann, "Böttcher," 104.
19. Cf. Nedelcho Milev, "Eisenstein, Bazin und der moderne Film," *Filmwissenschaftliche Beiträge* 1 (1968): 141–67. Here, Bulgarian critic Milev argues that André Bazin and Siegfried Kracauer have made contributions to film theory worth considering but are nevertheless inferior as theorists when compared to the Soviet Union's Sergei Eisenstein.
20. See Michael Opitz, "Benjamin, Walter," in *Metzler Lexikon DDR Literatur: Autoren—Institutionen—Debatten*, ed. Michael Opitz and Michael Hofmann (Stuttgart: Verlag J. B. Metzler, 2009), 33.
21. "Benjamins Schriften spielten für die theoretische Fundierung einer sich etablierenden marxistischen Literaturwissenschaft in der DDR keine Rolle" (Opitz, "Benjamin," 33).
22. Benjamin, "Work of Art," 220–24.
23. Ibid., 223.
24. The exception being early portrait photography, which acquired its aura through the cult value of a portrait of a loved one as a remembrance aid. See ibid., 226.
25. Ibid., 224.
26. See Miriam Hansen, "Benjamin, Cinema and Experience: 'The Blue Flower in the Land of Technology,'" *New German Critique* 40 (1987): 187.
27. Hansen, "Benjamin, Cinema and Experience," 189.
28. Cf. Joshua Feinstein, *The Triumph of the Ordinary: Depictions of Daily Life in the East German Cinema 1949–1989* (Chapel Hill: University of North Carolina Press, 2002), 57–59; and Hodgin, "Alternative Realities," 291.
29. Angela Dalle Vacche, "Introduction," in *The Visual Turn: Classical Film Theory and Art History*, ed. Angela Dalle Vacche (New Brunswick: Rutgers University Press, 2003), 28. The date of this essay is listed as unknown in both the original French and the translated English editions of *What Is Cinema?*, but Angela Dalle Vacche places it between 1943 and 1951.
30. Bazin, "Ontology," 11.

31. In addition to *Van Gogh*, Resnais made several other short films about artists and their art, projects that he called "visits." Though positive confirmation is not forthcoming, there is reason to suspect that Böttcher was also aware of Resnais' films, as he made a "visit" short of his own—*Hermann Glöckner: A Short Visit* (*Kurzer Besuch bei Hermann Glöckner*, 1984).
32. Bazin, "Painting," 165–166.
33. Bazin, "*Picasso Mystery*," 3.
34. Bazin, "Ontology," 12.
35. Ibid.
36. Ibid., 16.
37. Ibid.
38. Ibid., 8.
39. Bazin, "*Picasso Mystery*," 3.
40. Ibid., 4.
41. Ibid., 5.
42. Bazin, "Painting," 165.
43. Ibid.
44. Ibid., 166.
45. Ibid.
46. Ibid.
47. Among Warsaw Pact nations, East Germany stood out for its adherence to this artistic mode well after others, including the USSR, had slackened their own restrictions.
48. Quoted in Löser, "Jürgen Böttcher," 44.
49. For more on these unsanctioned experimental films, see Howes, *Moving Images on the Margins*; Löser, *Strategien der Verweigerung*; and *Counter Images: GDR Underground Films 1983–1989: The Nonconformist Super-8 Scene* (Amherst: DEFA Film Library, 2008), a DVD compilation by Löser of ten such films.
50. Small contends that experimental films and videos also function as theoretical texts using their images and symbols to convey ideas in place of words. Edward S. Small, *Direct Theory: Experimental Film/Video as Major Genre* (Carbondale: Southern Illinois University Press, 1994).
51. Ginnalberto Bendazzi, *Animation: A World History*, vol. 2: *The Birth of a Style—The Three Markets* (Boca Raton: CRC Press, 2016), 241.
52. A selection of ten of these films are available in the DVD compilation *Counter Images*.
53. Löser, "Jürgen Böttcher," 44. Brakhage, in fact, had a hand in the creation of the films, having encouraged Böttcher to realize the concept when the two met at a film festival in Amsterdam. See Hodgin, "Alternative Realities," 290.

Bibliography

Allan, Seán. "Jürgen Böttcher: A Brief Visit." Essay in accompanying booklet, *ART | WORK Six Shorts*, directed by Jürgen Böttcher, 1–9. Amherst: DEFA Film Library, 2011. DVD.

———. *Screening Art: Modernist Aesthetics and the Socialist Imaginary in East German* Cinema. New York: Berghahn Books, 2019.

Barthes, Roland. "The Problem of Signification in Cinema." In *Signs and Images: Writings on Art, Cinema and Photography*, edited and translated by Chris Turner, 21–34. London: Seagull Books, 2016.

Bazin, André. "The Ontology of the Photographic Image." In *What Is Cinema?* Volume 1. Translated by Hugh Gray, 9–16. Berkeley: University of California Press, 1967.

———. "Painting and Cinema." In *What Is Cinema?* Volume 1. Translated by Hugh Gray, 164–69. Berkeley: University of California Press, 1967.

———. "*The Picasso Mystery*." In "A Bergsonian Film: *The Picasso Mystery*." Translated by Bert Cardullo. *The Journal of Aesthetic Education* 35, no. 2 (2001): 1–9.

Bendazzi, Giannalberto. *Animation: A World History*. Volume 2: *The Birth of a Style—The Three Markets*. Boca Raton: CRC Press, 2016.

Benjamin, Walter. "The Work of Art in the Age of Mechanical Reproduction." In *Illuminations*, edited by Hannah Arendt and translated by Harry Zohn, 217–51. New York: Schocken Books, 1969.

Blümlinger, Christa. "Postcards in Agnès Varda's Cinema." In *Between Still and Moving Images*, edited by Laurent Guido and Olivier Lugon, 275–89. New Barnet: John Libbey, 2012.

Böttcher, Jürgen. "Jürgen Böttcher: Der Moment, der ist." In *Dokumentarisch Arbeiten*, interview by Christoph Hübner, edited by Gabriele Voss, 10–27. Berlin: Vorwerk 8, 1996.

Dalle Vacche, Angela. "Introduction." In *The Visual Turn: Classical Film Theory and Art History*, edited by Angela Dalle Vacche, 1–29. New Brunswick: Rutgers University Press, 2003.

Feinstein, Joshua. *The Triumph of the Ordinary: Depictions of Daily Life in the East German Cinema 1949–1989*. Chapel Hill: University of North Carolina Press, 2002.

Hansen, Miriam. "Benjamin, Cinema and Experience: 'The Blue Flower in the Land of Technology.'" *New German Critique* 40 (1987): 179–224.

Hartmann, Britta. "Böttcher, Jürgen." In *The Concise Routledge Encyclopedia of Documentary Film*, edited by Ian Aitken, 104–6. London: Routledge, 2013.

Hodgin, Nick. "Alternative Realities and Authenticity in DEFA's Documentary Films." In *DEFA at the Crossroads of East German and International Film Culture: A Companion*, edited by Marc Silberman and Henning Wrage, 281–303. Berlin: de Gruyter, 2014.

Howes, Seth. *Moving Images on the Margins: Experimental Film in Late Socialist East Germany*. Rochester, NY: Camden House, 2019.

Kilbourn, Richard. "The Documentary Work of Jürgen Böttcher: A Retrospective." In *DEFA: East German Cinema 1946–1992*, edited by Seán Allan and John Sandford, 267–82. New York: Berghahn Books, 2003.

Löser, Claus. "Jürgen Böttcher: Filmography/Filmographie." In *Jürgen Böttcher: Films/Filme 1957–2001*, edited by Kraft Wetzel, 35–47. Berlin: Nirwana Edition, 2002.

———. *Strategien der Verweigerung: Untersuchungen zum politisch-ästhetischen Gestus unangepasster filmischer Artikulationen in der Spätphase der DDR*. Berlin: DEFA Stiftung, 2011.

Milev, Nedelcho. "Eisenstein, Bazin und der moderne Film." *Filmwissenschaftliche Beiträge* 1 (1968): 141–67.

Opitz, Michael. "Benjamin, Walter." In *Metzler Lexikon DDR Literatur: Autoren—Institutionen—Debatten*, edited by Michael Opitz and Michael Hofmann, 33–34. Stuttgart: Verlag J. B. Metzler, 2009.

Small, Edward S. *Direct Theory: Experimental Film/Video as Major Genre*. Carbondale: Southern Illinois University Press, 1994.

Tannert, Christoph. "Von Vortönern und Erdferkeln: Die Filme der Bildermacher." In *Gegenbilder: filmische Subversion in der DDR, 1976–1989: Texte, Bilder, Daten*, edited by Karin Fritzsche and Claus Löser, 25–60. Berlin: Janus Press, 1996.

Filmography

Born in '45 (*Jahrgang 45*). Directed by Jürgen Böttcher. Potsdam: DEFA-Studio für Spielfilme, 1966.

Counter Images: GDR Underground Films 1983–1989: The Nonconformist Super-8 Scene. Amherst: DEFA Film Library, 2008. DVD.

Hermann Glöckner: A Short Visit (*Kurzer Besuch bei Hermann Glöckner*). Directed by Jürgen Böttcher. Potsdam: DEFA-Studio für Dokumentarfilme, 1984.

The Kitchen (*Die Küche*). Directed by Jürgen Böttcher. Potsdam: DEFA-Studio für Dokumentarfilme, 1986.

Potter's Bull (*Potters Stier*). Directed by Jürgen Böttcher. Potsdam: DEFA-Studio für Dokumentarfilme, 1981.

The Rabbit Is Me (*Das Kaninchen bin ich*). Directed by Kurt Maetzig. Potsdam: DEFA-Studio für Spielfilme, 1965.

Shunters (*Rangierer*). Directed by Jürgen Böttcher. Potsdam: DEFA-Studio für Dokumentarfilme, 1984.

Three of Us—A Film for the Sixth Party Conference of the SED (*Drei von uns—Ein Film zum VI. Parteitag der SED*). Directed by Jürgen Böttcher, Heinz Fischer, and Heinz Müller. Potsdam: DEFA-Studio für Dokumentarfilme, 1962.

Trace of Stones (*Spur der Steine*). Directed by Frank Beyer. Potsdam: DEFA-Studio für Spielfilme, 1966.

Van Gogh. Directed by Alain Resnais. Paris: Panthéon Production, 1947.

Venus According to Giorgione (*Venus nach Giorgione*). Directed by Jürgen Böttcher. Potsdam: DEFA-Studio für Dokumentarfilme, 1981.

Woman at the Clavichord (*Frau am Klavichord*). Directed by Jürgen Böttcher. Potsdam: DEFA-Studio für Dokumentarfilme, 1981.

Chapter 6

The Promise of Agency

Photographs and Value in *Tattoo* (2002)

Cynthia Porter

Tattoos are both at the heart and in the title of Robert Schwentke's 2002 German crime-thriller *Tattoo*. Set in Berlin, *Tattoo* follows homicide detectives Minks and Schrader as they investigate a series of crimes that are linked by one primary detail: each dead body they discover is missing a large swath of tattooed skin. Minks, the case's lead detective, hand picks Officer Schrader, the black sheep of the police academy, because the younger officer has insider knowledge of alternative, underground cultures, where the killer might be lurking. Soon the pair learn about a recently deceased tattoo artist named Hiromitsu whose artwork connects all the cases, as do fringe social groups. After the complicated suicide of the prime murder suspect, Schrader discovers information about a digital black market, where the flayed, tattooed skins of victims are being auctioned. The motivation for the auction website becomes clear: the high-brow art world is embracing tattoos as its new, highly prized commodity to be bought, sold, and collected.

Schwentke's *Tattoo* has yet to be paid the thorough scholarly attention it deserves. While it has been tied to a short story written by Roald Dahl and discussed through the lens of gender politics and its undertones of Nazi ideologies, the film remains largely overlooked within German and Film Studies criticism.[1] However, the film is worthy of sustained critical scrutiny because it deploys the photographic medium in ways both expected and unexpected for the crime genre. In the plot, photographs assist the police duo working to solve a series of murders: these images preserve innocence and love; record proof and documentation; present danger and threats; capture embarrassment and shame. Ultimately, though, in juxtaposing the medium of the photograph with the moving image, the film posits the ways in which photography poses different arguments and judgments of its subject, calling for the consumer to interpret and invest in the contents of a photograph in a particular way.

By exploring photography's multiple functions, this chapter illustrates how *Tattoo* invites viewers to assess the medium's evidentiary aspects, varying contexts, and how photographs can influence assignments of value and cultural perception. By featuring photographs of tattooed bodies in gallery exhibition catalogs, the film elevates the body-art practice to high art—troubling the association of tattoos with the underground body-art scene or with the inhumane practices of Nazi Germany. The chapter concludes with a discussion of how the film addresses the subject of tattoos appraised as art across the span of social class before closing with an examination of how Tattoo Studies approaches this task.

Driving the Plot and Illuminating Characters: Photos in *Tattoo*

Photography in Schwentke's film is often presented as an unflinching medium that provides evidence of significant events and moments in time. This becomes clear when the detectives visit the morgue to learn more about the recently murdered Lynn Wilson. When Wilson's charred and disfigured corpse is pulled out from a refrigerated cabinet, the rookie Schrader quickly turns away in disgust. Viewing the body directly is too much for him to handle. Thus, for most of the sequence, an uneasy Schrader stands at a distance with his back to the corpse, Minks, and the autopsy technician (see figure 6.1). The rookie stands in medium close-up profile, filling most of the frame while the veterans face each other in conversation to the right in soft focus. It is only later while viewing photographs of the woman's burnt corpse that Schrader is able to bear the sight of her. Sitting in the passenger seat of Minks' car, Schrader can casually flip through a large photo binder, where each gruesome image has its own page and protective plastic sleeve. One full-page photograph shows a close-up of the corpse's charred head, open mouth, and forked tongue, which serves to confirm that the victim was active in Berlin's body-modification scene. On the opposite page of the binder and framed within a long shot, another photograph captures the body on a metal table in the morgue, giving Schrader more

Figure 6.1. *Tattoo.* Directed by Robert Schwentke. Munich: Lounge Entertainment AG, 2002. Screen capture by Cynthia Porter.

visual context for the close-up image. Viewed through a car window as Schrader and Minks drive from Wilson's apartment, the photographs are presented through a layering of transparent barriers—first of the window and then the protective plastic sleeve of the binder. Each level provides the viewer more distance from the brutal yet flat images.

This distancing is precisely what Schrader needs to effectively regard the violence and mutilation subjected to the victim. Coupled with their presentation in a photo binder, the indirect witnessing provided by the photographs gives them a clinical and emotionally mute tone, which renders them more objective. Photographs are of more value to the detectives because they offer a detached visual record of evidence. However, this detachment does not mean that the significance assigned to the images is in any way diminished. Instead, the removed perspective might assist in coming to terms with images and experiences that are otherwise emotionally overwhelming. In this way Schrader benefits from the flatness and cold detachment offered by the photographs of Wilson's corpse—they enable him to do his job; he can do more with the photographic evidence than he could with direct access to the corpse.

However, contrasting with the cold objectivity of autopsy photographs, the film also employs photographs in a personal and emotional manner. For example, as Minks begins to trust Schrader and his skills, the older detective gives his partner a photo of an eight- or nine-year-old girl. In the picture, a grinning, school-aged girl with her hair split into two braids is shown in a medium close-up, one hand cupping the side of her face in a clearly staged pose that communicates childhood innocence. The older detective instructs

Figure 6.2. *Tattoo*. Directed by Robert Schwentke. Munich: Lounge Entertainment AG, 2002. Screen capture by Cynthia Porter.

Schrader to keep a look out for this girl, who he claims is the daughter of a friend. It is only later, inside Minks' home, that Schrader recognizes the young girl's face in numerous family portraits hanging on a wall (see figure 6.2). When he finds his younger partner staring at the portraits, the previously icy Minks shows a more tender, vulnerable side. The girl in the photos is Marie, Minks' daughter, who distanced herself from him years ago. These photographs for Minks are frozen moments from a better time in his life, preserving the innocence of his daughter while simultaneously connecting him to a period when his family was still intact—before the death of his wife. A hard-bitten detective while at work, Minks at home quickly becomes filled with loss and regret when in the presence of his photographic shrine to his former life.

The photograph of Marie as a child functions as a catalyst for Schrader, who views it as a piece of a bigger puzzle that needs to be solved. After realizing that he likely could not find Marie on his own, he passes the photo along to his roommate, Meltem, who is then able to successfully identify Marie and bring the two together. The passing on of the photograph exemplifies the mobility of the medium while also presenting how easily it disseminates the information it contains. In this case, Meltem, a disc jockey who performs at clubs and navigates the same social circles as Schrader, does not require much contextual information before she is able to identify Marie while working a gig. After seeing a heavily crumpled and folded photograph of Marie as a child, Meltem directs Schrader to a woman at the bar. Meltem easily recognized the grown-up Marie from the picture of her as a child—something Schrader proves unable to do on his own.

The two sets of aforementioned photographs function in different ways. The manner in which the images of Wilson are presented communicates a cold professionalism because they are packaged in an officious binder of photo evidence that Schrader and Minks consult to solve the mystery of Wilson's murder. These photos are large, protected, and provide a close-up of Wilson's corpse for further investigative scrutiny. Alternatively, while Marie's photo is handed to Schrader while he is on the job, the investigation of her whereabouts is officially off the books. The search for Marie, like the presentation of her childhood photograph, is personal. Rather than being housed in a binder, like the harsh and gruesome pictures of Wilson, Marie's photograph is transported in pockets and handled directly with bare hands. The photo passes from one person to the next in an almost casual manner despite the sense of urgency to find its subject. The effective dissemination of information contained by Marie's photograph then also shows its ease in mobilizing action to find its subject within the communities in which it is circulated.

This is not a new function of the medium, as photography has been broadly and historically employed to find missing or wanted persons. In the case of *Tattoo*, the photo of Marie operates in a similar manner and successfully accomplishes the task of bringing Schrader together with its subject. Unlike the flat and emotionally void photographs that are featured in criminal files in the film, the photo of Marie communicates connection. Before passing it on to Schrader, Minks carries this image around with him, which can be read as an expression of love and the preservation of the innocence of a child that has since grown into an independent adult.

In contrast to preserving love and innocence, the use of photography to document and categorize criminal files is common in crime films, and Schwentke's *Tattoo* is no exception. Beginning their investigation, Minks and Schrader go to the morgue, where they learn that all of the victims were killed by the same murderer: Norbert Günzel. Günzel is first introduced to the viewer through his criminal file, complete with a black-and-white mugshot. Unlike the photographs of Wilson's corpse or Marie, Günzel's photo is printed on a piece of paper and housed in a file folder that is simply tossed onto Schrader's bed. When the audience first sees Günzel's mugshot, it is revealed in what seems like a POV shot with the camera tilting down from a long shot of a seated Minks to the criminal's photograph. The camera here racks focus to a close-up of Günzel's file, complete with bureaucratic details and the mugshot. Shown in profile with the back of his head pressed against some kind of stabilizing device, the criminal is presented clinically, objectively, and shirtless, which displays what Minks considers his most identifiable physical trait: a heart-shaped tattoo located on his right upper arm. Deemed dangerous and low-class through his prior convictions, the file—and the photograph housed within it—is handled more dismissively than any other photograph in the film. The combination of a mugshot and criminal file visually tags Günzel as a potential threat and serves as an identification tool that later proves useful in the film as Schrader comes face-to-face with the killer.

Rather than Minks, it is Schrader who appears to be the constant consumer of photographs in *Tattoo*. Although Schrader does not spend a large amount of time looking at each image, he views photographs as absolute truths, or at least as platforms from which contextual narratives are built. Providing Schrader with evidence of truth in different ways, Wilson's photos reaffirm the level of violence that her murderer is capable of and assist in unearthing a crime ring on the dark web; Marie's photo confirms a connection to Minks that makes finding her personal, communicating an urgency that she must be found; and Günzel's mugshot provides evidence of a suspect capable of extreme brutality and contributes to later identifying the criminal. Each photographic genre seen in the film, ranging from the casual and seemingly mundane to the official and devoid of emotion, offers insight into how Schrader reads and assigns meaning to these images.

One theme throughout the film involves the accurate identification of a photographed subject outside the confines of the medium. Schrader, for example, is consistently given photographs throughout the film—photographic documentation, the photo catalog of Hiromitsu's tattoos, and even photos from Wilson's apartment—and while he does successfully use them to either track down the subjects or those responsible for the subject's demise, the process of translating isolated moments of time into the reality of his everyday life challenges the detective. He finds himself struggling with how the contents of the photographs reflect the dark motivations behind murders: illegal bidding on body parts and the sinister side of a city in which he is an active participant.

As Schrader pieces together that all twelve of the people who bore tattoos created by Hiromitsu are either reported as dead or missing, the viewer is presented with another function of photography within the film: photography of goods for sale. While inspecting evidence from Günzel's last crime scene, Schrader finds transactional information for a number of gruesome sales. Günzel has been selling the tattooed skin of—and off—his victims through an anonymous chat room on the dark web. A lawyer, collector, and active bidder in this black-market chat room, Frank Schoubya, provides details of how some tattoos are sold for exorbitant amounts of money and often placed for sale by a user under the pseudonym Irezumi, which means "tattoo" in Japanese. Irezumi is then pegged as the instigator of the murders, circulating orders for fulfillment, which then lead to the deaths of those who previously carried the desired ink. Through the accidental self-incriminating behavior of Schoubya, revealed by jumping for the bait of what had been Wilson's Hiromitsu tattoo, Minks and Schrader are provided with the information they need to attempt to capture the criminal operating under the username Irezumi.

The incriminating photographs found on Günzel's computer also serve as evidence of the violence done to his victims before their tattoos are posted for sale. The photographs that are taken and uploaded in the black-market chat room show the victims shackled, chained, abused, and exposed, thus exhibiting their tattoos as being accessible and available for purchase. When Minks and Schrader search Günzel's home, they find his basement transformed into a type of brutal workstation where he presumably brought his victims and forcibly separated them from their tattoos. In the basement, Schrader notices what is later determined to be Wilson's tattoo submerged in a preserving liquid. Later confirming their suspicions, Schrader finds the photos and associative information on Günzel's personal computer.

When used in the chat room, the medium of photography is then selected for not only communicating proof of possessing something of value, in this case being tattoos still on the bodies of their original owners, but also presenting them for sale. The photos provide proof of a predetermined value that is then assessed and renegotiated in a bidding war. Yet, aside from the monetary terms that are assigned to each photographed piece, the aesthetic of these photographs and how it informs how the images will be received is also important. Most of the photos of the victims found in Günzel's computer appear to be helpless, abused, and perhaps even drugged. However, there is a starkly different tone to the photos of Maya Kroner, who is both a friend of the deceased Wilson and who has a publicly unknown Hiromitsu tattoo on her body.

In another convoluted plot twist, Schrader attempts to capture Irezumi by recreating photographs of a tattooed body to be sold on the dark web. To trap Irezumi, Schrader and his team stage their photographs of Kroner with the same kind of violent and grungy atmosphere depicted in previous photographs of Günzel's victims. They post the recreated photos to the anonymous chat room and wait for the bidding to begin, hoping that Irezumi will see them and place a bid. Most importantly, however, what they have not yet realized is that the person they are trying to entrap (Irezumi) in the online auction is actually the person they're using as bait (Kroner) in the photographs. But their self-assured confidence in the evidentiary power of a photograph—that the viewer of the photo will believe what they see—reflects the folly of their own understanding of the medium and how they use it. Thus, they exaggeratedly focus on the external details—use of a similar camera, handcuffs, and how the nude body is presented. Kroner's duplicity, however, works in a way that leverages the instability of photographic evidence.

Connected to a more general visual literacy, this section of the film reflects the police's failure to look past external appearances projected by people as well as images. The detectives are so confident in their ability to seek out truth, evidence, and proof that they overlook the possibility that they too can be duped. A naive belief in the evidentiary nature of photography and their interest in using Kroner as an object make them fail to consider her as a subject. Because of her appearance as a successful, white, upper-middle class, blonde, German woman—cultural tags of innocence[2]—the detectives did not recognize her as a potential suspect. Kroner, now revealed as a femme fatale, uses photography to assist in camouflaging and recreating a narrative that enables her to hide in plain sight.

In *Tattoo*, photographs provide more advantages than disadvantages as the plot progresses. As previously mentioned, the film avoids the topic of how easily a photograph can be manipulated but rather focuses on how it can be used to manipulate the perceptions of others. By double-crossing Schrader, Kroner exemplifies how consumers of photography can be manipulated by its contents. But Kroner's reveal as a villain succeeds in the film precisely because the medium itself is so consistently framed as providing a reliable image of what is in front of the lens. In each instance of photography in *Tattoo*, the photos provide a point of departure for further investigation either in the multiplying cases of murder or in personal relationships. Schrader largely performs the heavy lifting that leads to the further uncovering of the backstory each photo presents in the plot. He interacts with photograph images as absolute, self-contained snapshots of truth. In *Tattoo*, the truth contained in the photos is presented in such a way that makes photos appear more accessible because of their finitude of communication. There is a lack of conversation around and about them. Instead, Schrader silently (and effectively) consumes the photographs as points of reference and assistance in accomplishing his job.

In marked contrast to the consideration of photos lending themselves to multiple and various interpretations, Schrader and Minks handle photos in the film as if they are simplistic and provide just enough information to be productive without oversaturating their consumer. In comparison to the moving images—experienced in the form of video pornography in the film—Schrader and Minks appear overwhelmed and discomfited by what the moving image offers them. After learning that their prime suspect created pornographic films, the duo watches a sampling of Günzel's work on screen before quickly agreeing that the medium of film, at least in this case, did not present the ideal approach to learning more about him. Instead, they abandon the moving image and opt to find the director of the pornographic films to determine Günzel's whereabouts. Yet it is the backdrop of a fake city skyline—a photograph—featured in the sex scene that aids in identifying the set of the pornographic production. Here, we see Minks and Schrader back within their comfort zone of using photographic images as evidence to effectively get closer to catching Günzel. Throughout the film, photographs are continuously proven productive and effective resources as they serve a variety of functions—largely in regard to proving theories and suspicions in the plot.

As discussed in this section, the photographs in *Tattoo* clearly fulfill a spectrum of functions and are embedded in almost every corner of the plot: from the preserving of innocence and love to the recording of proof and documentation, the assignment of diverse types of value, as well as being used as a tool for manipulating others. The film uses photography as a medium that provides information that cannot merely be taken at face value. While photographs are simply passed from one character to the next and are not explicitly scrutinized in the film, they instigate investigation by presenting catalysts to question perceptions of truth, intention, and value.

The Power of Photography

The use of photographs in *Tattoo* forces questions about how they contribute to the storyline and how, by including them, the film communicates a stance on the topics of art and class. This section examines how *Tattoo*'s use of photography intersects with debates in the field of photography theory. Ideas put forth by Roland Barthes, Fred Ritchin, and Susan Sontag contextualize the relationship between the personal and professional uses of photographs in the film, the multivalence of photographs that blur the line between truth (and therefore evidence) and fiction, the role of the witness, and the exhibitory value of photographs as they are used in the film.

Discussing one of the many functions fulfilled by photographs in his book *Camera Lucida*, Roland Barthes comments on the way photographs lend themselves to providing proof in varying situations. According to Barthes, the photograph gives its consumer a sense of connection between the object of the image and its relationship with reality. "By attesting that the object has been real," he observes, "the photograph surreptitiously induces belief that it is alive, because of that delusion which makes us attribute to Reality an absolutely superior, somehow eternal value; but by shifting this reality to the past ('this-has-been'), the photograph suggests that it is already dead."[3] Barthes' statement relates to some of the core functions of photographs presented in *Tattoo*: the ability of a photograph to simultaneously exhibit what happened (therefore serving as evidence in this genre) while also anticipating what will happen—namely, death.

This is especially on display when Schrader examines the photographs of Wilson's corpse. Their relationship to Barthes' "that-has-been" is indicated by their content as well as their context: the photographs prove that a human named Lynn Wilson existed at a certain time and place in the past, but their context (collected in a binder that the detective Schrader flips through) transforms this pastness into evidence, thereby allowing Schrader to regard them as "true." The photographs of Lynne Wilson's body witness that a violent crime took place, the magnitude of that violence, and serve as evidence in their attempt to find the perpetrator. Clarifying what photography offers its viewer, Barthes notes, "The Photograph does not necessarily say *what is no longer*, but only and for certain *what has been*."[4] The "that-has-been" photographs of the corpse are used to determine precisely how and why the death occurred; the content and context of these images are employed to learn more about a past reality.

As demonstrated previously, in addition to their evidentiary role in the plot, photographs can also be used as devices in films to provide more insight into the characters by drawing upon emotions and common cultural practices. This is most apparent in the way that the photograph of Minks' daughter circulates, which evokes another aspect of Barthes' "that-has-been." The photograph of Marie tells us more about the detectives than about Marie herself, who appears in the film mainly in the form of this image. Freed from the glass picture frame, Marie's photograph is passed by hand from Minks to Schrader and then on to

Schrader's roommate, Meltem. The photograph evokes Mink's longing for his innocent daughter before he lost her, his memory of the death of his wife, his fear of the death of his daughter, and his suspicion that their reconciliation will never happen. What both the viewer and Schrader see in the image is a frozen moment in Minks' life when his perception of family and life was better than in the filmic present. Put simply, when the photo was taken, Marie was safe and connected in a family unit with Minks and his wife, who was still alive at the time. While Minks has since lost his wife in an auto accident, he now fears the demise of Marie. Carrying around the photograph, he holds onto the hope that his lost daughter, first lost solely through the inability to locate her, will not worsen to the feared loss of her life—removing any possible chance for reconciliation. Thus, the "that-has-been" of a single image illuminates and motivates so much in the film—characters, their pasts, their hopes, and their plans.

As much as photographs in this film point back to a comfortable past, they also assert the possibility of an unwanted, inevitable future. In providing Schrader with his daughter's photograph, Minks is hoping to forestall something that he fears: the possibility that Marie is already dead. This distressing prospect, an unwelcome attendant of the image, is what Barthes would call the photograph's punctum. Providing a salient example of the relationship between the photograph, its punctum, and death, Barthes reflects on an image from 1865 of Lewis Payne waiting to be hanged for his assassination attempt of Secretary of State W. H. Seward. Barthes writes:

> The photograph is handsome, as is the boy: that is the *studium*. But the *punctum* is: *he is going to die*. I read at the same time: *This will be* and *this has been*; I observe with horror an anterior future of which death is the stake. By giving me the absolute past of the pose (aorist), the photograph tells me death is in the future. What *pricks* me is the discovery of this equivalence. In front of the photograph of my mother as a child, I tell myself: she is going to die: I shudder . . . *over a catastrophe which has already occurred*. Whether or not the subject is already dead, every photograph is this catastrophe. . . . there is always a defeat of Time in them: *that* is dead and *that* is going to die.[5]

When Marie's image is passed around in the film, the viewer is able to distinguish what Barthes calls its *punctum*, which is featured in the "pricked photograph."[6] The punctum is what we, the consumer of the photo, "add to the photograph and *what is nonetheless already there*."[7] In his home, Minks acknowledges to Schrader that he fears for Marie's life. After explaining that Marie is his daughter, the scene closes with Minks asking for Schrader's assistance in finding her, stating, "If she is still here . . . find her."[8] Here, Minks communicates both interpretations of Marie as "lost." He asks Schrader to locate her as he holds onto the hope that she is still alive and, therefore, still "here." Minks wants to foreclose the possibility that his daughter will exist for him only as an image, a someone "that-has-been" instead of someone who simply "is."

Barthes' reading of photography in terms of its relationship to time (the past and the future) and death demonstrates how Minks' motivation is explicitly expressed in his use of photography both to long for and find his daughter. After she spots Marie, Meltem shows Schrader that Minks' daughter is indeed still "here"; Marie is both still alive and found working as a bartender at one of the clubs that they frequent. As Minks suspected, Marie is located in the same social scene in which Schrader is an active member. It is shortly after Schrader finally makes contact with her (when Schrader learns the truth behind Marie's estrangement with her father) that Marie is murdered by Irezumi. Minks is confronted then with his greatest fear: his hopes of finding his daughter come true only after it is too late to save and reconcile with her. When she is murdered, the inevitability of death that had been anticipated in the photograph proves too real and Minks takes his own life in response.

Conclusion

Robert Schwentke's *Tattoo* is located within the generic expectations of crime films in German cinema—a genre that spans from Fritz Lang's groundbreaking 1931 film *M* to the Netflix blockbuster *Babylon Berlin* (2017). A central characteristic of these films is located in the tension created by the ability of photographs both to document events and to expand time: they serve as evidence, as witnesses that drive the plot, and also as sites that provide access into the motivations, feelings, pasts, futures, and dreams of the characters without much narrative exposition. In general, the juxtaposition of photographs with the moving image in crime films invites the viewer to question how concepts like truth and value are associated with the medium of photography, a question also posed in *Tattoo*. But the use of photographs in *Tattoo* also merges debates about tattoos, their significance in the Western world, and their relationship to art.

In *After Photography*, Fred Ritchin responds to the multivocality quality of photographs and their relationship to their historical context. He explains:

> If every photograph, as part of an evolving conversation informed by the dialectics of history and culture, can be considered multivocal, with a diversity of meanings, then there is no pretense at a single reality or a single interpretation. As a result, there is no idolatry that subsumes complexity. The photograph can no longer be read according to the simplistic notion that "the camera never lies," that there is only one concretized reality.[9]

Although Ritchin's argument might be applied to all photographs, he is referring specifically to digital photographs, which is also relevant to how the digital images in *Tattoo* circulate and can be comprehended. The photographs in *Tattoo*—photographs of tattoos on people's bodies that circulate on the dark web—assign artistic status to the tattoos by allowing them to be exhibited in galleries and viewed within the context of Western art. For example, Schrader gains a better understanding behind the interest in the Hiromitsu tattoos in a visit to Kroner's apartment. Showing him the art catalog of Hiromitsu's collective tattooed works, Schrader's immediate reaction is to classify them as "real works of art" (*echte Kunstwerke*), acknowledging their aesthetic value and categorizing them on the same level as other, more conventional examples of art. Viewing other photographs as evidentiary in nature, Schrader shows a range in how they can be read and assigned informational significance. Through photographs, *Tattoo* presents how the discourse in the West surrounding tattoos and their cultural reception have changed and how these reconsiderations influence how tattoos are read and culturally appraised for their value.

Susan Sontag clarifies the relationship between photography and art, declaring, "Photography, though not an art form in itself, has the peculiar capacity to turn all its subjects into works of art."[10] According to Sontag, the presentation of the photographic image serves as a classification and justification of its subject to be considered art. This is exemplified as Schrader sees the collection of Hiromitsu's tattoos published in a high-quality exhibition catalog typically found in a museum. Having also seen Wilson's tattoo on her [removed] skin, Schrader does not classify the tattoo as art until he sees the photograph of it in the Hiromitsu catalog. Sontag's argument explains how *Tattoo* presents the power of artistic assignment made evident through photography.

With Sontag's reading in mind, photography is presented in *Tattoo* as the medium that assigns artistic status. Other, more traditional parameters are placed as a counterbalance to the debatable medium of tattooing—the rarity of art pieces, Hiromitsu's classification as a master practitioner of his craft, the presentation of the tattoos in a gallery setting, and finally, the explicit label of art assigned by Schrader upon seeing photographs of Hiromitsu's collected works in a published catalog. Despite being presented with each of the building-block classifications of what easily designates other artistic expressions as art, it is not until Schrader sees the photographs of the tattoos that he freely and confidently identifies Hiromitsu's works as such. This suggests that even nonexpert detectives can recognize the high stakes and artistic value of the crime they are investigating. Released during the recession that followed German reunification, *Tattoo* presents an alternative avenue for income for working-class Germans in the film—by selling their tattoos—to make up for the high unemployment rate of 8 percent that, in reality, lasted from 1993 to 2007.[11]

Tattoo directly references the established art of tattooing in Japan with its mention of Irezumi (the username of the online bidder), which means "tattoo" in Japanese and also relates to Yasuzô Masumura's 1966 film *Irezumi,* which has a similar plot. These direct references to the long-established Eastern traditions of tattooing correspond to conversations around the intersection of tattoos and art that have been debated in a Western context since the tattoo renaissance began in the 1990s.[12] According to Juliet Fleming, a tattoo scholar who looks specifically at what some call the 1990s tattoo renaissance, the tattoo/art-conflict is rooted in terms of class. She states: "On the one hand, it advances serious claims to be considered a 'high' art whose products are governed by canons of taste and knowledge, and shown in galleries and museums. On the other hand, tattooing remains, in theory and in fact, a demotic practice whose products include prison- and home-made tattoos, as well as those done in commercial studios to more or less standard designs."[13] The breadth of tattooing genres, similar to the breadth of art genres, begets an assortment of artistic qualitative parameters that were not in place prior to the 1990s. Clarifying the shift that took place during the tattooing renaissance, Fleming explains how "[u]nlike earlier or less elite tattooists, artists of the tattoo renaissance may have professional art training and some association with the larger art world."[14] In this case, the overlap into the world of art is approached from the standpoint of a particular training rooted in established artistic parameters.

In her engagement of the many qualifiers and disqualifiers that raise and demote tattoos from artistic consideration, Fleming explains some of the same struggles found in active contemporary discussions around tattoos in a Western context that are applicable to *Tattoo*. It is apparent in the tension between the brutality that is done to the bodies of the victims who are forcibly stripped of their tattoos and the possessive, colonizing attention that often accompanies the identification and labeling of artistic value. Additionally, Fleming argues that because tattoos can represent the psyche, they can be elevated into the category of artistic expression in the West.[15] This is coupled with the fact that art, as expressed by Walter Benjamin, has a particular aura that is tied to its authenticity and lack of reproducibility.[16] It is the attribute of aura tethered to art that makes the concept applicable to tattoos due to their presentations on the living, moving medium of the body and thus no two tattoos can be the same.[17]

In the way tattoos are handled and utilized in *Tattoo*, the film frames them as potential qualifiers of the label-assignment of art. This is accomplished through the background of the tattoos being created by someone who is tagged as having artistic training, the lack of reproducibility due to their placement on the living canvas of the body, and the use of photography to capture and present Hiromitsu's tattoos as creative pieces worthy of artistic scrutiny. While *Tattoo* engages with the question of what qualifies as art throughout the plot, the whole argument could not have been accomplished if the use of photography was not employed to reinforce its arguments. *Tattoo* invites the viewer, wherever they stand on the social-class spectrum, to engage in the tattoo/art debate by providing a range of figures with whom they may be able to identify. In a plot that uses photographs to assign significance, urgency, and communicate perceptions of truth, the constant appraisal and value consideration of tattoos captured in these photos contributes to the discussion of how the category of art is assigned to them. This is one way *Tattoo* participates in conversations pertaining to the assignment of artistic value and how tattoos show an eligibility that is often dismissed.

Cynthia Porter is a visiting instructor at Denison University and a graduate student in the Department of German, Russian and East European Studies at Vanderbilt University, where she is completing her dissertation that explores how the practice of tattooing participated in systems of identity-formation in the wake of moments of perceived cultural rupture and transition in German twentieth- and twenty-first century history. Cynthia received a Digital Humanities Fellowship in the Vanderbilt Center for Digital Humanities (2017) and is a member of the inaugural cohort for the Comparative Media Analysis and Practice (CMAP) joint PhD program.

Notes

1. See Roald Dahl, "Skin," in *Skin & Other Stories* (London: Puffin, 2017), 1–21; and Verena Hutter, "Only for Convicts, Loose Women and Sailors? The Tattoo as Social, Political and Literary Practice in Germany from the 19th Century to Today" (PhD diss., University of California, Davis, 2012).
2. bell hooks states, "For we have always known that the socially constructed image of innocent white womanhood relies on the continued production of the racist/sexist sexual myth that black women are not innocent and never can be." bell hooks, "Madonna," in *Black Looks: Race and Representation* (Boston: South End Press, 1992), 159–60.
3. Roland Barthes, *Camera Lucida: Reflections on Photography* (New York: Hill and Wang, 1981), 79.
4. Barthes, *Camera Lucida*, 85—emphasis in the original.
5. Ibid., 96—emphasis in the original.
6. Ibid., 49.
7. Ibid., 55—emphasis in the original.
8. "Wenn sie noch . . . hier ist. Finden Sie sie." *Tattoo*, directed by Robert Schwentke (Munich: Lounge Entertainment AG, 2002).
9. Fred Ritchin, *After Photography* (New York: W. W. Norton & Company, 2010), 71.
10. Susan Sontag, *On Photography*, (New York: Farrar, Straus and Giroux, 1977), 149.
11. Oliver Lipps and Daniel Oesch, "The working class left behind? The class gap in Life Satisfaction in Germany and Switzerland over the Last Decades," *European Societies* 20, no. 4 (2018): 553.
12. Victoria Pitts-Taylor, *In the Flesh: The Cultural Politics of Body Modification* (New York: Palgrave Macmillan, 2003), 3.
13. Juliet Fleming, "The Renaissance Tattoo," in *Written on the Body: The Tattoo in European and American History*, ed. Jane Caplan (Princeton: Princeton University Press, 2000), 61.
14. Ibid.; for more on the tattoo renaissance, see Margo DeMello, "Appropriation and Transformation: The Origins of the Renaissance," in *Bodies of Inscription: A Cultural History of the Modern Tattoo Community* (Durham, NC: Duke University Press, 2000), 71–96.
15. Fleming, "The Renaissance Tattoo," 65.
16. Walter Benjamin, "The Work of Art in the Age of Mechanical Reproduction," in *Illuminations*, ed. Hannah Arendt, trans. Harry Zohn (New York: Schocken Books, 1968), 217–51.
17. Fleming, "The Renaissance Tattoo," 65.

Bibliography

Barthes, Roland. *Camera Lucida: Reflections on Photography*. New York: Hill and Wang, 1981.

Benjamin, Walter. "The Work of Art in the Age of Mechanical Reproduction." In *Illuminations*, edited by Hannah Arendt, translated by Harry Zohn, 217–51. New York: Schocken Books, 1968.

Dahl, Roald. "Skin." In *Skin & Other Stories*, 1–21. London: Puffin, 2017.
DeMello, Margo. "Appropriation and Transformation: The Origins of the Renaissance." In *Bodies of Inscription: A Cultural History of the Modern Tattoo Community*, 71–96. Durham, NC: Duke University Press, 2000.
Fleming, Juliet. "The Renaissance Tattoo." In *Written on the Body: The Tattoo in European and American History*, edited by Jane Caplan, 61–82. Princeton: Princeton University Press, 2000.
hooks, bell. "Madonna." In *Black Looks: Race and Representation*, 159–60. Boston: South End Press, 1992.
Hutter, Verena. "Only for Convicts, Loose Women and Sailors? The Tattoo as Social, Political and Literary Practice in Germany from the 19th Century to Today." PhD diss., University of California, Davis, 2012.
Lipps, Oliver, and Oesch, Daniel. "The Working Class Left Behind? The Class Gap in Life Satisfaction in Germany and Switzerland over the Last Decades." *European Societies* 20, no. 4 (2018): 549–71.
Pitts-Taylor, Victoria. *In the Flesh: The Cultural Politics of Body Modification*. New York: Palgrave Macmillan, 2003.
Ritchin, Fred. *After Photography*. New York: W. W. Norton & Company, 2010.
Sontag, Susan. *On Photography*. New York: Farrar, Straus and Giroux, 1977.

Filmography

Tattoo. Directed by Robert Schwentke. Munich: Lounge Entertainment AG, 2002.
Irezumi: The Spider Tattoo. Directed by Yasuzo Masumura. Japan: Daiei Motion Picture Co (Kyōto), 1966.

Chapter 7

Curating the Image

Visual Intertextuality in *The Baader Meinhof Complex* (2008)

Reinhard Zachau

Uli Edel's 2008 film *The Baader Meinhof Complex* (*Der Baader Meinhof Komplex*) is one of the most ambitious attempts to represent on film Germany's Red Army Faction (RAF) and the history of its first generation from 1967 to 1977.[1] The terrorist activities of the RAF overshadowed West German politics until the group was finally dissolved in 1998 in the wake of German unification. In the years following the fall of the Berlin wall in 1989, Germany's coming to terms with its past—or *Vergangenheitsbewältigung*, as it has been known since the 1960s—once again became the focus of the country's identity discussion that included the Holocaust, a divided and reunited Germany, the *Gastarbeiter* program, and the activities surrounding the RAF.[2] These debates established the country's memory culture of the 1990s, but the unresolved traumatic core of the RAF debate still resurfaces whenever a public event or major film—such as the 2005 KunstWerke exhibit *Regarding Terror: The RAF-Exhibition* (*Zur Vorstellung des Terrors: Die RAF*), Edel's 2008 *The Baader Meinhof Complex*, or Andreas Veiel's 2011 film *If Not Us, Who?* (*Wer wenn nicht wir*)—attempts to define the extent to which the RAF constituted a threat to the foundation of the Federal Republic.[3] This chapter examines how *The Baader Meinhof Complex* in particular remediates the visual legacy of the RAF via photography in order to probe, present, and process the unique convergence of violence, ideology, and representation that the organization represented in German culture.

A Visual Heritage

Since the 1990s, when films reenact historical moments to provide consensus-driven affirmative messages that leave few questions answered, they are often labeled "heritage films," a term that originated in British film making about its pre-World War II history.[4] The term was first introduced to German filmmaking by Lutz Koepnick who used 1990s German films about the Holocaust to demonstrate how heritage filmmaking moves toward "the production of usable and consumable pasts, of history as a site of comfort and orientation."[5] Koepnick sees German heritage filmmaking as part of a "postmodern nostalgia" and warns that these movies are increasingly linked to a reinterpretation of twentieth-century German history with its "historical minefield, structured by Germany's peculiar history of violence, displacement, and division."[6] According to Sabine Hake, *The Baader Meinhof Complex* can be understood within the generic parameters of heritage films as a nostalgic period piece alongside films like *Downfall* (2004)—also produced by Bernd Eichinger.[7] Heritage films tend to appeal to viewers with their lavish production value, star power, intense close-up scenes, powerful musical score, and, in the case of *The Baader Meinhof Complex*, "the ever-present blast of gunpowder."[8] Not surprisingly, the film became more successful than other German films in 2008 and was nominated as Germany's Academy Awards entry that year. As a consensus-driven heritage film, *The Baader Meinhof Complex* has also been criticized for its sensationalism, glorification of violence, and lack of critical reflection,[9] as well as its move from "politics to pornography."[10]

Yet, given the film's dizzying array of speaking parts and characters, dates, and events spanning over a decade without a central narrative, *The Baader Meinhof Complex* might be said to fail as a heritage film if the goal is, as mentioned previously, "the production of usable and consumable pasts, of history as a site of comfort and orientation."[11] However, its most consumable past is represented through famous photographs that simultaneously speak to those who remember them and orient those who are new to the story. In this way, the film can also be understood within the context of *postmemory*, a term coined by Marianne Hirsch to refer to the relationship between the current generation, the "generation after," to the trauma the previous generation experienced and transmitted through their memories.[12] By using photographs as its principal structuring device, *The Baader Meinhof Complex* shifts the emphasis away from political proclamations and connects the viewer to the protagonists emotionally, not rationally. In so doing, the film attempts to convey the multidimensional and generational trauma associated with the first generation of the RAF and its legacy.

The film utilizes various strategies to appeal to or reaffirm the shared heritage of multiple generations of viewers. Given that film is a visual medium composed of many images, and given that heritage films necessarily conflate historical events and images—whether documentary or reconstructed photographs—a key feature of heritage films is also how images are presented, recreated, and edited to establish the historical events in the collective memory. Yet collective memory is always heterogeneous, especially in Germany—a deep rift exists between the older generation raised during Nazi totalitarianism and the first post-World War II generation brought up in a democratic state. On the one hand, Rainer Werner Fassbinder's staged interview with his mother in the 1978 film *Germany in Autumn* (*Deutschland im Herbst*) remains one of the most chilling examples of this debate, given how his mother longs for a "benevolent dictator" to counter the country's inability to deal with the RAF crisis. On the other hand, a significant number of citizens sympathized with the RAF's intent to expose the nefarious past of Germany's leading officials—at the height of its popularity, around a quarter of young West Germans (Fassbinder included) expressed some sympathy for the group.[13] The passage of time has gradually obfuscated why the RAF was ever popular, and the post-9/11 generation no longer seems to know why they ever appealed to intelligent and sensitive people. Edel's film attempts to work with all these generations at once.

Although *The Baader Meinhof Complex* was based on Stefan Aust's 1985 book by the same name—a text that relies on numerous documentary sources to provide multiple perspectives and to drive its narrative—the film develops its narrative primarily via images. Catriona Firth has criticized Edel's film for whittling down the multiperspective approach of Stefan Aust's book to a single point of view that assumes an "air of authenticity and authority,"[14] but Edel expressed a desire to convey the spirit of this period to his children who grew up in the United States and knew "next to nothing" about what happened in Germany between 1967 and 1977.[15] The film may not provide the "true" historical or political story of the RAF, yet it capitalizes on the truth value associated with documentary photographs to create an air of authenticity while simultaneously manipulating the photograph to incorporate the visual legacy of the RAF in art, literature, and cinema. Thus, while incorporating the visual legacy of the RAF that would be understood by generations who experienced it, they are also indoctrinating a new generation into the postmemory of their representation of the RAF. Edel and Eichinger use photographs as the means through which they attempt to link generations and demographics, and any discussion of the images in *The Baader Meinhof Complex* therefore needs to include the history and resonance of those images.

In the large body of films about the RAF that began in 1975 with Volker Schlöndorff and Margarethe von Trotta's *The Lost Honor of Katharina Blum* (*Die verlorene Ehre der Katharina Blum*), it is evident that the focus has shifted away from a discussion of political goals and iconoclasm of the art film tradition of the New German Cinema and has been replaced by reproduction of iconic photographic images that have become part of Germany's collective memory. According to Svea Bräunert, bolstering the RAF mourning process via film works well in Germany's consensus-driven society that interpreted terrorism as part of the foundational trauma on which to build a unified Germany.[16] In his review of *The Baader Meinhof Complex,* Ulrich Kriest points out that the film focuses mostly on characters and images rather than on narrative and questions, and wonders whether popular images can communicate the complex political ideas the RAF stood for.[17] Kriest touches on the critical issue many Germans had with the movie: its avoidance of the ideological discussion about terrorism that earlier movies had attempted, such as Rainer Werner Fassbinder, Alf Brustelin, and others' 1978 film *Germany in Autumn* (*Deutschland im Herbst*) or Margarethe von Trotta's 1981 film *Marianne and Juliane* (*Die bleierne Zeit*). Earlier RAF films centered on more specific aspects, such as the relationship between the Ensslin sisters (*Marianne and Juliane,* 1981), Baader's biography (*Baader,* 2002), RAF members hiding in the GDR (*The Legend of Rita,* 2000), the assassination of Alfred Herrhausen (*Black Box BRD,* 2001), and, most often, the events surrounding 18 October 1977 including the kidnapping of Hanns-Martin Schleyer and the hijacking of the Lufthansa plane (*Mogadischu,* 2008; *Germany in Autumn,* 1978; and *Endgame,* 1997). As the first movie to attempt a comprehensive exploration of the RAF from 1967 to 1977 and beyond against the critical prowess of the New German Cinema, the stakes for *The Baader Meinhof Complex* were high from the beginning.

Instead of relying on strategies of iconoclasm, *The Baader Meinhof Complex* recreates and relies on media photographs with intervisual references that reflect the visual history of the RAF movement. Firth calls these images "doubly remediated" as they evoke not private, personal memories but public media images that make up a vast collective pictorial memory.[18] As Thomas Elsaesser argues, the result is a renewed mediated reality, a "double-coding" in which reality and copy can no longer be separated.[19] But this move to represent photographs of the RAF and their associative potential without exploring the history and politics of the group in depth is characteristic of many projects in RAF representation that have not been so harshly criticized, as demonstrated in the 2005 KunstWerke exhibit that featured many of them. The visual intertextuality demonstrated in the film's reworking of the media photographs produces the purported effects of heritage films; the interwoven images offer "usable and consumable pasts" and provide access to "history as a site of comfort and orientation"[20] while simultaneously blurring the group's history to highlight instead the convergence of violence, ideology, and representation in the history of the RAF. Before moving to a discussion of the photographs themselves, this chapter will address the *The Baader Meinhof Complex*'s remediation of the literary and cinematic influences on RAF members and in RAF representation.

Stylizing the Image

The visual history of the RAF depicted in the film directly relates to the group's own self-stylized image and their concern for the mythic proportions of their struggle. The first generation's attempt to defeat the leviathan of government and their inevitable failure was understood early on by the members themselves. During their imprisonment in the high-security Stammheim Prison, both Gudrun Ensslin and Ulrike Meinhof recognized the tragic element of the RAF's monomaniac reach for power in Herman Melville's 1851 novel *Moby Dick*.[21] In her journals, Ensslin adopted an epic perspective when considering the group and its goals and portrayed the RAF as a heroic experiment of shaping history.[22] She gave each member of the core group (except Meinhof) a code name based on Melville's novel: Ahab stood for Baader; Starbuck for Holger Meins; and the carpenter stood for Jan-Carl Raspe, to name a few. Ensslin—a pastor's daughter—likely also understood the connection between the great American novel and the biblical saga of Ahab and Leviathan. By linking the RAF to her perception of history producing heroic images based in classical iconography, she created one of the first mythologies of the group and elevated the RAF story to a timeless tragic tale of man versus providence that is on display in *The Baader Meinhof Complex* and through the group's literary, cinematic, and visual legacy.

While Ensslin created her own mythology by recalling images from the literary cannon, other members had their own aspirations that were also infused into the film. Andreas Baader was a cinephile who aspired to look fashionable and who had also attempted to write movie scripts inspired by French *nouvelle vague* films, such as Jean-Luc Godard's 1960 film *Breathless*. A scene in his favorite movie, Gillo Pontecorvo's 1966 *The Battle of Algiers*, became the model for the RAF bank raids where three banks were robbed simultaneously, as Baader's biographers Klaus Stern and Jörg Herrmann have noted.[23] With his interest in avant-garde cinema, Baader lived in his own artificial world of movie characters that included James Dean, Jean Paul Belmondo, and Marlon Brando.[24] Belmondo's character Michel in *Breathless* along with Clyde Barrow in *Bonnie and Clyde* became models for Baader and later also for Ensslin during their time in Paris.[25] Ensslin and Baader appeared to be kindred spirits in their obsessions with fast cars, avant-garde fashion, and epic struggles. From early on, they seemed to want to be characters in a *novelle vague* film.

The Baader Meinhof Complex taps into this cinematic iconography by citing Baader's and Ensslin's cinematic references that also appealed to the post-World War II generation brought up on the same fast-paced action movie fantasies. For example, Elsaesser suggests that the scene with the baby carriage that stopped Schleyer's car seems copied from a scene in Sergei Eisenstein's 1925 film *Battleship Potemkin*.[26] With its compilation of references to iconic film scenes, *The Baader Meinhof Complex* imitates Baader's and Ensslin's view of the world as a fantasy battleground for enacting their own violent political goals. But their fantasies were not limited to cinema. They also seemed to want to turn West Germany into a stage for a didactic play in the Brechtian tradition where they saw themselves as actors in a grand, revolutionary play.[27] Much like Baader and Ensslin imitated art in their life, *The Baader Meinhof Complex* (re)turns their life to art while also keeping in mind the long history of RAF films in their mise-en-scène and the tradition of representing significant moments in the RAF history that were not photographed.

The most formative memory in the origin of the RAF—when Ulrike Meinhof escaped out the window with Andreas Baader at Berlin's Institute for Social Studies in 1972—was not captured on television. However, as a well-known journalist who often appeared on television, Meinhof was known to the public from their living rooms and within the frame of a television. *The Baader Meinhof Complex* references this visual history by also representing Meinhof in a frame and using this moment as an important structuring device to highlight the turning point in Meinhof's biography when, by jumping, she left her regular life behind her to begin her career as an underground terrorist. Because no image was available, the film's recreation of this event replaced a representation that had only been imagined. Meinhof's jump out of the window defined her energy at the beginning of her RAF engagement, but the different approach to the portrayal of her arrest communicates her apathy, her disillusion, and her disinterest in continuing the battle.

The original arrest photo of Meinhof seems raw and unrefined with the flash highlighting her face, along with the jagged and crude gestures of the arresting police officer that clearly demonstrate the oppressive manner in which she was arrested and presented to the media. Volker Schlöndorff captured this incredulity in the scene of Katharina Blum's arrest for his movie *The Lost Honor of Katharina Blum* (1975), which itself was based on the original photograph of Ulrike Meinhof's arrest. However, in *The Baader Meinhof Complex*, Edel portrays Meinhof's arrest differently. Instead of a harsh flash, she is illuminated in uniform light with only a single police officer touching her arm lightly to support her sagging torso. Focusing on Meinhof's seemingly subdued expression, Edel portrays her arrest as a mental and physical resignation.[28] Unlike the original photo and Schlöndorff's movie, Edel's Meinhof does not show any reaction but exhaustion. According to Daniel Kothenschulte, instead of representing weakness, the tears that she sheds at her arrest represent her humanity.[29] Edel's attempt to alter Meinhof's revolutionary posture comes at an important part of the film; it conveys that the fight was over and demonstrates his attempt to imbue her representation with a sense of mourning that haunts the first generation.

Many of the iconic photographs of the RAF seem to have been carefully selected to resonate within a recognizable and strangely familiar aesthetic that evoked their lasting threatening presence in German society. To list some of the many examples, Charlotte Klonk points out that photos of Ulrike Meinhof often show her as a reinterpretation of a saintly image;[30] Carrie Collenberg explores the aesthetic significance of the 1974 deathbed photograph of Holger Meins that was published in *Stern* magazine and how it resonates with art-historical representations of Jesus Christ, Freddy Alborta's 1967 autopsy photograph of Che Guevara, and Käthe Kollwitz's 1919–20 woodcut "In Memorium Karl Liebknecht" ("Gedenkblatt für Karl Liebknecht")[31]—an observation echoed by Gerd Conradt with his description of the autopsy photograph of Holger Meins as "Ikone des Gegners" (icon of the opponent)[32]—and Eric Kligerman marks the aesthetic similarities between the 1977 photograph of a dead Andreas Baader that was published in *Stern* magazine (and later repainted by Gerhard Richter) with "Ecce Homo 1945" (the well-known image of a Holocaust victim printed in Gerhard Schoenberner's 1960 book *The Yellow Star* [*Der gelbe Stern*]).[33] These aesthetic connections are further emphasized in monumental tributes to the RAF's visual legacy such as Gerhard Richter's 1988 cycle of paintings *October 18, 1977* and the aforementioned 2005 KunstWerke exhibition *Regarding Terror: The RAF-Exhibition*. *The Baader Meinhof Complex* draws on this established iconography in its remediation of many documentary photographs of the RAF throughout the film.

By reenacting some of the most iconic photographs, *The Baader Meinhof Complex* connects older viewers with authentic photos they should recognize from when they originally saw them on television. In the process, they reaffirm this visual heritage by recreating the story of the photographs' creation and emphasize that the history of the RAF is the history of these photographs. When the film portrays student leader Rudi Dutschke's speech at the February 1968 Vietnam Congress at the Berlin's Free University, the film freezes in a gesture that simulates capturing a snapshot of him. The film's saturated colors in the frame transition to black and white to evoke the memory of the historic photo of Dutschke. Once the freeze frame and the image it references can register on the viewer, color returns to the still and the flow of time resumes. By recreating the most iconic photograph of the era, the film sparks a memory of the image's original context, which enables the viewer to feel more connected to the film. In citing well-known images and capitalizing on the recognition associated with them, the film additionally embeds these photographs in cinematic tropes that were important to RAF members and their generation.

These recontextualized images in *The Baader Meinhof Complex* include both their historic dimension and their impact on the film's narrative. One such example can be seen in the recreation of Jürgen Henschel's iconic 2 June 1967 photograph depicting the death of Benno Ohnesorg at the hands of the police. As the first fatal shooting by a police officer in post-World War II Germany, this moment is considered the birthdate of Germany's cultural revolution that created the RAF. Henschel's well-lit, dramatic photo remains one of best-known images of the German student movement with its focus on the woman's face, Friederike Dollinger, that clearly reflects her despair and her cry for help. Henschel's photo also resonates within an established aesthetic tradition in the pietá-like composition of the shot to show Dollinger, turned to the photographer with an expression of desperation, as she holds the dying Ohnesorg in her arms. Other photographs of the same moment—like the one by Bernard Larssen—miss what Roland Barthes refers to

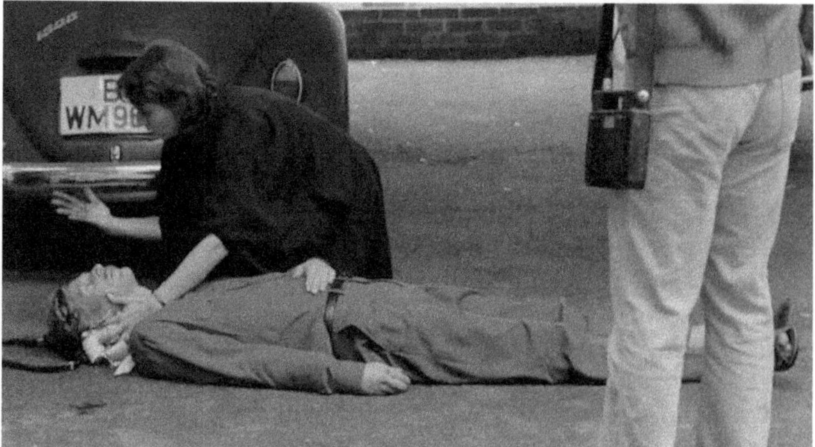

Figure 7.1. *The Baader Meinhof Complex (Der Baader Meinhof Komplex)*. Directed by Uli Edel. Munich: Constantin Film, 2008. Screen capture by Reinhard Zachau.

as the "pregnant moment," because Dollinger had already turned her head back to the dying Ohnesorg.[34] Larssen's photo shows the scene from a wider angle that includes spectators looking down on the dying Ohnesorg, as does the woman, whose face we only see from the side. *The Baader Meinhof Complex* capitalizes on the shock the entire nation felt about police brutality that brought back strong memories of Nazi violence that is reflected in Henschel's photograph. But a closer examination shows that it is not an exact copy of the original. The film's recreation of the iconic photograph also anchors the representation in a larger cinematic tradition and emphasizes its mediated status.

In recapturing and reenacting this scene, Edel does not use Henschel's bright flash but immerses the scene in a uniquely diffused light that removes the unevenness of the flash. Edel explains: "I wanted to avoid what most filmmakers do in genre films. Therefore no 'movie light!' . . . We followed the rules of cinéma verité, not the rules of standard fiction films."[35] To reproduce a *nouvelle vague* look, cameraman Rainer Klausmann recreated authentic lighting copied from press photos by using digital film technology.[36] Frank Schirrmacher calls the lighting effect "heartbreaking" because it "softens the viewer—even the light is remarkable, slightly hazy, like the morning sun after a deep sleep."[37] The cool and distancing light is also reflected in the actress's expression that no longer shows the shock of the original photograph. As the sequence further demonstrates, Klausmann frames the shot with the original photographer inserted into the scene, thereby reminding the current viewer that they are watching a mediated event. A similar pattern is also apparent in the film's portrayal of the arrest of Andreas Baader, Holger Meins, and Jan Carl Raspe.

In the film, the arrest of Baader, Meins, and Raspe on 1 June 1972 is framed from the perspective of a girl taking photos of the event. We witness a sequence of shots: first the advance of the police; then Raspe's arrest followed by Baader's and Meins' retreat into one of the garages; then the shooting of Baader; and finally the arrest of Meins and Baader. In order to extract Meins and Baader from the garage where they had barricaded themselves, the police in the film use teargas that blurs the arrest scene. Earlier, by focusing on Meinhof's face, the camera invited identification and sympathy with the victim that was reinforced by her submissive expression, without any hint of aggression, in contrast to the original photograph. However, in the arrest scene of Baader, Meins, and Raspe, the camera does not close in, but pulls back for a long shot that obscures Baader's arm with his gun in a foggy scene induced by teargas. By cutting between the arrest scene and the scene with the girl as its point of view, the movie does not offer the identification it did with Meinhof's arrest scene: the proximity of the Meinhof scene has been replaced by distance.[38] Instead of referencing cinematic strategies, this time the film seems to reference the work of Gerhard Richter and his 1988 painting cycle entitled *October 18, 1977* and known for its blurred depictions of the same scene: "Arrest 1" and "Arrest 2" (*Festnahme 1* and *Festnahme 2*).[39]

Mourning the Image

After Baader, Ensslin, and Raspe were found dead in their prison cells on 18 October 1977, Richter began to collect images of the group. His paintings were made in a multistep process, starting with the photograph projected onto the canvas, where it was traced for form. To replicate the look of the original picture, Richter takes his color palette from the photo. His hallmark "blur" is achieved with a light touch of a soft brush, or a hard smear with a squeegee. While Richter treated the arrest images with his soft blur, the movie replaced his technique with tear gas that produced a similar effect, with one exception: Baader is clearly visible in the film shot that is needed for cinematic continuity while Richter blurred the figure of the terrorist that made Baader all but disappear. Richter's focus on death in his cycle evokes the sorrow for "the people who died so young and so crazy, for nothing."[40] As an East German who fled to the West, Richter likely understood the larger context of their death within "the illusion that unacceptable circumstances of life can be changed by this conventional expedient of violent struggle."[41] Frances Guerin argues that Richter's repainted police-commissioned photographs of the RAF revived Germany's repressed trauma by following the sequence of historic events. Since many of the RAF photographs were no longer accessible to the public, these recovered images were an important agent in the process of addressing the trauma.[42] Richter's cycle triggered a collective mourning response that even resonated abroad when it was purchased by the New York Museum of Modern Art in 1995 and then returned to Berlin with the "Das MOMA in Berlin" exhibition in 2005–6, just two years before *The Baader Meinhof Complex*. The wave Richter initiated in the RAF mourning process is integral to the visual history of the RAF that then subsequently informed the film as well.

Uli Edel's representation of Gudrun Ensslin's suicide in her Stammheim prison cell evokes another painting in Richter's cycle, entitled "Hanged" (*Erhängte*). The police photo that Richter based his painting off of is a medium shot of Ensslin hanging by her neck from the bars of her jail cell in front of a window. There is a black curtain on her left and a bright white wall along the right side of the frame. When the photograph originally appeared in *Stern* magazine, Ensslin's body was depicted in a full-frontal shot in which all but the window frame behind her and the ground beneath her feet was cropped with a tape measure running the length of her body. The blurred effect in Richter's painting is so pronounced that only the barest details of the photograph remain visible. Edel shows the scene in a carefully balanced framed shot, including the attending physician on the left, covering up the mirror or window frame, and the prison guard in the right foreground, covering up the bright wall. While Richter's obscured image strains the eye and forces the viewer to search for clues in order to comprehend (or recognize) the image, Edel achieves a similar effect by balancing the scene and with his subdued cinematic lighting reminiscent of the lighting used on the reenactment of the Ohnesorg photograph.

Death and its relationship to stillness and motion is an essential element of the RAF story and their representation and is fundamental to twentieth-century photographic and cinematic theory. In *The Still/Moving Image: Cinema and the Arts*, Eivind Røssaak explores Roland Barthes' influence on photography and filmmaking. Barthes' view of the opposition between the moving and the still image contradicts the traditional concept that cinema addresses emotions while photography offers a more rational approach.[43] Barthes reverses this order by admitting to being more affected by still photos than by moving images. When facing a photograph, the immobilized past or that which "has been" seems to have an emotional effect, as Barthes illustrates with a photo of his mother who had passed away: "It is as if the photograph always carries its referent," the person being photographed.[44] This process involves a passage into immobility, as if the person being photographed prepares for a "metonymical death," where the person turns into an object fixed on a glass plate or a paper print, "anesthetized and fastened down, like butterflies."[45] André Bazin described photography in a similar way as an opposition to film, where life is halted at a set moment where it is freed from its destiny, as if it were embalmed in time.[46] According to Bazin, a movie cannot preserve an object or a person as a still photo can that enshrouds instantaneous moments, like bodies of insects in amber.[47] As Richter's cycle ends with a painting of the dead Ulrike Meinhof, the movie ends with a similar still image of the dead Hanns-Martin Schleyer on a pillow of dry autumn leaves bathed in subdued amber light; a light that resembles the color palette of the happy family scene with Ulrike Meinhof at the beginning.[48] *The Baader Meinhof Complex* unites victims and perpetrators in its epitaph for the dead and ignites retrospection and mourning within postunification memory culture.

Conclusion

The Baader Meinhof Complex can also be understood as an attempt to enshroud the photographs of the RAF—and all that their accompanying associations and multidimensional potential implied—within the context of the film and thus invites the viewer to participate in the historical process of *Vergangenheitsbewältigung*. It might be assumed that the film attempts to cast the characters in more detail, to create a hyperreal portrayal instead of washing out distinct features as Richter does with his characteristic blur. However, despite the illusion of authenticity demarcated by captions, dates, and supposed reenactments of documentary photographs, the film structures the narrative around photographs that are well-known as examples of multidimensional and highly referential surfaces. The images examined in this chapter and their cinematic, literary, and aesthetic resonance subsequently blur any semblance of truth or history of the group, except the one that exists in the image itself and its exchange with the viewer. In this way, Edel evokes Richter's cautious articulation of the political purpose behind his cycle that refers to "ideological motivation [and] the tremendous strength, the terrifying power that an idea has, which goes as far as death."[49] As such, *The Baader Meinhof Complex* is a heritage film that reminds and reinitiates a multigenerational and international audience into a complex visual heritage located at the convergence of violence, ideology, and representation.

Reinhard Zachau is Professor Emeritus of German at Sewanee: University of the South. His research explores East German and Nazi literature. He has authored several books that address German writers opposing the Nazis: *Hans Fallada als politischer Schriftsteller* (1990), *Heinrich Böll: Forty Years of Criticism* (1994), *Stefan Heym: Socialist, Dissenter, Jew* (2002), and *Topographie und Literatur: Berlin und die Moderne* (2009). Zachau's pedagogical work has resulted in several textbooks, including *German Culture through Film: An Introduction to German Cinema* (2005); *Berliner Spaziergänge: Literatur, Architektur, Film* (2009); and *Cineplex: German Language and Culture Through Film* (2014).

Notes

1. The editors of this volume have helped differentiate this chapter from ideas put forth in two previous publications: Reinhard Zachau, "*The Baader Meinhof Complex*," in *German Culture Through Film: An Introduction to German Cinema*, ed. Reinhard Zachau, Robert C. Reimer, and Margit Sinka, 2nd ed. (Newburyport: Focus, 2017), 329–37; and Reinhard Zachau, "Death Images in *The Baader Meinhof Complex*," *Glossen* 33 (Nov. 2011). I am especially indebted to Svea Bräunert and Christine Gerhardt for their papers and our discussions at the 2009 GSA panel on RAF films and to Carrie Collenberg-González for her paper at the 2009 SAMLA conference.
2. Inge Stephan and Alexandra Tacke demonstrate the significance of the RAF in twentieth-century German history by dedicating an entire volume to the RAF in *NachBilder*, their three-volume series on the visual representation of traumatic periods in recent German history alongside the Holocaust and German unification. Inge Stephan and Alexandra Tacke, eds., *NachBilder der RAF*, vol. 2 (Cologne: Böhlau, 2008).
3. Klaus Biesenbach, ed., *Zur Vorstellung des Terrors: Die RAF*, 2 vols. (Göttingen: Steidl, 2005).
4. See Andrew Higson, *Waving the Flag: Constructing a National Cinema in Britain* (New York: Oxford University Press, 1995).
5. Lutz Koepnick, "Reframing the Past: Heritage Cinema and Holocaust in the 1990s," *New German Critique* 87 (2002): 51.
6. Ibid., 53.

7. Sabine Hake, "Historisierung der NS-Vergangenheit: *Der Untergang* (2004) zwischen Historienfilm und Eventkino," in *NachBilder des Holocaust*, ed. Inge Stephan and Alexandra Tacke (Cologne: Böhlau, 2008), 214.
8. Genevieve Yue, "World Gone Wrong," *Reverse Shot*, 20 August 2009.
9. Catriona Firth, "The Concealed Curator: Constructed Authenticity in Uli Edel's *Der Baader Meinhof Komplex*," in *Exhibiting the German Past: Museums, Film, and Musealization*, ed. Peter M. McIsaac and Gabriele Mueller (Toronto: University of Toronto Press, 2015), 88.
10. "[D]er letzte Schritt von der Politik zur Pornografie." Ulrich Kriest, "Der Baader Meinhof Komplex: 'Action speaks louder than words.' Oder: Warum niemand den Film *Der Baader Meinhof Komplex* braucht," *Film-Dienst*, 19 December 2008.
11. Koepnick, "Reframing the Past," 51.
12. Marianne Hirsch, *The Generation of Postmemory* (New York: Columbia University Press, 2012), 5.
13. "Who Were the Baader-Meinhof Gang?" *BBC News*, 12 February 2007.
14. Firth, "The Concealed Curator," 88.
15. Katja Eichinger, *Der Baader Meinhof Komplex: Das Buch zum Film* (Hamburg: Hoffmann und Campe, 2008), 34.
16. Svea Bräunert, *Gespenstergeschichten: Der linke Terrorismus der RAF und die Künste* (Berlin: Kulturverlag Kadmos, 2015).
17. Kriest, "Der Baader Meinhof Komplex."
18. Firth, "The Concealed Curator," 94.
19. Thomas Elsaesser, *Terror und Trauma* (Berlin: Kulturverlag Kadmos, 2007), 85.
20. Koepnick, "Reframing the Past," 51.
21. Stefan Aust, *Der Baader Meinhof Komplex* (Hamburg: Hoffmann und Campe, 2008), 390–95.
22. Ibid., 390. See also Gerd Conradt, *Starbuck Holger Meins* (Berlin: Espresso, 2001), 68.
23. Jörg Herrmann and Klaus Stern, eds., *Andreas Baader: Das Leben eines Staatsfeindes* (Munich: Deutscher Taschenbuch Verlag, 2007), 104–5.
24. Stephan and Tacke, *NachBilder der RAF*, 69–70.
25. Yue, "World Gone Wrong."
26. Elsaesser, *Terror und Trauma*, 83.
27. Ibid., 100.
28. See Zachau, "*The Baader Meinhof Complex*," 334–35.
29. Daniel Kothenschulte, "Belmondo Baader," *Frankfurter Rundschau*, 17 September 2008.
30. Charlotte Klonk, "Bildterrorismus: Von Meins zu Schleyer," in *NachBilder der RAF*, ed. Inge Stephan and Alexandra Tacke (Cologne: Böhlau, 2008), 199.
31. Carrie Collenberg, "Dead Holger," in *Baader Meinhof Returns: History and Cultural Memory of German Left-Wing Terrorism*, ed. Gerrit-Jan Berendse and Ingo Cornils (Amsterdam, NY: Rodopi, 2008), 78.
32. Conradt, *Starbuck Holger Meins*, 68.
33. Eric Kligerman, "Transgenerational Hauntings: Screening the Holocausts. Gerhard Richter's *October 18, 1977* Paintings," in *Baader Meinhof Returns*, ed. Berendse and Cornils, 61.
34. "The pregnant moment is just this presence of all the absences (memories, lessons, promises) to whose rhythm History becomes both intelligible and desirable." Roland Barthes, *Image Music Text*, trans. Stephen Heath (London: Farrar Strauss & Giroux, 1977), 73.
35. "Ich wollte in diesem Film alles vermeiden, was man als Filmemacher sonst im Genrekino tun würde. Also: Kein 'Kinolicht'! . . . Wir sind den Gesetzen des 'Cinéma

Verité' gefolgt und nicht denen des Fiktionsfilms." Eichinger, *Der Baader Meinhof Komplex*, 42–43.

36. Ibid., 42–47.
37. "Dieser Film macht seinen Zuschauer sehr empfindlich, auch das Licht in ihm ist sonderbar, leicht blendend, wie die Morgensonne nach der Rekonvaleszenz." Frank Schirrmacher, "Der Baader Meinhof Komplex," *Frankfurter Allgemeine Zeitung*, 14 September 2008.
38. See Zachau, "*The Baader Meinhof Complex*," 335.
39. See Christina Gerhardt, "Terrorism and Memory: Gerhard Richter's *October 18, 1977* (1989) and the Kunst-Werke Exhibit (2005)," in *Screening the Red Army Faction: Historical and Cultural Memory* (New York, NY: Bloomsbury, 2020), 233–56.
40. Dietmar Elger and Hans Ulrich Obrist, "Interview with Gregorio Magnani (1989)," in *Gerhard Richter: Text, Writings, Interviews and Letters 1961–2007* (London: Thames & Hudson, 2009), 222.
41. Ibid., 213.
42. Frances Guerin, "The Gray Space between: Gerhard Richter's 18. Oktober 1977," in *The Image and the Witness: Trauma, Memory and Visual Culture*, eds. Frances Guerin and Roger Hallas (London: Wallflower Press, 2007), 115
43. Eivind Røssaak, *The Still/Moving Image: Cinema and the Arts* (Latvia: Lap Lambert, 2010).
44. Ibid., 5.
45. Ibid., 57.
46. André Bazin, "The Ontology of the Photographic Image," in *What Is Cinema?*, trans. Hugh Gray (Berkeley: University of California Press, 1967), 14.
47. Ibid., 14–15.
48. See Zachau, "*The Baader Meinhof Complex*," 335.
49. Gerhard Richter, *The Daily Practice of Painting: Writing and Interviews 1960–1993* (Cambridge, MA: MIT Press, 1995), 194.

Bibliography

Aust, Stefan. *Der Baader Meinhof Komplex*. Hamburg: Hoffmann und Campe, 2008.

Barthes, Roland. *Image Music Text*. Translated by Stephen Heath. London: Farrar Strauss & Giroux, 1977.

Bazin, André. "The Ontology of the Photographic Image." In *What Is Cinema?* Translated by Hugh Gray, 12–16. Berkeley: University of California Press, 1967.

Biesenbach, Klaus, ed. *Zur Vorstellung des Terrors: Die RAF*. 2 volumes. Göttingen: Steidl, 2005.

Bräunert, Svea. *Gespenstergeschichten: Der linke Terrorismus der RAF und die Künste*. Berlin: Kulturverlag Kadmos, 2015.

Collenberg, Carrie. "Dead Holger." In *Baader Meinhof Returns: History and Cultural Memory of German Left-Wing Terrorism*, edited by Gerrit-Jan Berendse and Ingo Cornils, 65–81. Amsterdam, NY: Rodopi, 2008.

Conradt, Gerd. *Starbuck Holger Meins*. Berlin: Espresso, 2001.

Eichinger, Katja. *Der Baader Meinhof Komplex: Das Buch zum Film*. Hamburg: Hoffmann und Campe, 2008.

Elger, Dietmar, and Hans Ulrich Obrist. *Gerhard Richter: Text, Writings, Interviews and Letters 1961–2007*. London: Thames & Hudson, 2009.

Elsaesser, Thomas. *Terror und Trauma*. Berlin: Kulturverlag Kadmos, 2007.

Firth, Catriona. "The Concealed Curator: Constructed Authenticity in Uli Edel's *Der Baader Meinhof Komplex*." In *Exhibiting the German Past: Museums, Film, and Musealization*, edited by Peter M. McIsaac and Gabriele Mueller, 81–99. Toronto: University of Toronto Press, 2015.

Guerin, Frances. "The Gray Space between: Gerhard Richter's 18. Oktober 1977." In *The Image and the Witness: Trauma, Memory and Visual Culture*, edited by Frances Guerin and Roger Hallas, 113–28. London: Wallflower Press, 2007.

Hake, Sabine. "Historisierung der NS-Vergangenheit: *Der Untergang* (2004) zwischen Historienfilm und Eventkino." In *NachBilder des Holocaust*, edited by Inge Stephan and Alexandra Tacke, 188–218. Cologne: Böhlau, 2008.

Herrmann, Jörg, and Klaus Stern. *Andreas Baader: Das Leben eines Staatsfeindes*. Munich: Deutscher Taschenbuch Verlag, 2007.

Higson, Andrew. *Waving the Flag: Constructing a National Cinema in Britain*. New York: Oxford University Press, 1995.

Hirsch, Marianne. *The Generation of Postmemory*. New York: Columbia University Press, 2012.

Kligerman, Eric. "Transgenerational Hauntings: Screening the Holocausts. Gerhard Richter's *October 18, 1977* Paintings." In *Baader Meinhof Returns: History and Cultural Memory of German Left-Wing Terrorism*, edited by Gerrit-Jan Berendse and Ingo Cornils, 41–63. Amsterdam, NY: Rodopi, 2008.

Klonk, Charlotte. "Bildterrorismus: Von Meins zu Schleyer." In *NachBilder der RAF*, edited by Inge Stephan and Alexandra Tacke, 197–215. Cologne: Böhlau, 2008.

Koepnick, Lutz. "Reframing the Past: Heritage Cinema and Holocaust in the 1990s." *New German Critique* 87 (2002): 47–82.

Kothenschulte, Daniel. "Belmondo Baader." *Frankfurter Rundschau*. 17 September 2008.

Kriest, Ulrich. "Der Baader Meinhof Komplex: 'Action speaks louder than words.' Oder: Warum niemand den Film *Der Baader Meinhof Komplex* braucht." *Film-Dienst*, 19 December 2008. Retrieved 6 June 2020 from http://www.filmzentrale.com/rezis2/baadermeinhofkomplexuk.htm.

Richter, Gerhard. *The Daily Practice of Painting: Writings and Interviews 1960–1993*. Cambridge, MA: MIT Press, 1995.

Røssaak, Eivind. *The Still/Moving Image: Cinema and the Arts*. Latvia: Lap Lambert, 2010.

Schirrmacher, Frank. "Der Baader Meinhof Komplex." *Frankfurter Allgemeine Zeitung*. 14 September 2008. Retrieved 26 July 2020 from https://www.faz.net/aktuell/feuilleton/kino/der-baader-meinhof-komplex-diese-frau-brauchte-mich-ganz-199463.html.

Stephan, Inge, and Alexandra Tacke, eds. *NachBilder der RAF*. Volume 2. Cologne: Böhlau, 2008.

"Who Were the Baader-Meinhof Gang?" *BBC News*. 12 February 2007. Retrieved 10 July 2021 from http://news.bbc.co.uk/2/hi/europe/6314559.stm.

Yue, Genevieve. "World Gone Wrong." *Reverse Shot*. 20 August 2009. Retrieved 20 August 2020 from http://www.reverseshot.org/reviews/entry/361/baader_meinhof_complex.

Zachau, Reinhard. "Death Images in *The Baader Meinhof Complex*." *Glossen* 33 (Nov. 2011). Retrieved 20 August 2020 from http://blogs.dickinson.edu/glossen/archive/most-recent-issue-glossen-332011/reinhard-zachau-glossen-33/.

Zachau, Reinhard, Robert C. Reimer, and Margit Sinka. *German Culture Through Film: An Introduction to German Cinema*. 2nd edition. Newburyport: Focus, 2017.

Filmography

Baader (*Baader*). Directed by Christopher Roth. Almería: Leading Edge Producciones, 2002.

The Baader Meinhof Complex (*Der Baader Meinhof Komplex*). Directed by Uli Edel. Munich: Constantin Film, 2008.

The Battle of Algiers (*La battaglia di Algeri*). Directed by Gillo Pontecorvo. Algeria: Casbah Film, 1966.

Battleship Potemkin (*Bronenosets Potemkin*). Directed by Sergei M. Eisenstein. Moscow: Goskino, 1925.

Black Box BRD (*Black Box BRD*). Directed by Andres Veiel. Berlin: Zero Film. 2001.

Bonnie and Clyde. Directed by Arthur Penn. Los Angeles: Warner Brothers, 1967.

Breathless (*A Bout de Souffle*). Directed by Jean-Luc Godard. France: Les Film Impéria, 1960.

Downfall (*Der Untergang*). Directed by Oliver Hirschbiegel. Munich: Constantin Film, 2004.

Endgame (*Todesspiel*). Directed by Heinrich Breloer. Hamburg: Multimedia Gesellschaft für Audiovisuelle Information, 1997.

Germany in Autumn (*Deutschland im Herbst*). Directed by Rainer Werner Fassbinder, Alf Brustelin, and others. New York: IBS Filmproduktion, 1978.

If Not Us, Who? (*Wer wenn nicht wir?*). Directed by Andreas Veiel. Berlin: Zero Film, 2011.

The Legend of Rita (*Die Legende von Rita*). Directed by Volker Schlöndorff. Potsdam-Babelsberg: Babelsberg Film, 2000.

The Lost Honor of Katharina Blum (*Die verlorene Ehre der Katharina Blum*). Directed by Volker Schlöndorff and Margarethe von Trotta. Munich: Bioskop Film, 1975.

Marianne and Juliane (*Die bleierne Zeit*). Directed by Margarethe von Trotta. Munich: Bioskop Film. 1981.

Mogadishu (*Mogadischu*). Directed by Roland Suso Richter. Berlin: TeamWorx Produktion, 2008.

Chapter 8

Re-presenting German Heritage Films

Photographic Memory in *Aimée & Jaguar* (1999), *Good Bye, Lenin!* (2003), and *Almanya: Welcome to Germany* (2011)

Carrie Collenberg-González

As a style of filmmaking that began in the late twentieth century, German heritage films can be understood as part of Eric Rentschler's "cinema of consensus"[1] through their distinct approach to history as opposed to the films of New German Cinema that came before them. Instead of the critical and iconoclastic strategies of their predecessors, German heritage films appeal to the public through loving recreations of historical periods, lavish production values, remediation of known cultural media, and star power.[2] Photographs are often embedded within these generic parameters yet their integral role as structuring agents and analogies for historical trauma and memory often goes unacknowledged. This chapter explores the photographic dimensions of German heritage films, specifically in Max Färberböck's *Aimée & Jaguar* (1999), Wolfgang Becker's *Good Bye, Lenin!* (2003), and Yasemin Şamdereli's *Almanya: Welcome to Germany* (*Almanya: Willkommen in Deutschland*, 2011). Through photographs, each of these films presents a self-enclosed world that serves the construction of a national cinema by using consensus-driven strategies to represent significant (and marketable) historical periods in twentieth-century Germany—respectively, World War II and the Holocaust; the German Democratic Republic (GDR) and the *Wende*; and Turkish immigrants and the West-German *Gastarbeiter* (guestworker) program.

In an article on 1990's German heritage films about the Holocaust, Lutz Koepnick observes that the films present historical epochs "from the perspective of post memory" and that they use various forms of cultural transmission to do so, including photographs.[3] While Marianne Hirsch's definition of *postmemory* often refers to how the Holocaust is remembered and represented by the children and grandchildren of survivors, her definition can also be applied to the "guardians" of any "traumatic personal and generational past . . . and that past's passing into history or myth."[4] From Oliver Wendell Holmes' claim in 1859 that photographs are a "mirror with a memory"[5] to the sustained use of photographs in albums, journalism, and social media, photographs have been connected to memory and postmemory in various ways.[6] Although this chapter cannot accommodate a longer discussion of the intricate relationship between photographs and memory, it acknowledges the photograph as a critical visual tool in German heritage films to represent the past and its transition into history and myth. In a consensus-driven genre, it follows that consensus-driven strategies and assumptions—like those that connect photographs to memory—will be employed because they will be understood on a visual level by a popular audience. German heritage films make a nostalgic appeal to the audience in their use of photographs to represent the past but also re-present the past by emphasizing the nonlinear structure of memory, photographs, and trauma.

In German heritage films that depict traumatic twentieth-century events from the World Wars to reunification, photographs serve as analogies that reveal the workings of trauma and its nonlinear structure. In *Spectral Evidence*, Ulrich Baer notes that the connection between the promise of the indexical nature of a photograph (the idea of relationship between what is depicted as a record of what happened) and the inevitable gap in knowledge experienced by the viewer mimics the distortion inherent in screen memories and the associated ideas of belatedness (*Nachträglichkeit*) in understanding traumatic events and their imprint on the psyche and on memory.[7] With Baer's connection in mind, the photographs examined in the three films below demonstrate the link between personal, cultural, and national approaches to trauma. Their privileged role in the narrative of the films suggests that memory in German heritage films is indeed photographic; but not in the colloquially understood eidetic sense that every detail is remembered. Rather, photographic memory in German heritage films seems to rely on the memory of a personal photograph that masks a deeper historical trauma and that emphasizes the connection between the past, present, and future.

Divided into three sections, this chapter shows how photographs structure the plot in all three films, provide the characters and audience access to imagined pasts and futures, enable access to otherwise inaccessible spatial–temporal dimensions, and structurally connect the personal experiences of the characters to historical trauma. The first section demonstrates how the plot of *Aimée & Jaguar* is a series of flashbacks that reanimate the photographs Lilly Wust took of Felice Schragenheim; the second section focuses on chiastic transitions in *Good Bye, Lenin!* between moving and still images of Berlin and Christiane Kerner that highlight Alex's coming of age and coming to terms with the death of his mother and the GDR; and the third section addresses how photographs convey optically unconscious elements of familial representation and postmemory in *Almanya: Welcome to Germany*. Together, the use of photographs in these films serves as an analogy for the representation of history and working of trauma that is specific to German heritage films.

Reanimated Photographs in *Aimée & Jaguar* (1999)

Based on Erica Fischer's best-selling book, Max Färberböck's *Aimée & Jaguar* (1999) is one of the most well-known German heritage films of the 1990s and was Germany's submission to the 1999 Academy Awards for Best International Feature Film.[8] When praised, the film represents a liberating view that celebrates lesbianism, female spaces, and German and Jewish symbiosis. When criticized, the film is representative of a consensus-driven, sentimental, and nostalgic view of history that features a German woman whose proprietary view of her Jewish lover denies her lover any agency and panders to national fantasies of symbiosis and redemption. Profiting from and responding to the "memory boom"[9] and subsequent emergence of trauma studies of the 1990s, both the book and film can be understood as memory projects that depict German Lilly Wust's (Aimée) memory of her relationship with Jewish Felice Schragenheim (Jaguar) from 1942 to 1944, before Felice was arrested and eventually murdered in a concentration camp. The frame narrative—beginning and ending with Lilly taking photographs—brackets the film's structure as a series of flashbacks based on the reanimation of photographs from Lilly's private collection that transmit her memory of Felice to the viewer.

Although Lilly's camera and the many pictures she takes throughout the film do not go unnoticed by critics, their structural role as establishing shots that frame the film's narrative as a series of flashbacks is often underestimated.[10] The frame narrative establishes the significance of photographs throughout the film: the film begins with Lilly behind the camera, taking a picture of her son with Felice; the final scenes parallel the first with Lilly behind the camera, again taking a picture of Felice. The structuring role of photographs is further emphasized in the first few scenes. The first scene after the initial shots depicts Lilly as an eighty-four-year-old German woman who has just moved into a retirement community where she meets her old friend Ilse, one of the only people in the world who might remember Lilly's lesbian relationship with the Jewish woman Felice and her complicit role in Felice's death. This meeting triggers Lilly's memories, which the film then presents in flashbacks structured around photographs. The viewer is first transported to the recent past in Lilly's apartment before her move, where she sells everything except a chair and her photographs of Felice. Next, the film moves deeper into the past to her time with her lover, focusing on the reanimation of the photographs in Lilly's collection. Examining the relationship between cinematic flashbacks and memory, Maureen Turim writes: "the flash image of memory by which films represent the actual process of memory are best seen as figures, metaphors for memory fragments."[11] These memory fragments—delivered in the form of reanimated photographs—represent Lilly's mediated understanding of the past. In this manner, the narrative structure and character of memory in the film is built upon flashbacks and the reanimation of photographs, highlighting the photographic character of Lilly's personal memories and her inability to move beyond them.

The relationship between Lilly's personal collection of photographs and their historical context is established immediately. After the opening credits and this initial flashback, the scene fades to black. A voice suddenly speaks: "Berlin has always been one of Germany's most important cities, a center. And right here in these rooms, you're in the center of the center, so to speak." Soon, it becomes clear that a group of people is being led through an estate sale at Lilly's modern-day apartment located in the capital of postunified Germany. The camera, meanwhile, pans over a suitcase of clothes and a large stack of photographs tied together with a ribbon, lingering on one of them taken at a New Year's Eve party. Continuing its meandering path through the house, the film camera leads to a young boy who, along with his mother, discovers Lilly seated in a corner smoking a cigarette. Lilly says unsentimentally: "The photos and the chair are mine. You can burn the rest." Aware of her own mortality, Lilly wants to take her photographs and a chair where she can presumably sit and look at them with what time she has left. Near the end of the film, Lilly says that she only thought of "one face, one name" for the last fifty years, doubtlessly the photographed face of Felice, memorialized in the New Year's Eve party image from the film's beginning. Throughout the film, the viewer is invited to sit next to Lilly in her chair and look through her photographs as they come to life.

The nonlinear structure of photographs is emphasized during the last flashback and reanimation of Lilly's photographs. As Ilse takes Lilly's hand to lead her into the blurry green of the large park, the film flashes back one final time to a joyous evening of Lilly and Felice together with friends around a table. Like the beginning of the film, the sequence opens with Lilly holding a camera. Their conversation continues, and while talking about true love and what they want out of life, Felice says, "I don't want forever! I want now! Now! Now! Now! I want loads of nows, and I want them until I turn old and gray. And besides, I want more cake." At this moment, Lilly snaps two photographs of Felice and the image cuts to black to end the film with the information that explains Felice's likely death in a concentration camp. Lilly's memory of Felice, as portrayed in the film, is thus photographic: the memories conveyed recreate the photographs in Lilly's "book of tears";[12] Felice's face that she refuses to leave and cannot process reanimates a personal and national trauma that she cannot penetrate. Baer writes, "Because trauma blocks routine mental processes from converting an experience to memory or forgetting, it parallels the defining structure of photography, which also traps an event during its occurrence while blocking its transformation into memory."[13] Throughout *Aimée and Jaguar*, photographs are revealed as the device Lilly uses to remember Felice, to establish her eternal presence and the "now!" of her memory (and life), but also to elide the historical severity of Lilly's and Germany's complicit role in Felice's death and the Holocaust.

Revealing the film's photographic structure and its relationship to trauma complements various readings of the film. It explains the emphasis on Lilly's scopophilia by revealing the source of her memory as photographs and explains Lilly's privileged narration and the flatness of Felice's character that is literally reduced to an image. Koepnick writes, "The film's final images may thus reanimate the victims of history, but they do so under conditions that mystify rather than reveal what makes this resurrection possible."[14] However, if one suspends common assumptions of time and allows for multiple temporalities to exist simultaneously, then the "now" of the film's final images and their status as the last photograph taken before Felice's death can be seen or felt on equal terms as the "now" of Lilly's present and her historical knowledge and guilt despite the amount of time between them. Baer writes, "Only if we abandon or substantially revise the notion of history and time as inherently flowing and sequential will we recognize what we see or fail to see in these photographs."[15] The prevalent use of photographs in German heritage films can be read as a structural analogy for how trauma is perceived and makes sense in a style of filmmaking that emerged in the midst of a memory boom and a reemergence of trauma studies in postunified Germany.

Chiastic Strategies in *Good Bye, Lenin!* (2003)

Wolfgang Becker's *Good Bye, Lenin!* (2003) is one of the most popular and critically acclaimed post-*Wende* films about life in the German Democratic Republic (GDR). It is often used in German classrooms as an accessible and nuanced approach to help students develop a preliminary understanding of East Germany, and it is frequently thought of in terms of nostalgia or its cute, specifically East-German counterpart *Ostalgie* (nostalgia for the east), or as "Heimat-folklore and post socialist kitsch."[16] The film production and marketing appeal, coupled with the encapsulation of an important historical period, places the film well within the parameters of heritage films. As in the case of *Aimée and Jaguar*, the photographs in *Good Bye, Lenin!* are often acknowledged but rarely given sustained critical attention in scholarship. This section will show how the photographs in the opening and closing sequences of the film link its narrative goals to a chiastic transition between moving and still images that highlight Alex's coming of age and coming to terms with the death of his mother and the GDR.

The film leads with Super-8 footage of Alex and his sister at their family's *Datsche* (cabin) in the summer of 1978, evoking the past and nostalgia associated with the media. The footage is intercut with still images in the form of seven GDR postcards of buildings, cars, and street scenes of East-Berlin. The opening sequences with the home footage and the postcards reappear later at important moments in the film's narrative. During a later trip to the same *Datsche*, Alex's mother reveals the true story of what happened with their father and why she devoted herself to the GDR, rendering Alex's quest to save her futile and

Figure 8.1. *Good Bye, Lenin!* Directed by Wolfgang Becker. Berlin: X-Filme Creative Pool, 2003. Screen capture by Carrie Collenberg-González.

subverting the innocence associated with the nostalgic Super-8 footage from earlier. The postcards also reappear at the end of the film but in an altered form. After they have sent his mother's ashes into space, the same soft piano music of Yann Tiersen from the beginning of the film accompanies three wide-angle street scenes of East-Berlin in 1990 that subvert the idyllic visions of the GDR depicted on the postcards at the beginning. The Berlin of the former GDR has been transformed: the postcard images become moving images in the present moment of Berlin as a unified city and the capital of a newly reunited Germany. While Berlin is transformed from the past of the postcard image to the present of the moving footage, a similar visual language transforms Alex's mother from the present to the past.

After the closing street scenes of a unified Berlin fade, the film replays Super-8 footage of Alex's mother taking a photograph that was shown earlier in the film. In this early scene, Christiane Kerner is shown setting up a camera and then hurrying to pose with her children until the timer captures the picture. Then, at the end of the film and directly following the postcards that have just been transformed into live street scenes, the same Super-8 footage of Alex's mother taking a picture is shown. Except this time, the camera freezes when the photograph is taken and remains still for nearly ten seconds until the shot fades to black and the credits roll. The final shot of the film is this photograph of Alex's mother (see figure 8.1). During the first sequence, the narrator Alex describes his mother as "a passionate crusader for the concerns of common people"; but by the end, his idealism of his mother and the GDR has changed. He says, "The country my mother left behind was a country she believed in, a country we kept alive until her last breath, a country that never existed in that form, a country that, in my memory, I will always associate with my mother." In a visual and chiastic gesture, the static and idyllic East-Berlin depicted on the postcards is returned to the living, united Berlin and allowed to change and transition while the recently deceased mother and the country she represented are suspended in time in the form of still images.

In many ways, the emphasis on this photograph echoes the Winter Garden photograph in Roland Barthes' *Camera Lucida*.[17] The second part of the book embraces the subjectivity inherent in understanding the power that photographs have by focusing on Barthes' search to find the one photograph of his mother that captures her essence, and he believes he is successful. His chapter on the photograph opens with this remembrance: "There I was, alone in the apartment where she had died, looking at these pictures of my mother, one by one, under the lamp, gradually moving back in time with her, looking for the truth of the face I had loved. And I found it."[18] Barthes' description of the photograph of his mother in *Camera Lucida* is strangely similar to the picture that Alex's mother takes of them in *Good Bye, Lenin*: "The brother and sister, united, as I knew, by the discord of their parents, who were soon to divorce, had posed side by side, alone, under the palms of the Winter Garden."[19] Although Barthes did not print the photograph of his mother in his book, the director of *Good Bye, Lenin!*, Becker, included his at the beginning and end of the film in a more deictic gesture appropriate to the visual medium of film. Exploring the dialogue between Becker's use of photographs and Barthes' approach to the Winter Garden photograph in *Camera Lucida* sheds light on the significance of photographs in *Good Bye, Lenin!*

Told through Alex's perspective, the film is a coming-of-age story recounted as a flashback that shows how he comes to terms with the simultaneous end of the GDR and the death of his mother as he grapples with the power of representation to manipulate reality. While both Barthes and Alex remain trapped in the inability to understand the female characters around them, to understand the lives their mothers had lived when their existence was not defined by the presence of their sons, Barthes is able to locate (or at least thinks he does) the true essence of his mother. By choosing a picture of her as a young girl, he has chosen a time before his existence:

> Or again (for I am trying to express this truth) this Winter Garden Photograph was for me like the last music Schumann wrote before collapsing, that first *Gesang der Frühe* which accords with both my mother's being and my grief at her death; I could not express this accord except by an infinite series of adjectives, which I omit, convinced however that this photograph collected all the possible predicates from which my mother's being was constituted and whose suppression or partial alteration, conversely, had sent me back to these photographs of her which had left me so unsatisfied. These same photographs, which phenomenology would call "ordinary" objects, were merely analogical, provoking only her identity, not her truth; but the Winter Garden Photograph was indeed essential, it achieved for me, utopically, *the impossible science of the unique being*.[20]

There are more similarities between Barthes and Alex here. Jennifer Creech writes that "*Good Bye, Lenin!*'s narrative and cinematic strategies position the viewer as simultaneously sympathetic and critical, constructing the female protagonist as the site of contradiction between ideology and dialectics, real existing socialism and the utopian impulse at its heart."[21] Here, the photograph of Christiane Kerner and everything she represents is this liminal site, this "utopically . . . impossible science of the unique being." The associative power of photography and meaning is also inherent in the use of piano music to accompany the essence and grief of their mothers. Barthes writes about Schumann's *Gesang der Frühe* while Yann Tierson's music plays over Alex's photograph. Tierson, the composer of the music for Jean-Pierre Jeunet's *Amélie* (2001) just two years before *Good Bye, Lenin!*, entitled the piece "Summer 78." This refers to the year in which Sigmund Jähn became the first German in space and the year in which the film begins, but it also happens to coincide with the time between the death of Roland Barthes' mother (1977) and the writing and publication of *Camera Lucida*, which happened to be the same year Barthes died (1980). Whether the connections are intentional or not, the associative dialog is something enabled by the photograph and the potential spaces it can inhabit and transcend.

For Alex, his mother's essence remains at the subjective level. His Winter Garden picture, so to speak, is one that depicts her sovereign gaze but also one that holds her hostage in an oppressive web of representation. The truth of Alex's photograph is the innocence and childish reverence with which he looks at his mother and not the impossible science of the unique being she was. Alex's photograph of his mother does not entirely parallel the moment described by Barthes who, by choosing a picture of his mother as a young girl, chose a time before his existence. For Alex, his memory of his mother is defined by his gaze because the real subject of the photograph and film is Alex and his gaze, his understanding of the world and of death. After sending off his mother and his country into space, Alex willingly relinquishes his own innocence to the past and allows himself to move forward into new spaces. His chiastic coming-of-age story can be understood as the attempt of a generation to come to terms with systems of authority and representation—both private and public—and see where they stand in the face of upheaval and where they will go.

Postmemory in *Almanya: Welcome to Germany* (2011)

Yasemin Şamdereli's *Almanya: Welcome to Germany* (2011) is a critically acclaimed heritage film whose uncanny timeliness emphasizes the significance of migration and integration in Germany at the fifty-year anniversary of labor migration in Germany and presages the waves of refugees from the Syrian Civil War who began arriving in Europe in 2014.[22] Like *Good Bye, Lenin!*, the accessible and domesticated portrayal of an important historical period is often used in classrooms to help students gain a deeper understanding of the guestworker program as well as the social and cultural debates about multiculturalism and identity associated with it.[23] This section will focus on the significant role photographs play in the narrative as a way to link the film's utopian visions to discourses surrounding cultural practices of familial representation, postmemory, and trauma. According to Marianne Hirsch: "'Postmemory' describes the relationship that the 'generation after' bears to the personal, collective, and cultural trauma of those who came before—to experiences they 'remember' only by means of the stories, images, and behaviors among which they grew up. But these experiences were transmitted to them so deeply and affectively as to seem to constitute memories in their own right."[24] *Almanya* relies on strategies of photographic memory as a means to structure and unfurl the narrative and to emphasize the postmemory and weight of intragenerational trauma.

Almanya tells the story of four generations of the Yilmaz family—a Turkish family from Anatolia—and spans three time periods. Beginning in the film's present moment in 2011, the narrator goes back in time to tell the story of when their grandparents met in Turkey, when the grandfather Hüseyin came to Germany as a guestworker in 1964, how he returned to Turkey to retrieve his family, and their trip back to Germany together. The story then converges with the present moment where the family takes a pivotal trip to Turkey together and then returns to Germany, changed forever. In the process, we are introduced to Hüseyin and his wife, Fatma; their children, Veli, Muhamed, Leyla, and Ali (born in Germany); and eventually the children's partners and children. Ali is married to a German woman named Gabi and they have a six-year-old boy named Çenk. Leyla's daughter, Çanan, is pregnant. The central conflict of the narrative begins when young Çenk, confused, asks whether they are Turkish or German. At this point, Çanan takes over as narrator and tells the story of her family and how they are both Turkish and German. Sweeping across nearly fifty years, *Almanya* uses photographs to portray a seemingly utopian vision of harmony and reconciliation that weaves together the past, present, and future—eliding time and space, history and subjectivity in a gentle and comedic confrontation with trauma and acceptance of hybrid identities.

The pervasive use of photographs throughout the film finds much of its power by playing on the optical unconscious in representations of the family. While Walter Benjamin's approach to the "optical unconscious" is concerned with what the camera and photograph expose that the eye does not see,[25] Marianne Hirsch uses the term to justify close readings of photographs—especially family photographs—to uncover more about the family and how reliant it is on the "invisibility of its structuring elements."[26] *Almanya* opens and closes with vintage, white-rimmed family photographs of young family members laid out on a tapestry and in an album that anchor the photographs in both Turkish and German contexts. The photographs depict images of the Yilmaz children participating in "normal" German activities like carrying *Schultüten* (a gift given to children to celebrate their first day of school) or dressing up for *Fasching* (Mardi Gras), but it is significant to recognize that the children are first-generation Turkish children who had not grown up with these traditions and for whom these traditions were new. These framing photographs on the tapestry and in the album document the children's seemingly successful integration into and participation in German cultural rites and create the illusion of a successful integration on private and public levels.

Almanya combines whimsical details with photographic representation to comment on the injustice and arbitrariness of representation, framing, commemoration, and memory. One such example can be seen in the cinematic manipulation of the iconic historical photograph of the one-millionth guest worker who arrived in Germany in 1964, a Portuguese man named Armando Rodrigues de Sá, who was honored and celebrated in the media. In the film, Hüseyin arrives alongside de Sá but, with a polite gesture, allows him to go ahead of him. As such, de Sá becomes the celebrated one-millionth guestworker in the iconic photograph while Hüseyin is the one-million-and-first. By politely letting de Sá go ahead of him, Hüseyin does not become the subject of the iconic picture of the one millionth guest worker to arrive and be celebrated. Instead, he is just one of many workers in the background of the historical footage and photographs, curious about but oblivious to the commotion and its historical significance. During this scene, the filmmakers juxtapose reenactments that insert Hüseyin into historical footage alongside actual historical footage, thereby inserting Hüseyin's personal story into historical representation. By literally inserting Hüseyin and his family's story into the historical representation of Germany, the directors demand that a space be claimed and that the personal stories of the guestworkers and their families be acknowledged at a public level of discourse, as is later emphasized when he is invited by Angela Merkel to give a speech. This gesture relates the epigraph of the film, a quotation from Max Frisch that states: "We called workers. People came."[27]

Photographs also provide insight into how the characters feel and serve as narrative devices that are used as portals to other spaces and times. In one example, Hüseyin keeps photographs of his wife, three children (at the time), and a postcard of a Turkish landscape tucked into the bunk bed mattress above his bed while he is living alone in Germany. He keeps these images next to letters and his toothbrush, which shows how essential they are to his emotional well-being, health, and daily routine. In another example, Çanan and Çenk look at an old, creased, black-and-white photograph of a young goat that comes to life and provides them access to the countryside where their grandparents first met. They look at this photograph at a family dinner that takes place after Çenk has had a bad day at school and is confused about whether he is Turkish or German, a question that also draws ambiguous answers from his family. Once they enter the photograph, Çenk learns more about his past and begins to see the present as something inevitably imbued by the past. During the funeral scene at the end of the film, Çenk sees each of his family members standing next to past versions of themselves and seems to grasp the potential of fluid temporal and spatial planes that his father referred to when describing how water can exist as a liquid, gas, and solid. In these examples, photographs exceed their indexical referents and provide a platform for the oldest and youngest members of the Yilmaz family to connect with the past, present, and future.

Photographs play a significant role in the formation of postmemory to show how Çanan and Çenk internalize and process the memories of their grandparents, which forms the motivation of the entire narrative. The postmemory of the Yilmaz past is bookended with two family photographs: one of the nuclear family together on the couch that is used to market the film on posters; and another of the extended family taken by a young boy during the family trip to Turkey. While the first shot depicts an ostensibly happy family, the unconscious optics reveal that they are in the midst of incredible and disconcerting change: the children want to celebrate Christmas; Fatma is pregnant with Ali; Leyla questions why her father has a mustache when no other German men do; and Veli and Muhamed speak to each other in a language Hüseyin cannot understand. After this picture is taken, Hüseyin decides to take the family back to Turkey only to realize that they no longer fit in there either. The second family picture is taken approximately forty years later, after Cenk's question about their identity, after Hüseyin and Fatma have just received their German citizenship, and during another trip to Turkey where Hüseyin has purchased a home. It shows them together for the last time before Hüseyin dies, in his homeland, where he can no longer be buried because he relinquished his citizenship. The film catches up to itself temporally here—the retelling of their story and the present diegesis of the film merge in the photograph, and the family continues, together, into the future. Even though Hüseyin has died, his character still accompanies them as a living presence, and although he is portrayed as a safe and comforting escort, he is also representative of lived trauma that Çanan will carry forward and recount as postmemory to the child she is carrying.

In the examples provided above, the photographs structure the narrative, provide insight into the characters, transfer memory from one generation to another, anchor their private lives in the historical, and serve as an analogy for the family's shared trauma. Superficially, the photographs depict innocuous young goats or ostensibly happy families and children participating in middle-class cultural activities. Like the film itself, these images can be understood on the surface as examples of a light-hearted, comedic, and endearing vision of harmony and integration. However, the photographs and the film itself also represent the anxiety of integration and identity as well as the marginalization of the lives of so many workers who left their families and countries and retrieved their families—issues that remain as much a part of the present and future as they do the past. The photographs in the film provide a model that relates the personal to the political in their representation that on the surface depicts the Yilmaz family while indicating a deeper connection to contemporary politics and the many other families in Germany who have endured, are enduring, and will endure similar struggles.

Conclusion

The examples explored in this chapter reveal the photographic character of memory in German heritage films and function as a type of a *mise en abyme* that links the personal stories of the characters with their historical contexts. In *Aimée & Jaguar*, the photographs that form the structure of the flashbacks are first addressed in Lilly's apartment, which is located in Berlin—"the center of the center"—and link Lilly's personal memory of the past to the new capital of a postunified Germany. Alexander's coming-of-age story in *Good Bye, Lenin!* also places the photograph of him looking at his mother within the postcard images of East-Berlin that transition to the streets of a unified Berlin and a new future. And in *Almanya: Welcome to Germany*, Hüseyin's personal narrative is inserted into the historical (and therefore recognizable) visual rhetoric of guestworkers and refugees. As German heritage films, these films belong to a larger body of memory work that concerns itself primarily with representation and the understanding of the self and its positioning in history vis-à-vis the photograph. By using photographs or by evoking cultural practices of looking at photographs, the films appeal to *consensus-driven markets*, a term often used negatively to imply that the history represented is somehow inaccurate, embedded within hegemonic systems of power and oppression—and therefore dangerous or banal. In any case, it is not the photograph that should be condemned but the photographic structure of our modern memories and the relationship between history and representation that should be explored.

The German heritage films addressed in this chapter show that the representation of memory is indeed photographic—not eidetic but related to actual photographs and the practice of photography that impact the narrative with regard to both form and content; structuring, informing, and progressing the narrative, these guiding structures are second nature enough that they are hardly ever noticed. German heritage films also respond to postunification notions of *Vergangenheitsbewältigung* (coming to terms with the past) that respond to a cultural skepticism regarding authenticity and history that privileges personal narratives and memory, of which photographs play an integral role. Our increasing reliance on the visual and the digital—which explodes the already exploded temporal and spatial planes of the photograph—to represent ourselves and history only makes photographs more important as an object of study to examine how the representation of history is inextricably linked to the history of representation. Understanding how photographs work in German heritage films as a structural analogy for trauma that simultaneously links personal and historical representation is a productive start that enhances our understanding of German national cinema and its reliance on photographs to represent the past.

According to Kaja Silverman, "Photography is the vehicle through which . . . profoundly enabling but unwelcome relationships are revealed to us, and through which we learn to think analogically. It is able to disclose the world, show us that it is structured by analogy, and help us assume our place within it because it, too, is analogical."[28] Her approach leads to uncanny conclusions that confront viewers with their insistence on linear narratives that separate the past from the present and future instead of understanding them as one, as photographs demonstrate. The rupture inherent to photographs in German heritage films and the affective modes they initiate aid in the construction of meaning and can also help us better understand and be in the world. Instead of garnering meaning based on the examination and listing of the indexical depiction of a photograph or how it works formally, we might allow these differences to work together and simultaneously to consider larger patterns inherent to photography and the intersection of photographs and German cinema as a vantage point from which to draw larger conclusions about German culture and the traumas it has endured.

Carrie Collenberg-González is Assistant Professor and Section Head of German and director of the *Deutsche Sommerschule am Pazifik* at Portland State University. She has published on Heinrich von Kleist, German cinema, immersion instruction, and the aesthetics of terrorism. Her most recent articles include "Rape Culture and Dialectical Montage: A Radical Reframing *People on Sunday* (1930)" in *Feminist German Studies* (2020) and "The Daisy Oracle: A New *Gretchenfrage* in Goethe's *Faust*" in the *Goethe Yearbook* (2021). She is coauthor of *Cineplex: German Language and Culture Through Film* (2014), and her coedited volume *Heinrich von Kleist: Artistic and Philosophical Legacies* is forthcoming.

Notes

1. Eric Rentschler, "From New German Cinema to the Post-Wall Cinema of Consensus," in *Cinema and Nation*, ed. Mette Hjort and Scott MacKenzie (New York: Routledge, 2000), 260–77. Rentschler's article does not include heritage films as a critical term but distinguishes between popular films of the 1990s (to which heritage films belong) and New German Cinema.
2. Heritage films were first approached in British cinema but have since been related to many national cinemas. See Andrew Higson, *Waving the Flag: Constructing a National Cinema in Britain* (Oxford: Clarendon Press, 1995); Belén Vidal, *Heritage Film: Nation, Genre and Representation* (New York: Wallflower Press, 2012); and Lutz Koepnick, "Reframing the Past: Heritage Cinema and the Holocaust in the 1990s," *New German Critique* 87 (2002).
3. Koepnick, "Reframing the Past," 78.
4. Marianne Hirsch, *The Generation of Postmemory: Writing and Visual Culture After the Holocaust* (New York: Columbia University Press, 2012), 1.
5. Oliver Wendell Holmes, "The Stereoscope and the Stereograph," in *Soundings from the Atlantic* (Boston: Ticknor and Fields, 1859), 129.
6. See Olga Shevchenko, ed., *Double Exposure: Memory and Photography* (New Brunswick: Transaction Publishers, 2014); and Marianne Hirsch, *Family Frames: Photography, Narrative, and Postmemory* (Cambridge, MA: Harvard University Press, 1997).
7. Ulrich Baer, *Spectral Evidence: The Photography of Trauma* (Cambridge, MA: MIT Press, 2002), 8.
8. Erica Fischer, *Aimée und Jaguar: Eine Liebesgeschichte, Berlin 1943* (Cologne: Kiepenhauer und Witsch, 1995).
9. The "memory boom" refers to a surge in memory studies that took place in many disciplines in the 1990s and was largely related to repercussions of the Holocaust. See Jay Winter, "The Generation of Memory: Reflections on the 'Memory Boom' in Contemporary Historical Studies," *Canadian Military History* 10, no. 3 (2012).
10. Lutz Koepnick opens his essay with a description of Lilly behind the camera and refers to her "scopophilia" (Koepnick, "Reframing the Past," 49); Muriel Cormican writes: "Farberbock keeps the viewer aware that the events portrayed are the acts of memory of people other than Felice and that memory and the recounting of the past are privileges denied those who lost their lives to the Holocaust." Muriel Cormican, "*Aimée und Jaguar* and the Banality of Evil," *German Studies Review* 26, no. 1 (2003): 107.
11. Maureen Turim, *Flashbacks in Film: Memory and History* (New York: Routledge, 1989), 209.
12. "Book of tears" is the name Lilly Wust uses to refer to her diary, a scrapbook where she keeps letters and poems the two wrote to each other along with the photographs she developed after 1945 (Fischer, *Aimée und Jaguar*, 148–49).
13. Baer, *Spectral Evidence*, 9.
14. Koepnick, "Reframing the Past," 50.
15. Baer, *Spectral Evidence*, 1.
16. Anke Pinkert, *Film and Memory in East Germany* (Indiana: Indiana University Press, 2008), 207.
17. Roland Barthes, *Camera Lucida: Reflections on Photography*, trans. Richard Howard (New York: Hill and Wang, 2010).

18. Barthes, *Camera Lucida*, 67.
19. Ibid., 69.
20. Ibid., 70–71.
21. Jennifer Creech, "A Few Good Men: Gender, Ideology, and Narrative Politics in *The Lives of Others* and *Good Bye, Lenin!*," *Women in German Yearbook* 25 (2009): 101a.
22. See Sabine Hake and Barbara Mennel, "Introduction," in *Turkish German Cinema in the New Millennium: Sites, Sounds, and Screens*, ed. Sabine Hake and Barbara Mennel (New York: Berghahn Books, 2012), 1.
23. For example, both *Good Bye, Lenin!* and *Almanya: Welcome to Germany* are featured in the second-year German textbook *Cineplex: Intermediate German Language and Culture Through Film*, ed. Reinhard Zachau, Jeanne Schuller, and Carrie Collenberg-González (Cambridge, MA: Focus, 2014).
24. Hirsch, *The Generation of Postmemory*, 5.
25. Walter Benjamin, "The Work of Art in the Age of Mechanical Reproduction," in *Illuminations*, ed. Hannah Arendt (New York: Schocken, 1969).
26. Hirsch, *Family Frames*, 117.
27. "Wir haben Arbeitskräfte gerufen, und es sind Menschen gekommen."
28. Kaja Silverman, *The Miracle of Analogy: or The History of Photography, Part 1* (Stanford: Stanford University Press, 2015), 11.

Bibliography

Baer, Ulrich. *Spectral Evidence: The Photography of Trauma*. Cambridge, MA: MIT Press, 2002.

Barthes, Roland. *Camera Lucida: Reflections on Photography*. Translated by Richard Howard. New York: Hill and Wang, 2010.

Benjamin, Walter. "The Work of Art in the Age of Mechanical Reproduction." In *Illuminations*, edited by Hannah Arendt, 217–51. New York: Schocken, 1969.

Caruth, Cathy. "Trauma and Experience: Introduction." In *Trauma: Explorations in Memory*, edited by Cathy Caruth, 3–11. Baltimore: Johns Hopkins University Press, 1995.

Cormican, Muriel. "*Aimée und Jaguar* and the Banality of Evil." *German Studies Review* 26, no. 1 (2003): 105–19.

Creech, Jennifer. "A Few Good Men: Gender, Ideology, and Narrative Politics in *The Lives of Others* and *Good Bye, Lenin!*" *Women in German Yearbook* 25 (2009): 100–26.

Elsaesser, Thomas. *Weimar Cinema and After: Germany's Historical Imaginary*. New York: Routledge, 2000.

Fischer, Erica. *Aimée und Jaguar: Eine Liebesgeschichte, Berlin 1943*. Cologne: Kiepenhauer und Witsch, 1995.

Hake, Sabine, and Barbara Mennel, eds. *Turkish German Cinema in the New Millennium: Sites, Sounds, and Screens*. New York: Berghahn Books, 2012.

Higson, Andrew. *Waving the Flag: Constructing a National Cinema in Britain*. Oxford: Clarendon Press, 1995.

Hirsch, Marianne. *Family Frames: Photography, Narrative, and Postmemory*. Cambridge, MA: Harvard University Press, 1997.

———. *The Generation of Postmemory: Writing and Visual Culture After the Holocaust*. New York: Columbia University Press, 2012.

Holmes, Oliver Wendell. "The Stereoscope and the Stereograph." In *Soundings from the Atlantic*. Boston: Ticknor and Fields, 1859.

Koepnick, Lutz. "Reframing the Past: Heritage Cinema and the Holocaust in the 1990s." *New German Critique* 87 (2002): 47–82.

Pinkert, Anke. *Film and Memory in East Germany*. Indiana: Indiana University Press, 2008.

Rentschler, Eric. "From New German Cinema to the Post-Wall Cinema of Consensus." In *Cinema and Nation*, edited by Mette Hjort and Scott MacKenzie, 260–77. New York: Routledge, 2000.

Shevchenko, Olga, ed. *Double Exposure: Memory and Photography*. New Brunswick: Transaction Publishers, 2014.

Silverman, Kaja. *The Miracle of Analogy: or The History of Photography, Part 1*. Stanford: Stanford University Press, 2015.

Turim, Maureen. *Flashbacks in Film: Memory and History*. New York: Routledge, 1989.

Vidal, Belén. *Heritage Film: Nation, Genre and Representation*. New York: Wallflower Press, 2012.

Winter, Jay. "The Generation of Memory: Reflections on the 'Memory Boom' in Contemporary Historical Studies." *Canadian Military History* 10, no. 3 (2012): 57–66.

Zachau, Reinhard, Jeanne Schuller, and Carrie Collenberg-González, eds. *Cineplex: Intermediate German Language and Culture Through Film*. Cambridge, MA: Focus, 2014.

Filmography

Aimée & Jaguar. Directed by Max Färberböck. Berlin: Senator Film Produktion, 1999.

Almanya: Welcome to Germany (*Almanya: Willkommen in Deutschland*). Directed by Yasemin Şamdereli. Munich: Roxy Film, 2011.

Amélie (*Le fabuleux destin d'Amélie Poulain*). Directed by Jean-Pierre Jeunet. Paris: Canal+ Group, 2001.

Good Bye, Lenin! Directed by Wolfgang Becker. Berlin: X-Filme Creative Pool. 2003.

Chapter 9

IMAGING THE "GOOD LIFE"

Destabilizing Subjecthood and Conceptions of the Normative Family in *Ghosts* (2005)

Simone Pfleger

The image of a child looms large in Christian Petzold's 2005 film *Ghosts* (*Gespenster*),[1] whose narrative revolves around an orphaned teenager, Nina, and Françoise, a mother searching for her long-lost daughter Marie with only a photograph of the young girl as a toddler to guide her. In this picture, a roughly two-year-old girl, presumably Marie, looks into the camera. She sits on a blanket next to a picnic basket in a park. Because this image appears only briefly at a point early in the film, the audience does not get to look at it for long. The image then features more prominently toward the end when viewers finally get time to see the photograph of the toddler juxtaposed with a series of four computer-generated (CG) images, extrapolated from Marie's face as portrayed in the first image. Thus, it is not the photograph itself but rather the CG sequence of faces that holds particular significance for the ways in which the film constructs and comments on familial relationships. Indeed, *Ghosts* employs photographs to explore how the normative family unit is visualized as well as how a sense of relationality within, a belonging to, and a desire for this normative family unit is constructed and critiqued.

In order to examine the film's depiction of the normative family, this chapter foregrounds Nina's ambivalent longing for physical and emotional closeness to another human being and for inclusion in a traditional familial configuration of a monogamous, heterosexual couple with child(ren). As such, *Ghosts* and Nina's attachment to and rejection of the "good life" comment on the tenuous stability of the hegemonic status of the heteronormative family in contemporary German society as well as the nation's need for normativity to secure the dominant status of certain identities and institutions against which all other subjects are compared. Petzold's film underscores that these sociocultural desires for normativity and anxieties of transgression are tied to a specifically German context with the movie's setting in the urban spaces of Berlin. However, the transnational tendency in the Berlin School in general and Petzold's oeuvre in particular points to the deconstruction of a specifically national cinema and emphasizes that cultural anxieties around nonnormative familial structures and queer relations are a global trend. Indeed, the film might be one way of thinking politically about the present in terms of how these anxieties exceed the local Berlin and the national German context and bespeak the entrenchment of hegemonic ideas of familiality and heteronormativity in Western societies.

In conversation with queer theorist Lauren Berlant, I seek to show how subjects cling to certain desires and fantasies of relations with others that present an obstacle to their thriving. Quickly summarized, Berlant's concept of "cruel optimism" denotes relations and wishes that seem positive for the individual but are in fact restrictive and normative.[2] These fantasies, testaments to the so-called "good life," merely appear to be favorable but are in fact symptoms of how neoliberalism is restructuring and dismantling social structures in ways that endanger precarious life-worlds or realities for many individuals. Engaging with this Berlantian notion of cruel optimism, this chapter underscores that the aesthetics of *Ghosts*—and particularly its use of CG photographs—allow us to interrogate what I term heteronormative familiality[3] and offer a potential escape from it.[4] By imaging—that is, by both visualizing and sparking Nina's imagination—the photographs in *Ghosts* enable Nina to construct a fantasy of belonging to and fitting into the kind of normative life that allows her to forge heterofamilial bonds. However, she ultimately relinquishes her desire to belong by literally discarding the photograph and the CG images, which together play a key role in the emergence and cultivation of her fantasies. Thus, *Ghosts* provides a sense of hope of belonging but stops short of suggesting that this embeddedness in normative family structures represents what is understood as an ostensibly "good life" and the only form of togetherness, which everybody desires.

Addressing the protagonists' investment in certain fantasies and bonds that reflect dominant sociocultural norms and conventions, I demonstrate how *Ghosts* visualizes Berlant's concept of the "good life,"[5] which they understand to be "that moral-intimate-economic thing"[6] that includes "upward mobility, job security, political and social equality, and lively, durable intimacy."[7] Thus, the film comments on how digital imaging technologies facilitate the construction of normative familial fantasies. In order to pursue this goal, this chapter is structured in two parts. Part one introduces what I call "projected familiality," which suggests that digital technologies and CG images in particular construct an artificial telos that enable the film's protagonists to construct a familial narrative. I examine how photographs are integral for the construction of the "good life" of heterofamilial bliss but also engender change. Part two then takes a closer look at the sequence toward the end of *Ghosts* when Nina is confronted directly with various images of a child. Due to the striking similarity with Nina—particularly the picture of a teenage girl—the young woman is prompted to negotiate questions of subjectivity, family belonging, and the desire to succumb to forging heterofamilial bonds.

Normative Fantasies and the Construction of Projected Familiality

The orphan Nina appears to struggle with her attachment to particular intersubject fantasies in terms of forming relationships, exemplified through her interactions with Françoise as well as Toni, a young woman who enters Nina's life suddenly and unexpectedly and with whom she experiences a fleeting moment of intimacy. In the vein of various other Berlin School films,[8] the narrative of *Ghosts* begins in medias res and introduces the viewer to Nina, who lives at a home for troubled youth. Nina meets Toni and Françoise, a woman in her early forties who comes to believe that Nina is actually her lost daughter Marie, who was kidnapped as a child. Because Nina possesses one of two specific physical markers that could confirm Nina's identity as Marie—she has a similar scar on her left ankle, but viewers never find out if she also has a mole on her back—Françoise offers Nina the promise of hope that she has a family and a place of belonging. However, it is not entirely clear whether Nina really believes in this fantasy. Although she follows Françoise and encourages the woman to tell her about her life and her past, Nina continues to appear affectless, which makes it difficult from the audience's perspective to tell whether Nina buys into Françoise's fantasy throughout the film. The possibility of Nina connecting with Françoise is ultimately ruptured when Françoise's husband Pierre forces his wife to return home from Berlin, thereby leaving Nina behind to walk through a seemingly empty and lifeless city alone.

By perpetuating the uncertainty whether Nina is indeed Marie, the film's photographic cues help construct heteronormativity. Combined with the family photograph of Marie, the CG images create a particular narrative and an identity that affirms the traditional familial configuration of the married couple with child, or, to borrow from Marianne Hirsch's book title *Family Frames*,[9] the picture of Marie frames the family. Hirsch's work, much like *The Familial Gaze*,[10] is mostly concerned with how family photos contribute to an identity while highlighting their role as entities that define the private and the public. Hirsch explores the role that conventions play in the process of constructing familial relationships through photographs.[11] Arguing that the images often represent an idealization and not the lived reality, Hirsch uncovers the potential that rests in family photos in creating and shaping personal and cultural memory.[12]

By including a variety of essays that interrogate family photos depicting "portraits of nursemaids, nannies, servants, or slave women (mostly black) holding white infant children on their laps," *The Familial Gaze*, according to Hirsch, aims at unsettling the "boundaries of the family."[13] While these efforts are certainly important advances into what has been heretofore perceived as *the* family by emphasizing the presence of racial and class differences and inequalities,[14] Hirsch's familial gaze fails to address family configuration beyond the normative, heterosexual, and monogamous couple. As such, *The Familial Gaze*, while attempting to trouble and subvert dominant ideologies and denaturalize what constitutes *the* family, falls short of doing so with an eye toward nonnormative genders and sexualities.

Different from Hirsch's approach, French sociologist Pierre Bourdieu's *Photography: A Middle-Brow Art* (1990) considers family photographs as possessing a social function insofar as they are a means to position individuals vis-à-vis society at large and depict what is deemed "photographable."[15] In this sense, the CG images embed the girl within the context of heterosexual intimacy, reproduction, and monogamous coupledom, thereby functioning as the arbiter of heteronormativity's generative force. In their dual function, the photographs thus visualize the fantasy of the desirable normative familial life—a fantasy that the image of Marie both embodies and promises.

Aside from conjuring up visions of the ideal, normative family, the photographs also destabilize the ostensible status quo of the heteronormative family unit represented by the heterosexual couple and the child. As Nina, Toni, and Françoise interact with each other, they forge and shatter affective relations that engender fantasies and desires of the "good life," which more broadly includes particular normative narratives of family structures, relationships, and identity that seemingly produce feelings of happiness but mask the ways in which they impede their thriving.

Such attachments to normativity are at the center of Lauren Berlant's theorization in their seminal work *Cruel Optimism*. In their book, Berlant considers a variety of relationships of an individual, "ranging from objects or scenes of romantic love and upward mobility to the desire for the political itself,"[16] and positions the concept of what they call "good life fantasies" at the center of inquiry. As many are attached to a certain idea of what constitutes a desirable life—such as attachments of "enduring reciprocity in couples, family, political systems, institutions, markets, and at work"[17]—Berlant examines lives in the present moment and tracks what happens to individuals once these idealizations begin to fray. They contend that when these fantasies collapse, they nevertheless keep us stuck in the present, deny any attachments to others, and block our vision of a future even though these fantasies are broken. Precisely this stuckness in an impasse or "time of dithering"[18] does not provide any assurance of our identity, place of belonging, or relations with others. Rather, the present moment urges us to "detach from a waning fantasy of the good life"[19] and to explore different ways of inhabiting the social world. In other words, we need to aim at recasting life in ways that allow us to experiment and to create new forms of being and belonging—even though we might fail in the process of doing so.[20]

Extrapolating from both Berlant's notion of cruel optimism and moving beyond the restrictiveness of Hirsch's "familial gaze" for communities that do not subscribe to heteronormative roles, I propose the notion of "projected familiality" as an attempt to hone in on the kinds of "good life" fantasies of nonnormative familial bonds created through Nina's encounter with Françoise in *Ghosts*. My concept seeks to capture new modes of belonging by taking into account the use of one photograph and three CG images, which taken together visualize and champion the fantasy of familial belonging; it is only through the photos that the kinship formation is substantiated. By relying on both a real photograph and digitally produced CG images, the type of relationality I describe here is grounded in the presence of two seemingly contradictory forces: mimesis (or imitation) and diegesis (or narrative).[21]

Positioning these two terms as emblematic for projected familiality, I understand the actual photograph of Marie, depicting her as a two-year-old toddler sitting on a picnic blanket, to possess a mimetic quality: that is, it depicts the child at a certain moment in time and functions as realia do by visualizing—both presenting and representing—Marie's body. It evinces the toddler's existence and, by extension, functions as a token, which, through the very act of being shown to others, establishes Françoise's status as a mother and the familial relationship between her and Marie. In this sense, it is an object that constructs not only Marie's identity, but it also aids in the affirmation of Françoise's subject position.

By contrast, the CG images that visualize the aging process from infant to teenager portray an imaginary progression that possesses a linear and forward advancing temporal arc. While the first image in the sequence is the face of Marie taken from Françoise's photograph of her child, the subsequent three are created by the computer program that simulates the aging process. Taken together, the four headshots construct a particular telos or fictional aging process of a two-year-old girl that rests on the fabrication of the facial features of the three different Maries through algorithms. In this sense, the CG images speak to the concern raised by Mary Ann Doane that the digital seems to threaten the "certainty of referentiality we have come to associate with photography."[22] Thus, the images indeed create a fictitious developmental narrative from toddler to teenage Marie. In doing so, they substantiate a body and thus a subject that may or may not exist, since Françoise does not have any clue whether or not Marie is still alive.

Based on this dual presence of mimesis in the photograph of Marie and diegesis in the CG images, my theorization of projected familiality in *Ghosts* points to the issue of referentiality: that is, the photograph is a copy of a person and affirms a person's existence which consequently enables the construction of Marie's maturation process. She exists because of the CG images, which substantiate a development from toddler to teenager. At the same time, the final CG image serves as the point of departure for a retrograde projection of familiality since the toddler Marie indeed has real-life parental figures embodied by Pierre and Françoise.

This way of generating heterofamilial fantasies is closely bound up with the existence of both the photograph and the CG images. Together, these pictures function as discrete points that generate a sequence or a force vector, which aims at two distinct directions. On the one hand, they construct a telos that allows for the emergence of the "good life" by materializing the potential corporeal features of Marie and thus substantiate the long-lost teenage child that possesses a family in the present. On the other hand, when reading the sequence of images backward, they construct an illusion of belonging, kinship, and a past for Nina that turns the orphan into a subject—more specifically the toddler Marie—whose picture was taken by her parents and who is thus firmly embedded in the normative family unit.

Because the film is so centered on restoring and fortifying the nuclear family unit by finding the lost child, *Ghosts* exhibits the power and persistence of heteronormative fantasies. My concept of "projected familiality" reveals that expressions of desire to forge kinship connections with others can be attributed to certain individuals and their wishes; to be sure, Françoise needs to find Marie, and Nina is willing to entertain the illusion that she is in fact the child. However, along with revealing the fantasy's potency and pervasiveness of belonging to a normative family beyond the microscopic level of individual subjects, projected familiality also serves as a cultural commentary on contemporary society. Considered from this macroscopic perspective, *Ghosts* exemplifies how the heterosexual family has become "the core institution of the nation-state"[23] that produces and encourages its citizens to reproduce the nuclear family unit as the epitome of a particular life that they ought to champion and replicate. The state does so not only through the unequal distribution of financial benefits for those who are in heterofamilial kinship structures, but also by assigning sociocultural value to certain people and recognizing certain forms of intimacy that yield heterofamiliality. In other words, through its depiction of projected familiality, the film critically interrogates the link between the state and the normalization of monogamous, committed, heterosexual couples that produce offspring.

Disruptions of Projected Familiality and the Rejection of Fantasies of Familial Bliss

When viewers are initially introduced to Nina, the teenage girl seems to epitomize many of the characteristics of an impassive and detached child. She lives at a public foster home, has no clear direction in life, and, as many Berlin School scholars have noted, embodies a ghostly presence.[24] This sense of detachment and impassivity is paramount when approaching the final sequence in *Ghosts*. The film's last scene depicts Nina back in the same park where she retrieves Françoise's wallet, which Toni earlier stole, emptied of money, and discarded in a trash can. The sequence is introduced through a long shot that depicts Nina walking up to the fork of a gravel path that is positioned approximately at the center of the bottom third of the frame where she stops. Although she has entered the frame via the left trail, following the tilt of her head and the direction of her gaze, it appears that Nina is looking down at the other path, which points toward the back right of the frame toward a place unknown to the viewer.

Based on this particular position at the fork of the path, Nina has two options as to how to continue her journey—in one literal sense, she walks through the park; while in a metaphorical sense, she tries to maneuver through the trials and tribulations of life. She is positioned at a fork and depicted at a standstill for a few moments during which she selects one of the two paths. This brief moment of inaction foregrounds a shift in Nina's actions (from progressively advancing to halting) and allows her to pause and contemplate the possibilities that lie ahead. In this instance, both gesture and pause emphasize not only the narrative significance of photographs in the film and Nina's orientation toward them, but also the body, its position, and its directionality in space. In other words, Nina stands out visibly from the environment she is in and has to reorient herself. This turn, both literally and phenomenologically, then directs her toward what is yet to come along the way.

This moment of pause reveals Nina's uncertainty about what to do and underscores how much is at stake in this very moment. She has to make a decision and is left with two choices: continue on the path, or turn and head to an unknown place that is spatially located at an angle behind her, which Nina seems to be contemplating. Choosing the first option means she does not change her directionality and remains on a known linear trajectory; selecting the second option implies a move away from the current position of the camera, away from the screen, and thus away from the viewer. It would turn her away from the *now* and return her—despite the difference in angle—to a more familiar place. In this sense, she would return to a cycle of what Valerie Kaussen calls, "compulsive repetitions, rituals that depend upon the ghostly status and the quasi-invisibility of the homeless teenager"[25]—a life of relationships that never fully grant her a way of belonging and of asserting her place in the world through bonds to other human beings. That is, a life in which she functions as a temporary placeholder, or in other words, a corporeal being that does not register as meaningful to others and whose sole purpose is to fill a gap or a void.

After pondering for a few seconds at the fork, Nina looks up and into the distance before moving somewhat briskly toward a place that is located to the left of the camera, beyond the frame. As she passes the

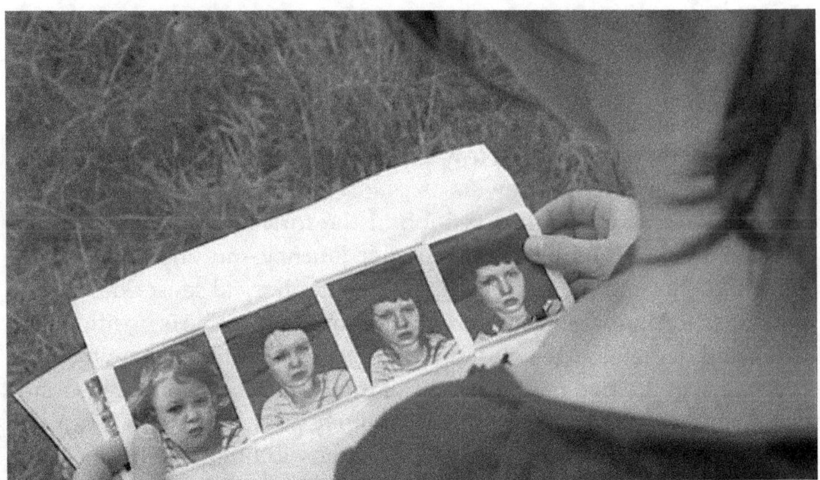

Figure 9.1. *Ghosts* (*Gespenster*). Directed by Christian Petzold. Berlin: Schramm Film Körner & Weber, 2005. Screen capture by Simone Pfleger.

camera, the film cuts to a shot of her walking toward the garbage can, reaching in, and taking out the wallet Toni earlier stole and discarded. An over the shoulder close-up allows the viewers to see Nina open the wallet and take out some pictures that were stored in one of the inside pockets. This act of unfolding the paper unveils the final image of a theoretical, teenaged Marie, who looks very similar to Nina (see figure 9.1). A cut to a medium close-up frontal shot of Nina's upper torso and her head tilted downward looking at the images depicts her hair and face—particularly her mouth—further enhances the resemblance between Nina and Marie. By cutting back and forth between the teenage girl looking at the images and the pictures of Marie, the sequence establishes a consistent, circular rhythm as its shot reverse shot editing between Nina and the pictures of Marie draws the viewers closer in. The close camera distance, the rather slow frequency of transition between each shot, and the long shot duration (of roughly five seconds per image and a total of twenty-eight seconds combined) generate an apparent elongation of the present that foregrounds the images both temporally and visually in a way that emphasizes a projected familiality that will soon be disrupted.[26]

By lingering on either Nina's face or the four faces in the images, the film constructs a mirroring effect that is linked to both the visual details of the image sequence and the editing choice in the sequence.

As the camera encourages the audience to stay with the pictures, it invites them to bring a range of stories to bear on the scene. While the arrangement of shots in this circular fashion encourages viewers to ponder whether Nina is Françoise's kidnapped daughter and whether she was indeed robbed of having a traditional family life, they also repeatedly jolt us out of constructing that particular narrative and remind the audience of Nina's presence. Quickly alternating between the actual person and the CG images that appear to index different moments in the past, the film encourages viewers to imagine a past whose telos is constantly interrupted by Nina's actual presence, thus foreclosing the creation of a seamless narrative of the girl's past.

This series of shots in the final scene evokes Berlant's notion of cruel optimism; or rather, Nina yearns with cruel optimism for a heterofamilial bond to overcome her solitude and experience a sense of connectedness with others. The possibility of the "good life," of Nina being Marie and of belonging to a conventional family unit, is underscored by the deployment of crosscuts that seem to reenforce visually a connection between Nina and the images of Marie. As such, these photos serve as indexical referents to a past that can only emerge when Nina engages with the images and invests in projected familiality. The presence of Nina's body serves as a material foundation unfolding an alternative world—that is, one in which Nina is given the opportunity to entertain the idea of being Marie and is integrated into the kinship relations created by normative family life.

As the resemblance is indeed striking, the editing choices mentioned above in this final scene together with the CG images fulfill a dual purpose: they keep Nina stuck in an impasse, but they also cause us to probe our own stuckness and attachment to the fantasy of belonging to a normative family unit with a heterosexual, monogamous, married couple that is constructed and performed in front of our very own eyes. By cutting back and forth between the teenage girl looking at the images and the pictures of Marie, the sequence emphasizes that Nina is pondering whether she might be Marie or not, whether she was indeed robbed of the "good life" about which she fantasizes and to which she is attached. And while this moment in the present is only rendered possible by the existence of the photographs and their technologies, she cannot do anything but engage with this particular illusion of believing in the possibility of being Françoise's kidnapped daughter and of having a family—a desire that leaves her longing but never offers her any chance of belonging.

This promise of potentially being able to project a sense of familial bliss not only allows Nina to construct a past that she might have experienced but was too young to remember; it also establishes a sense of her belonging to Françoise and Pierre's heteronormative familial configuration in and for the future. In this regard, affective attachments and a kinship bond to the couple are possible only if Nina is able to invest in a particular segment of time and its linear unfolding as suggested by the progression of CG images. In order to earn the status of a family member, however, Nina must rehearse a fictitious past that lacks any connection to her current life. This narrative of Nina as Marie affirms her presence by allowing her to imagine a past while denying her the ability to materialize as Marie because of the story's lack of substance; it relies on accepting a temporal progression from two-year-old Marie to teenage Marie but can only transform Nina into Marie if Nina reverses the same temporal sequence. She must move backward in time in order to become the two-year-old girl and then move forward through a past she never lived.

After contemplating the possibility of this past and her connection to Françoise and Pierre, Nina crumples up the pictures and tosses them back into the garbage. While Kurt Buhanan reads this scene as Nina having "no real recourse for establishing a relationship" with Françoise thereby "effectively render[ing] the photograph blank for her eye, devoid of meaning,"[27] Joy Castro disagrees and argues that "Nina recognizes the hopelessness of pursuing a relationship within a configuration that disempowers, dismisses, and misdiagnoses Françoise's persistent maternal desire."[28] Although she challenges Buhanan's reading that the images do not possess any significance for Nina, Castro suggests that Nina does not pursue a relationship with Françoise out of concern for the woman thereby leaving Nina's desire to reside with unquestioned heterofamilial structures.

Returning to this act of discarding the images, I propose an alternative to both Buhanan's and Castro's readings. Instead, I suggest that Nina—regardless of whether she is or is not Marie—actively uncouples herself from the fantasy of and an attachment to having a family, from having a fixed life narrative materialized through the CG images, and from having a distinct and concrete past as a consequence. In doing so, she appears to detach herself from the confines of lineage and linearity for defining her subjectivity as well as from conventional desires of sociality and belonging. Instead, she seems to reject Françoise's "good-life" fantasy in favor of inhabiting a position that turns her away from the normative heterofamilial narrative but does not automatically engender the possibility of forging bonds.

Upon discarding the pictures and, with them, the possibility of participating in the narrative of belonging to Françoise and Pierre's family, Nina continues down the same path that led her to the garbage can and appears to be headed toward an unknown point in the distance. This transition from engaging with the images to then walking away from them is emphasized on a formal level. After a medium shot of Nina's face, the camera then pans away from the young woman and transforms gradually into a long shot when the camera stops its movement as Nina keeps on walking with her back turned to the camera. The viewer is left behind to watch as the dark colors of Nina's clothes blend more and more with the dark green leaves of the trees, whose branches droop and partially obstruct the view.

While Marco Abel identifies Nina's desires and pursuit of a seemingly desirable life trajectory, of belonging, and of forming and maintaining relationships to be an overarching theme in Petzold's entire oeuvre, the final sequence of *Ghosts* supports a different reading. When she ultimately turns away from any connections to others and departs from the fantasy of being Marie, Nina seems to have no other choice but to turn away from the images that symbolize Nina's longing for a bond. She is forced to direct her physical body and her gaze toward a vast grassy area, devoid of any other human beings with whom she could interact. Cook, Koepnick, Kopp, and Prager comment on this particular kind of emptiness in various Berlin School films and understand *Ghosts* as one example "where Berlin is partly today's Berlin, insofar as it is under construction, but is also tomorrow's postindustrial city, its urban landscape a desert."[29] In other words, viewers know that the film is located in one of the largest German metropolitan centers, yet Nina's existence lacks any indicators that gesture toward the presence of others. She is headed toward a life that offers nothing but loneliness and isolation, lacking any relationships with which she might construct a shared or collective present or future.

While this final sequence appears to accentuate Nina's unfulfilled yearning for conventional and normative family bonds while emphasizing her stuckness, certain aesthetic characteristics of the Berlin School allow for a reading of the film's ending that is in conversation with the Berlantian concept of cruel optimism, but also considers the importance of the audience as active participants in the viewing experience. The final sequence in *Ghosts* permits an alternative reading, despite—or maybe because of—how it negotiates notions of physical and emotional attachment to what constitutes the "good life." Rather than valorizing Nina's act of resistance to and refusal of a certain idealized version of how to relate to others as progressive and liberated, Petzold instead underscores the viewer's own investment in her dismissal of normative fantasies. In other words, the film seeks to illustrate the audience's tendency to idealize struggle and opposition.

In this sense, when Nina wads up and throws the images away, it signals her active and conscious decision to relinquish the desire to be a part of Françoise's family. If the medium shot of Nina's face before she discards the pictures urges us to construct a fantasy that ties the girl to Françoise and her husband, the subsequent over-the-shoulder close-up of Nina's hands tossing the wallet and the images stresses her action rather than her body and her surroundings. The downward tilt of the camera encourages the audience to align with Nina's point of view; we watch the items dropping into the garbage instead of inhabiting a position from which to observe Nina. To be more precise, viewers bear witness to the moment when Nina decides to face the images directly one last time before she lets go of them completely, turns away, and walks off.

Viewers watch Nina's body move through an area of the park that lacks signs of the Berlin cityscape in the background, thereby suggesting complete social isolation. Her back is to the camera and the audience can hear only ambient noise, such as the wind rustling in the trees in the park. This final sequence invokes an affirmative rejection and abandonment of normative family life evoked by the combination of Françoise's narrative and the pictures; both the lack of extradiegetic sound and the abrupt ending of the movie deny the viewer the chance to sentimentalize this moment. Instead, in an excessively long take of thirty-eight seconds, the viewer's attention is drawn to Nina's blue T-shirt and jeans because the outfit creates a stark contrast to the soft green grass and foliage of the trees, thereby rendering her hyper visible and emphasizing her physical presence. As her body moves forward, the camera stays with her. The audience is forced to linger and watch her figure gradually become smaller and smaller without any references that indicate what is yet to come.

While walking away could signal Nina's determination to abandon normative conceptions of heterofamilial bonds along with their attendant modes of procreation and reproduction so that she might completely detach and move on freely, the scene's aesthetics complicate such an attempt to idealize the film's ending. In particular, the combination of the shot duration and Nina's slow movement prevents us from glorifying Nina as a fully transformed, independent subject. Rather, the interplay between formal aspects, the mise-en-scène, and filmic characters evokes a sense of extension or prolonging of the present moment.

Without any reference to other diegetic objects or subjects that might point to a potential future in which she is able to forge relational bonds, Nina appears indeed alone and without any sense of belonging in that final sequence. On the one hand, she registers as completely isolated and detached from any relationships—while her clothes and her presence in the park echo her time with Toni and her engagement with the pictures in the wallet index the potential of being part of a normative family unit, the long shot duration of the final scene emphasizes her solitude and alienation from others. On the other hand, this lack or absence of buildings and other people suspends her from the present and its referents to a seemingly normalized social life with family and friends and allows her to embrace an alternative mode of being. This type of existence thus extends the promise of envisioning previously unexplored bonds of sociality and relationality, connections that stretch beyond the familiar to reimagine the familial.

Conclusion

In Petzold's *Ghosts*, the photograph of Marie and the CG images are integral for setting up cruelly optimistic attachments to heterofamilial desires that seemingly promise a particular kind of normative life and relationships, thereby demonstrating how family photos construct a particular telos and relationality that allow for the projection of a kinship formation. While it is only of secondary importance whether Nina believes she is Marie, whether Françoise truly believes Nina is Marie, or whether Toni was aware of Nina's infatuation with her, all these relationships raise important questions, such as how they can generate desires for and fantasies of certain kinds of bonds that indicate and comment on heterofamilial normativity as the sociocultural status quo in contemporary Germany in particular and the global North in general. Although these might create impasses that keep individuals stuck, the film's content and aesthetics underscore the potential for the refusal of succumbing to the desire to forge bonds, regardless of whether these relations register as normative or not.

Overall, the use of photographs in *Ghosts* is representative of Petzold's investment in the visual as well as techniques of surveillance in particular, and a recurrence of these and other motifs—such as the crumbling of interpersonal (romantic) relationships, ghostly presences, and disorienting spaces and places—in Berlin School films exemplifies and affirms themes in early twenty-first-century German national cinema while simultaneously addressing universal and transnational trends. The film employs particular editing and cinematographic strategies, such as long takes and long shots, not to reify a national identity and calcified notion of "German-ness," but to enable and even encourage the audience to pause in order to consider the prevalence of and harm done by championing the hegemonic status of heterofamiliality and normativity in most Western society. The use of the photograph of toddler Marie and the CG images encourages a queer reading of the film that destabilizes and denaturalizes the link between the photographs and heterofamilial bonds and thus refuses to offer redemption.

Simone Pfleger is Assistant Professor of Gender and German Studies at the University of Alberta. Their research is grounded in gender and queer theoretical methodologies and engages with notions of temporality, political subjectivity, affect, intimacy, and precarity in post-2000 German-language literature, film, and culture. They have published in *Feminist Media Studies*, *Feminist German Studies*, and *The German Quarterly*, among others. Simone is currently coediting a volume on transdisciplinarity in German Studies and working on a monograph on queer temporality and aesthetics in the cinema of the Berlin School.

Notes

1. Christian Petzold's *Ghosts* is the second film of the so-called "Ghost Trilogy," along with *The State I Am In* (*Die innere Sicherheit*, 2000) and *Yella* (2007).
2. Lauren Berlant, *Cruel Optimism* (Durham: Duke University Press, 2011), 2.
3. My use of the phrase "heteronormative familiality" delineates a particular kind of family constellation that idealizes the heterosexual, monogamous couple with child(ren) as the paragon of dominant mainstream society.
4. Sianne Ngai, *Ugly Feelings* (Cambridge, MA: Harvard University Press, 2007), 2–3. Additional scholarship on affect theory and several queer theorists have, however, shifted their focal point toward constructing avenues of exploration and theorizing that foreground "the aesthetics of the ugly feelings." Ngai argues that these "ugly feelings," which include affective responses such as irritation, envy, and paranoia, foreclose a cathartic relief for the subject and are often paired with "a general state of obstructed agency," and thus seem less powerful to a society that focuses on affirmative acts as expressions of progress and power (Ngai, *Ugly Feelings*, 3). Further investigations of the notion of "ugly feelings" feature prominently in writings of J. Jack Halberstam's *The Queer Art of Failure* (Durham: Duke University Press, 2011), Eve Kosofsky Sedgwick's *Touching Feeling: Affect, Pedagogy, Performativity* (Durham: Duke University Press, 2003), Sara Ahmed's *The Cultural Politics of Emotion* (New

York: Routledge, 2004) and *The Promise of Happiness* (Durham: Duke University Press, 2010), and Berlant's *Cruel Optimism*.

5. I will use quotation marks throughout this chapter to emphasize the constructed nature of what constitutes a good life. In this sense, I seek to draw special attention to the fact that those fantasies and desires that determine what is deemed a good life reflect and champion certain standards and ideals set by dominant culture.
6. Berlant, *Cruel Optimism*, 2.
7. Ibid., 3.
8. This particular way of introducing viewers to the film's narrative and its characters is also characteristic of Christoph Hochhäusler's *I Am Guilty* (*Falscher Bekenner*, 2005), Ulrich Köhler's *Windows on Monday* (*Montag kommen die Fenster*, 2006), Angelica Schanelec's *Afternoon* (*Nachmittag*, 2007), and Maria Speth's *The Days Between* (*In den Tag hinein*, 2001), among others.
9. Marianne Hirsch, *Family Frames: Photography, Narrative, and Postmemory* (Cambridge, MA: Harvard University Press, 1997).
10. Marianne Hirsch, *The Familial Gaze* (Hanover: University Press of New England, 1999).
11. Ibid., xi.
12. Hirsch, *Family Frames*, 10–12.
13. Hirsch, *Familial Gaze*, xiv.
14. Ibid.
15. Pierre Bourdieu, *Photography: A Middle-Brow Art*, trans. Shaun Whiteside (Stanford: Stanford University Press, 1990), 6.
16. Berlant, *Cruel Optimism*, 2.
17. Ibid.
18. Ibid., 5.
19. Ibid., 263.
20. The notion of failure as a springboard to reimagining and constructing the world features prominently in Halberstam's *The Queer Art of Failure*, 2–3, 11. Halberstam engages with the ideas of finding alternatives (1) to success that is defined according to the conventional frameworks of heteronormativity and capitalism; (2) to "academic legibility and legitimization" as well as academia's function in the "circulation and reproduction of hegemonic structures"; and (3) to archives that reaffirm the status of certain cultural artifacts as "high" culture. Failure, as Halberstam claims, "may in fact offer more creative, more cooperative, more surprising ways of being in the world" (Halberstam, *Queet Art of Failure*, 1).
21. My use of the terms *mimesis* and *diegesis* evokes Plato's understanding of the physical world as a model for beauty, truth, and the good, which he deemed most important to govern artistic production. The term *mimesis* further echoes literary critic Erich Auerbach's *Mimesis: Dargestellte Wirklichkeit in der abendländischen Literatur* (Mimesis: Reality Represented in Western Literature, 1946) in which the writer outlines a comprehensive theory of representation that spans from Homer's *Odyssey* to William Shakespeare, Molière, and Miguel de Cervantes Saavedra to twentieth-century writers like Virginia Woolf and Marcel Proust. David Green and Joanna Lowry, "From Presence to the Performative: Rethinking Photographic Indexicality," in *Where Is the Photograph?*, ed. David Green (Maidstone: Photoworks, 2003), 60. This particular duality of presentation and representation emphasizes Green and Lowry's claim that "[photographs] point to the real while reminding us that photography can never represent it." Photographs have a person or object or scenery as a real-world referent but fail to ever encompass fully the totality of that subject or object in question.

22. Mary Ann Doane, "Indexicality: Trace and Sign; Introduction," *differences: A Journal of Feminist Cultural Studies* 18, no. 1 (2007): 1. Doane's theorization leans on Barthes' observation that photographs depict an "absolutely, irrefutably present," and thus attributes an unequivocal and universal power to them that affirms the existence of the object or subject inside their frame. Roland Barthes, *Camera Lucida: Reflections on Photography*, trans. Richard Howard (New York: Hill and Wang, 1981), 77.
23. Elizabeth A. Povinelli, *The Empire of Love: Toward a Theory of Intimacy, Genealogy, and Carnality* (Durham: Duke University Press, 2006), 197.
24. Marco Abel, "Imaging Germany: The (Political) Cinema of Christian Petzold," in *The Collapse of the Conventional: German Film and Its Politics at the Turn of the Twenty-First Century*, ed. Jaimey Fisher and Brad Prager (Detroit: Wayne State University Press, 2010), 270; Anke Biendarra, "Ghostly Businesses: Place, Space, and Gender in Christian Petzold's *Yella*," *seminar: A Journal of Germanic Studies* 47, no. 4 (2011): 467–68; David Clarke, "'Capitalism Has No More Natural Enemies': The Berlin School," in *A Companion to German Cinema*, ed. Terri Ginsberg and Andrea Mensch (New York: Wiley Blackwell, 2012), 145–46; Jaimey Fisher, *Christian Petzold* (Chicago: University of Illinois Press, 2013), 5–6; Petra Löffler, "Ghost Sounds und die kinematographische Imagination," in *Kino in Bewegung: Perspektiven des deutschen Gegenwartsfilms*, ed. Thomas Schick and Tobias Ebbrecht (Wiesbaden: VS Verlag für Sozialwissenschaften, 2011), 72–73; Beate Ochsner, "Christian Petzold oder: die gespenstische Zeit des Films," in *Bilder in Echtzeit: Medialität und Ästhetik des digitalen Bewegtbildes*, ed. Isabell Otto and Tobias Haupts (Marburg: Schüren, 2012), 64–66; Johanna Schwenk, *Leerstellen—Resonanzräume: Zur Ästhetik der Auslassung im Werk des Filmregisseurs Christian Petzold* (Baden-Baden: Nomos, 2012), 73–74; Andrew J. Webber, "Topographical Turns: Recasting Berlin in Christian Petzold's *Gespenster*," in *Debating German Cultural Identity Since 1989*, ed. Anne Fuchs, Kathleen James-Chakraborty, and Linda Shortt (Rochester, NY: Camden House, 2011), 67–69. North American Germanists such as Marco Abel, Anke Biendarra, David Clarke, and Jaimey Fisher and also academics in Germany such as Petra Löffler, Beate Ochsner, and Johanna Schwenk identify a lack of presence in all the film's characters. Andrew J. Webber notes that in negotiating personal and collective identity, subjective as well as national memory, the film's protagonists appear ghostly as they interact with others and the urban cityscape in the postunification capital Berlin.
25. Valerie Kaussen, "Ghosts," in *Berlin School Glossary: An ABC of the New Wave in German Cinema*, ed. Roger F. Cook et al. (Bristol: Intellect, 2013), 156.
26. Jasmin Krakenberg, "Moving Portraits: Christian Petzold and The Art of Portraiture," *senses of cinema* 84 (Sep. 2017). Many contemporary German films categorized under the moniker Berlin School and are characterized by a distinct cinematography that often deploys long shots and long takes in order to give the audience the impression that filmic time is moving at a much slower pace compared to the typical, fast pace of mainstream (Hollywood) cinema; Christian Petzold's *Ghosts* is no exception. Indeed, Krakenberg suggests that the movement of the camera often stops completely and lingers on the film's mis-en-scène, revealing a distinct motionlessness and an aesthetics, which gestures toward that of other arts such as photography.
27. Kurt Buhanan, "What's Wrong with This Picture? Image-Ethics in Christian Petzold's Films," *The German Quarterly* 89, no. 4 (2016): 486.
28. Joy Castro, "'A Place without Parents': Queer and Maternal Desire in the Films of Christian Petzold," *senses of cinema* 84 (Sep. 2017).
29. Roger F. Cook et al., "Introduction: The Berlin School—Under Observation," in *Berlin School Glossary: An ABC of the New Wave in German Cinema*, ed. Roger F. Cook et al. (Bristol: Intellect, 2013), 13.

Bibliography

Abel, Marco. *The Counter-Cinema of the Berlin School*. Rochester: Camden House, 2013.

———. "Imaging Germany: The (Political) Cinema of Christian Petzold." In *The Collapse of the Conventional: German Film and Its Politics at the Turn of the Twenty-First Century*, edited by Jaimey Fisher and Brad Prager, 258–84. Detroit: Wayne State University Press, 2010.

———. "Intensifying Life: The Cinema of the 'Berlin School.'" *Cineaste* 33, no. 4 (2008). Retrieved 29 December 2018 from https://www.cineaste.com/fall2008/intensifying-life-the-cinema-of-the-berlin-school/.

Ahmed, Sara. *The Cultural Politics of Emotion*. New York: Routledge, 2004.

———. *The Promise of Happiness*. Durham: Duke University Press, 2010.

Barthes, Roland. *Camera Lucida: Reflections on Photography*, translated by Richard Howard. New York: Hill and Wang, 1981.

Berlant, Lauren. *Cruel Optimism*. Durham: Duke University Press, 2011.

Biendarra, Anke. "Ghostly Businesses: Place, Space, and Gender in Christian Petzold's *Yella*." *Seminar: A Journal of Germanic Studies* 47, no. 4 (2011): 465–78.

Bourdieu, Pierre. *Photography: A Middle-Brow Art*. Translated by Shaun Whiteside. Stanford: Stanford University Press, 1990.

Buhanan, Kurt. "What's Wrong with This Picture? Image-Ethics in Christian Petzold's Films." *The German Quarterly* 89, no. 4 (2016): 480–95.

Castro, Joy. "'A Place without Parents': Queer and Maternal Desire in the Films of Christian Petzold." *senses of cinema* 84 (Sep. 2017). Retrieved 29 December 2018 from http://sensesofcinema.com/2017/christian-petzold-a-dossier/queer-and-maternal-desire-christian-petzold/.

Clarke, David. "'Capitalism Has No More Natural Enemies': The Berlin School." In *A Companion to German Cinema*, edited by Terri Ginsberg and Andrea Mensch, 134–55. New York: Wiley Blackwell, 2012.

Cook, Roger F., Lutz Koepnick, Kristin Kopp, and Brad Prager. "Introduction: The Berlin School—Under Observation." In *Berlin School Glossary: An ABC of the New Wave in German Cinema*, edited by Roger F. Cook, Lutz Koepnick, Kristin Kopp, and Brad Prager, 1–25. Bristol: Intellect, 2013.

Doane, Mary Ann. "Indexicality: Trace and Sign; Introduction." *differences: A Journal of Feminist Cultural Studies* 18, no. 1 (2007): 1–6.

Duggan, Lisa. "The New Homonormativity: The Sexual Politics of Neoliberalism." In *Materializing Democracy: Toward a Revitalized Cultural Politics*, edited by Russ Castronuevo and Dana Nelson, 175–93. Durham: Duke University Press, 2002.

Fisher, Jaimey. *Christian Petzold*. Chicago: University of Illinois Press, 2013.

Green, David, and Joanna Lowry. "From Presence to the Performative: Rethinking Photographic Indexicality." In *Where Is the Photograph?*, edited by David Green, 47–60. Maidstone: Photoworks, 2003.

Halberstam, Jack (formerly Judith). *The Queer Art of Failure*. Durham: Duke University Press, 2011.

Hirsch, Marianne. *Family Frames: Photography, Narrative, and Postmemory*. Cambridge, MA: Harvard University Press, 1997.

———. "Introduction: Familial Looking." In *The Familial Gaze*, edited by Marianne Hirsch, xiv–xxv. Hanover: University Press of New England, 1999.

Kausesen, Valerie. "Ghosts." In *Berlin School Glossary: An ABC of the New Wave in German Cinema*, edited by Roger F. Cook, Lutz Koepnick, Kristin Kopp, and Brad Prager, 147–56. Bristol: Intellect, 2013.

Krakenberg, Jasmin. "Moving Portraits: Christian Petzold and The Art of Portraiture." *senses of cinema* 84 (Sep. 2017). Retrieved 29 December 2018 from http://sensesofcinema.com/2017/christian-petzold-a-dossierchristian-petzold-and-the-art-of-portraiture/.

Löffler, Petra. "Ghost Sounds und die kinematographische Imagination." In *Kino in Bewegung: Perspektiven des deutschen Gegenwartsfilms*, edited by Thomas Schick and Tobias Ebbrecht, 63–78. Wiesbaden: VS Verlag für Sozialwissenschaften, 2011.

Ngai, Sianne. *Ugly Feelings*. Cambridge, MA: Harvard University Press, 2007.

Ochsner, Beate. "Christian Petzold oder: die gespenstische Zeit des Films." In *Bilder in Echtzeit: Medialität und* Ästhetik *des digitalen Bewegtbildes*, edited by Isabell Otto and Tobias Haupts, 63–79. Marburg: Schüren, 2012.

Povinelli, Elizabeth A. *The Empire of Love: Toward a Theory of Intimacy, Genealogy, and Carnality*. Durham: Duke University Press, 2006.

Schwenk, Johanna. *Leerstellen—Resonanzräume: Zur* Ästhetik *der Auslassung im Werk des Filmregisseurs Christian Petzold*. Baden-Baden: Nomos, 2012.

Sedgwick, Eve Kosofsky. *Touching Feeling: Affect, Pedagogy, Performativity*. Durham: Duke University Press, 2003.

Webber, Andrew J. "Topographical Turns: Recasting Berlin in Christian Petzold's *Gespenster*." In *Debating German Cultural Identity Since 1989*, edited by Anne Fuchs, Kathleen James-Chakraborty, and Linda Shortt, 67–81. Rochester, NY: Camden House, 2011.

Filmography

Ghosts (*Gespenster*). Directed by Christian Petzold. Berlin: Schramm Film Körner & Weber, 2005.

The State I Am In (*Die innere Sicherheit*). Directed by Christian Petzold. Berlin: Schramm Film Körner & Weber, 2000.

Yella. Directed by Christian Petzold. Berlin: Schramm Film Körner & Weber, 2007.

Chapter 10

VIOLENCE, DEATH, AND PHOTOGRAPHS

Capturing the (Un)Dead in *Rammbock* (2010)

Melissa Etzler

Since the release in 2010 of Marvin Kren's zombie flick *Rammbock* (*Berlin Undead*), critics have consistently stressed the film's uniqueness, highlighting particularly its emotional core and the romantic dimension of this love story.[1] These reviews certainly do seem to describe aspects of the film's basic plot: the narrative focuses on Michael, or Michi, who is on a quest to win back the heart of his ex-girlfriend, Gabi. During a sudden outbreak of a virus that turns regular humans into aggressive monsters akin to zombies, Michi fights to survive long enough so that he can find Gabi, rescue her, and convince her that he deserves a second chance. In the penultimate sequence, the couple do reunite, though Gabi has been fully transformed into one of the violent horde. In what seems like a sacrificial act of love, Michi (who had been fighting off the infection after an injury) embraces Gabi tightly and allows his body to succumb to the virus, thereby reconnecting the zombie couple forever.

Although many reviews understand the film as a narrative of undying (or undead) love, lurking beneath the veneer of this zombie romance is a dark, pessimistic critique of control and power dynamics, exhibited most clearly by how characters use photographs and cameras in the film. To become a zombie is to waver between life and death and to undergo a forced forfeiture of free will and control. Because one's will is at stake, zombies in films are always, according to Chera Kee, an "allegory for the larger societal self" and reflect moments in which "people were caught up in events essentially in someone else's control."[2] Drawing upon this tension, this chapter outlines how characters use photographs in *Rammbock* to dominate others, control their identities, and rewrite their pasts. Generally speaking, these processes can be understood within larger generic and societal trends.

Before transitioning into close readings of the primary scenes in which photography plays a role, a more detailed summary of the narrative is necessary. *Rammbock* follows Michi, who has traveled from Austria to Berlin to win back his ex-girlfriend Gabi after she ended their seven-year relationship. Showing up in person at her apartment to return her keys, Michi almost immediately finds himself trapped within her space. Gabi is missing and everyone in and around the building has been infected with a mysterious disease. While the actual term "zombie" is not used within the film's fictional reality, the characteristics of the infected and the obvious allusions to the zombie-genre validate the comparison. Unable to relinquish his pursuit of Gabi after he realizes that she is not only romantically involved with her neighbor Kai but also infected with the zombie virus, Michi staves off the rampantly spreading infection within his body long enough to find Gabi and trap her in an embrace as he transitions into a zombie, locked in an altered state of a simultaneous past and present.

Two types of photographic images appear in the film: analog photographs and digital images, both of which reveal a problematic power dynamic and generational divide. The analog photographs are associated with Michi's thirtysomething generation who may also keep physical photo albums and occasionally long to return to an image from the past. Digital photography, by contrast, is associated with the teenage protagonist, Harper, who is also trapped in Gabi's apartment but saves himself by employing the camera as a weapon to ward off those who are infected. Photography reveals both the power dynamic in Michi and Gabi's relationship as well as Michi's attempts to control Gabi via her image. Gabi is introduced to the viewer through nondiegetic photographs rather than traditional flashbacks, and thus shown as an ideal image preserved in an undead state in Michi's memory as well as on her digital camera. Michi's control of Gabi, which is portrayed in his possession of her image and eventually his occupation of her apartment, sets the stage for a broader societal commentary on control and images as well as how they are related to violence and the past.

Analog Photography and the Invention of the Perfect Past

Michi reveals himself as a zombie-maker before the introduction of the literal zombies within the narrative in many ways. Speaking about zombies as a cultural construct, Suzanne Goodney Lea suggests that a zombie-maker is "incapable of negotiating the complexity of human interaction" and "to be a zombie-maker is to fully consume another," a position driven by "the wish that we might somehow have complete power over someone that still functions as a person."[3] By manipulating Gabi's photographic image and personal objects, Michi relegates her to the realm of the undead before the virus outbreak. In controlling Gabi by first commandeering her image and then her personal space, Michi zombifies Gabi into a position of enslavement, transforming her into someone who can be owned, controlled, or consumed (i.e., a zombie). His status as a zombie-maker is demonstrated by his approach to photographs, which open the film and which Michi manipulates in an attempt to invent the perfect past.

Beginning with the establishing shot, *Rammbock* reveals Michi's disconnection from reality. The viewer is presented with a medium close-up of Michi, a shot typically used to direct the viewer to the subject. However, this shot is disorienting because Michi switches his gaze upward at the sky at an off-screen object to his right, to the center, and then to the left. The viewer lacks auditory clues or visual contextualization that would give meaning and purpose to Michi's gaze. Already in the realm of the imaginary, suggested by his directed gaze toward the clouds, Michi's disconnectedness is underscored by the juxtaposition of a series of photographic images of him with Gabi. The shot of his face cuts to a photograph of Michi and Gabi in which she is smiling and her eyes are focused downward while Michi, standing behind her, kisses her cheek (see figure 10.1) The photograph fills most of the corner of the screen, but leaves enough empty space surrounding it to reveal a page that has been painted over with dark green paint. The green background seems to contain text, though it cannot be read because it has been blacked out (perhaps with a marker) before being painted over, leaving only the photograph. Michi has erased everything but what he wants to see—happy shots of him with Gabi. This once-happy relationship is simultaneously imbued with the veracity promised by the material document coupled with the mendacity of Michi's subjective projection and control over the image.

The juxtaposition of these photographs with Michi's gaze suggests a dissonance between the representation of a happy relationship in the photographs and Michi's current state of despair and longing for the past, which is emphasized by the editing and color palette. The film cuts after a moment to Michi still staring upward to his left. This is again intercut with another photograph, this time nearly filling the lower left portion of the screen with Michi embracing Gabi as he sits behind her

Figure 10.1. *Rammbock* (*Berlin Undead*). Directed by Marvin Kren. Berlin: Moneypenny Film, 2010. Screen capture by Melissa Etzler.

on a fallen tree in the woods. He has ventured into a nostalgic dream world related to the images of him and Gabi in the woods, a landscape that stands in stark contrast to the barren cityscape of Berlin. Michi's present consists of the dismal grey of his sweater and the melancholic blue of his jacket; both colors bleed into the beige and off-white palette of Berlin. Even though the photographs depict normative "happy" scenes, their colors create a warm, but ominous, connection to the world of the undead that he is nearing and the past that he cannot recover. The censorship of the context around the photographs, the juxtaposition, and the color palette place the photographs firmly in Michi's perspective; they are both framed and curated by him. The photographs reveal Michi's nostalgic attempts to gain confidence and overcome his anxiety regarding what may be lost. Michi conjures up the images as an attempt to actualize the past within the present, a futile effort. While this film will soon turn into a tale of the undead, the use of photographs in this sequence establishes the dichotomy between the mortality of those represented, the relationship they had, and Michi's attempt to resurrect them into the present.

As an affirmation that this relationship is irreconcilable, the disconnect between Gabi and Michi represented in the photographs is confirmed verbally. As the film cuts to Michi from the photographs, he looks forward but away from the camera and states: "I wanted to personally bring back your keys. Aren't you glad? . . . You can't just move out after seven years like it's nothing! Gabi, please. Gabi, I love you."[4] Each sentence is punctuated by the insertion of warm-colored photographs of them together. As Michi's voice rises in panic with the final three statements, the shot-reverse shot reveals that Michi is not speaking with Gabi but is practicing his speech with a male friend playing the role of Gabi. The sequence offers an example of the type of dialogue that J. L. Austin would refer to as "infelicitous," or a speech act that is achieved and yet remains hollow since it has landed in a void of misdirected dialogue.[5] Another term, which is more applicable in this context, that Austin employs for such a speech act is an "abuse."[6] The performance of a conversation, which Michi should share only with Gabi, removes her personhood: she, like the undead, is simultaneously present and absent. Her voice is silenced by Michi's friend roleplaying their anticipated conversation. Thus, Michi silences Gabi both rhetorically and through his control of her image.

Although Michi, the mild-mannered Austrian protagonist, might seem like a thoroughly unassuming individual or jilted lover, the misdirected speech that silences Gabi as well as the curated and censored photographs demonstrate an abusive control over Gabi. Here, Gabi's image and voice are controlled for the public—his male friend and the viewers. Michi's presentation of the photographs to the viewer is intended to gain the viewer's sympathy in his quest to reinstate his former, happy relationship. Michi demonstrates Gabi's wrongfulness in ending their relationship, yet she has no chance to share her side. Michi turns Gabi into a metaphorical zombie since he has removed her agency in his denial of her voice and perspective.

Taming the Digital Image and Overwriting Authenticity

The switch from analog photographs to digital photography extends the film's zombie plot, thereby further emphasizing the focus on the undead and control over the past. Michi's control of Gabi's image continues when he invades the private space of her apartment. His attempt to possess Gabi moves from the imagery space of Michi's photographic memories to his occupation of her apartment, her bedroom, and one key object within it: her digital camera. According to Kevin Boon, zombies have all "experienced a loss of something essential that previous to zombification defined them as human, usually this entails a loss of volition."[7] When Michi claims Gabi's space, he is once more proving himself a zombie-maker by denying Gabi's autonomy in his usurpation of the objects that intimately define her.

Gabi's identity is continually eroded by Michi's persistent attempts to reclaim his lost relationship, as illustrated by how he takes possession of her physical belongings. After hunkering down in the apartment, Michi encroaches on Gabi's most personal space, her bedroom. In another effort to resurrect Gabi despite her absence, Michi projects his affection onto metonymic replacements for Gabi: he cuddles Gabi's pet rabbit and then takes the liberty of scrolling through the images on her digital camera. Michi turns the camera awkwardly, suggesting to the viewer his lack of familiarity with the device. The digital photographs that Michi finds feature Gabi sewing a bear costume, followed by an image of animal costumes in progress, and Gabi posing in the brown bear costume. While the color of the bear costume harkens back to the earth-tone photographs of Gabi and Michi, they simultaneously underscore his distance since these images of Gabi have been taken by someone else. The warm brown tones once shared by Gabi and Michi are as representative of her new relationship with (presumed photographer and her new boyfriend) Kai as they are of her progression from analog to digital photography.

Gabi's separation from Michi, indicated by both her physical absence and also in her progression to digital photography from Michi's analog images, seems only to heighten his desire for her. Michi's desire and its relationship to the photographs of Gabi can be understood through Susan Sontag, who argues, "the sense of the unattainable that can be evoked by photographs feeds directly into the erotic feelings of those for whom desirability is enhanced by distance."[8] Michi's desire for Gabi indeed wavers in the realm of an uncanny, in-between state. He is comforted by his recognition of the woman in the photos and uses these images to feel a closeness to her. However, while the figure of Gabi on the camera is familiar, Michi must register the unfamiliar perspective since someone else has taken these images. Any sympathy the viewer might feel for the vulnerable, jilted Michi is undermined by his invasion of her privacy and private space.

Informed by Gabi's digital photograph, Michi seeks out her bear costume and puts it on to envelop himself in a softer version of her. The photograph of the costumed woman is a bridge, imbuing the physical costume with her unseen essence. Indeed, it is only because he finds the image of Gabi in the costume that the costume has any meaning for him. By covering his own body with the same costume that covered her body, he thinks he can reclaim her love for him in this pale replacement for the human connection he desires. Yet, this warm and furry costume has the same effect as the photograph in that it represents the dichotomy between the living and the dead, the familiar and the unfamiliar. The objectification of Gabi through the bear costume and photographs foreshadows the undead being she becomes. Thus, Michi's acceptance here of lifeless metonyms is extended when he later eagerly embraces her as a zombie, indicating that he desires her less as an individual than as an image, a replica of the original—something he can tame and control.

Michi's consumption and inhabitation of Gabi through images denies her agency, or any auratic presence in a Benjaminian sense. Although most frequently deployed to discuss replications of artworks and their subsequent devaluation, Walter Benjamin's claim that authenticity is tied to an object's physicality and historical testimony is applicable to Gabi here.[9] Up until this point, Gabi is presented solely through Michi's focus on metonymic replacements; his projected idea of Gabi is unsolicited, and he denies Gabi her authenticity. Another idea that helps contextualize Gabi's presence in the film in terms of her relationship to the photographs is Sontag's understanding of the "talismanic uses of photographs [that attempt] to contact or lay claim to another reality."[10] Presumably, Michi believes that if he continually gazes at Gabi's image and surrounds himself with her material objects, he will be able to magically reinvigorate their relationship. Thus, Gabi becomes the blank slate onto which Michi can enliven his fantasy of reconnection, even if it is only a replication of his imagined past. As long as Gabi only exists for Michi as photographs in his memory and on her camera, he can resurrect and insert himself into his historical version of Gabi.

The Battering Ram and the Photographic Hunt

Thus far, all the photographs and objects related to Gabi have illustrated Michi's desire to return to an ideal relationship that likely never existed, and the crux of the film, the scene in which the "battering ram" of the title is constructed, shows that Michi will stop at nothing to rekindle a relationship that is a fantasy. Michi and Harper plan to break through Gabi's bedroom wall to create an exit leading into her neighbor's apartment. Unbeknownst to Michi, Gabi's neighbor Frau Bramkamp provides him with direct access to Gabi, who has sought shelter in the attic with Bramkamp's son, her new love interest. To get into Bramkamp's room, Michi and Harper tie together objects from Gabi's room to cre-

Figure 10.2. *Rammbock (Berlin Undead)*. Directed by Marvin Kren. Berlin: Moneypenny Film, 2010. Screen capture by Melissa Etzler.

ate a battering ram. The device consists of planks of wood from her bed that are strapped together using a collection of Gabi's brassieres and undergarments. The violence done to Gabi's possessions reiterates Michi's demonstrative claim of Gabi by way of her belongings.

Michi not only intrudes upon Gabi by destroying her living space, he also inserts himself into her current life through her digital camera. To add insult to injury for Gabi, just as Michi prepares the phallic battering ram to bash through her bedroom wall and retrieve her, Harper, who is in possession of Gabi's digital camera, smiles mischievously and insists Michi hold still for a photo. Michi grabs a rope to balance the ram and poses for a shot that is eerily reminiscent of those taken of anglers next to suspended swordfish, eagerly displaying their prowess and ability to conquer nature's dangerous creatures. Even though Michi looks sheepish posing next to the ram, the image captured is reminiscent of both hunting and colonial expansion.

The photograph here commemorates a threshold moment, a picture of the battering ram (the title of the movie) and the last moment before Gabi's private space is thoroughly destroyed. Speaking to a similar memorialization of violence, Sontag notes that the "gun safari" has been exchanged for the camera in today's "ecology safari."[11] Given the irrevocable damage done to wildlife as part of the African safari,

Sontag argues that nature can be protected by replacing the shotgun with a camera to "shoot" wildlife in an ecological, sustainable manner. This photograph of Michi with the battering ram (figure 10.2) contains elements of both the gun safari and the ecological safari. In this analogy, although they have replaced the gun with a camera, the shot is still linked with the violence and "shooting" associated with the gun safari. Here, the photograph simultaneously commemorates the construction of the battering ram out of Gabi's most personal items while celebrating Michi's obstinate resolve just before he rams through the wall, thus thoroughly and violently destroying Gabi's space in yet another example of his determination to possess her. Unlike Sontag's hope that "people might learn to act out their aggressions with cameras,"[12] (consequently replacing actual violence with images of violence), Michi only becomes more aggressive. In fact, the camera in this scene is used to memorialize the impending act of aggression, not to replace it. Michi continues with his stubborn insistence to possess and destroy her, proving that he himself might be considered the "battering ram" of the film's title.

As this image suggests, Michi's conquest of Gabi's personal space can be understood in terms of colonialist endeavors. On a mission from Austria to Gabi's apartment in Berlin, Michi—the hero of the story—invades Gabi's personal space, claims her possessions as his own without her permission, and gains unauthorized access to unknown territory, the virtual realm of her digital camera and the images that it contains. It is not enough just to view the images, as he does previously. In this sequence, with Harper's help, Michi now inhabits her collection of private images. This insertion of the battering ram photograph into the camera's memory card further solidifies Michi as a penetrating colonizer within the film, as the image here suggests. With the acquisition of this final frontier, Michi is able to ram through the wall in his pursuit of Gabi while Harper has taken control of the camera.

After occupying her bedroom, being inserted into the memories on her digital camera, and then destroying the sheltering walls of her apartment, Michi finally locates and reattaches himself to Gabi for all time. As the film nears its end, Gabi, like the other zombies, is drawn out of the apartment building. She enters the shared courtyard where she finds Michi, who himself is in the early stages of infection. Once he spots her, he approaches and forcefully wraps her with his arms. As a gesture, this hug represents the culmination of Michi's previous controlling actions. Because he is holding her so tightly, the undead Gabi is

Figure 10.3. *Rammbock* (*Berlin Undead*). Directed by Marvin Kren. Berlin: Moneypenny Film, 2010. Screen capture by Melissa Etzler.

prevented from running away. When her punches on his back become less forceful, the camera rotates around the couple to reveal Michi's eyes also turning white, marking his own transition. He is becoming a zombie himself, meaning the pair can be together forever—Michi's dream and Gabi's nightmare. Similar to how Michi used his photographs of Gabi, here he also erases the woman's agency and individuality. She cannot exist unless Michi can play a role in her existence, alive or undead. Similar to the photographs that opened the film, director Marvin Kren's camera now entraps Gabi in an endless, liminal state, in-between life and death with Michi.

Although Michi's embrace represents his decision to yield to his inevitable zombification, other characters desperately run toward life by embracing violence. After Michi and Harper break through Gabi's wall and enter the adjoining apartment, Harper serendipitously discovers the aggressive power of photographic technology. To the duo's surprise, they are confronted by the neighbor Frau Bramkamp, who has become a zombie. Although Michi is able to escape, Harper is trapped on top of Bramkamp's kitchen cupboard. Harper uses Gabi's digital camera to take a picture to see if the coast is clear. As the flash fires, Bramkamp lunges at Harper in a sequence that reveals that the camera can transcend a purely evidentiary function. Physically harmed by the flash, she stumbles back, grabbing at her throat. While she is reeling, a

POV shot of the display on Gabi's digital camera (figure 10.3) shows a captured image of Bramkamp screaming with her head thrown back in pain, her hair disheveled and her virus-infected complexion washed out due to the flash, which makes her appear even more ghostly and translucent. Here, Harper realizes the power of the camera's flash to stun and debilitate the aggressive zombies long enough for him to escape. Thus, the camera takes on a new significance; it has become a necessary weapon and means of survival.

Rhetorically, symbolically, and historically, the violence inherent in taking photographs with cameras can be understood in terms of aggression and warfare, which motion pictures have underscored. As Friedrich Kittler points out: "The history of the movie camera coincides with the history of automatic weapons. The transport of pictures only repeats the transport of bullets. In order to focus on and fix objects moving through space, such as people, there are two procedures: to shoot and to film. . . . With the chronophotographic gun, mechanized death was perfected."[13] As a cultural construct, zombies represent the unidentified mass, the symbolic Other, the undead past that can be eliminated via machine guns and other automatic weapons. After the characters learn that sudden flashes from cameras seem to hurt the zombies, a Kittlerian sense of photographic violence comes to the fore. Once the harmful nature of the photographic flash becomes clear, the uninfected humans arm themselves with cameras and flashes to "focus on and fix" the infected humans around them.

Once reunited, Michi and Harper capitalize on this realization as they employ the destructive potential of the camera's flash to escape Berlin. They construct a makeshift vehicle/weapon out of a shopping cart, Gabi's digital camera, and a collection of camera flash units they have scavenged; this mobile weapon is intended to fire enough flashes to clear the streets of zombies so that their group can make their way to the Spree River and escape. Michi explains that during their escape, each person will be "armed" (*bewaffnet*) with a camera and will "shoot" (*schießen*) both to the front and the back. As they flee, Anita, a noninfected survivor the pair meets on the way, says she hopes that it "hurts really badly," and Harper responds with "yeah, really badly." The uninfected humans' only hope is the camera and its flash, with the flash functioning as a metonym for the larger process of photographically recording an image, a disruptive act that stuns, repels, and causes pain to the zombies. The small army of the living uses the camera and flashes as a type of automatic weapon to cut a path through—and cut down—the undead horde, with camera flashes replacing bullets.

Conclusion: Capturing the (Un)Dead

Zombie films, and horror films in general, are often read allegorically as commentaries on modern warfare and reflections of their national context. In the United States, George Romero's *Night of the Living Dead* (1967) is known for its political commentary on the Vietnam War, while his newer film *Diary of the Dead* (2007) can be seen as a response to the US occupation of Iraq and Afghanistan.[14] In a German context, horror films from *The Cabinet of Dr. Caligari* (1920) to *The Nightmare* (2015) respond to cultural anxieties that came about in response to national traumas. Jörg Buttgereit's oeuvre and especially *Nekromantik* 2 (1990) are examples of the German approach to unification and *Vergangenheitsbewältigung* (coming to terms with the past).[15] In *Nekromantik* 2, Monika M. digs up the past (in the form of her dead ex-boyfriend) and brings his exhumed corpse into her bedroom. Then, in an attempt to get over her interest in the past and her ex, she begins a relationship with a new, living boyfriend. However, she fails miserably. Her beheading of the living boyfriend during sex demonstrates her futile attempt to overcome the past—an idea that is then compounded when she replaces his head with the head of her dead ex-boyfriend, and then gets pregnant from this last sexual encounter. Her obsession with the past then becomes a horrifying portrayal of the reunification and the future of Germany in the form of her unborn child, who will be born of murder and trauma: an idea so horrible that *Nekromantik* 2 was the first film to be confiscated and prohibited to be owned or viewed in Germany since World War II.[16] Like Monika, Michi is also unwilling to relinquish the past.

Indeed, Michi's obsession with the glossy, two-dimensional Gabi is not far from necrophilia; he initially desires a former version of Gabi from the dead relationship represented in his memory by the old photographs. His interest here brings to mind what Roland Barthes observed in a 1977 interview: "What I really find fascinating about photographs . . . is something that probably has to do with death. Perhaps it's an interest that is tinged with necrophilia, to be honest, a fascination with what has died but is represented as wanting to be alive."[17] Michi desires a doubly objectified Gabi. She is an image in a digital photograph and an inauthentic individual hidden by the bear costume. Compared to Buttgereit's *Nekromantik* films, *Rammbock* is relatively tame, but Michi's own attachment to the past (i.e., his ex-girlfriend), his anxiety about the end of their relationship, and his failure to come to terms with the past can also be understood in a similar German national context. However, it is the use of cameras in *Rammbock* that more solidly sets the stage:

cameras are simultaneously a medium that commemorates the past as well as one that secures their power over it through the violent act of taking pictures, both in digital and analog formats.

The analog/digital divide in *Rammbock* also speaks to a national context. As Andrés Mario Zervigón writes, "The history of photography in Germany is the history of the country's troubled encounter with modernity, realized in visual form."[18] This troubled encounter with photographs in *Rammbock* corresponds to what he describes as Germany's current status as a "photo-mad country of promiscuous makers and users," which has "reconfigured the relationship between photography and Germany. Whereas in the nineteenth-century, the medium played an important role in defining the identity of Germany and the German, now it critically re-digests those terms on a mass scale for a global audience."[19] Although Zervigon acknowledges the international character of image making and admits that "no one quality can be isolated as distinctly German,"[20] the global scale he refers to might be seen in the context of the anxiety experienced around photographs, representation, and social media.

Michi's actions and Harper's use of the technology to control the zombies with the camera represent the social anxiety that came with social media: that one's identity can be created and undermined by photographs. Much like Michi's representation of his relationship with Gabi, social media offers individuals the opportunity to curate their identity and, as Annika Blau suggests, "present a cultivated and preferred simulation."[21] These tendencies of representation in *Rammbock* through Michi's conquest of Gabi are similar to the types of conquest Blau recognizes on social media. Blau argues that it was initially easy to differentiate between our online and real personas, but she claims we have now reached a "social media saturation point" whereby we cannot argue the online simulacrums are less real than ourselves. Michi adopts this point-of-view since the curated images of Gabi represent an absolute reality that needs reinstating. Gabi, however, has no say in the matter. Blau acknowledges that the digital, virtual relationships on social media help "define and affect our real relationships";[22] and Michi will not cease to express his agency by defining his relationship to Gabi through photographs as a way to reinstate his fantasy in their relationship.

Michi's attempt to reinstate his idealization of the perfect past depicted in his photographs of Gabi results in a series of violent actions related to photography that anchor the film in its national context. His curation of his memories of Gabi by way of her photographs, his battering ram, and his desperate embrace reflect his desire to control the past as well as the future and his necessary failure. When Michi embraces Gabi for the last time, he must finally understand the severity of the images he had used and their inevitable relationship to the death of the person depicted and their idealized relationship. The camera's persistent looping around the couple in a dizzying effect causes a brief feeling of vertigo in the viewer. While Gabi is trapped within the camera's circle, the viewer swoops around the couple with it. This metacritique is embedded in the generic conventions of postmodern horror films to which *Rammbock* belongs. We see how the film "constitutes a violent disruption of the everyday world," "transgresses and violates boundaries," questions "the validity of rationality," "repudiates narrative closure," and "produces a bounded experience of fear."[23] As Harper and Anita presumably escape along the Spree river, in a long shot of the city space a flash fires at no character in particular, revealing that the viewer is also entangled in a constellation of control and violence as perpetrator and victim that the photograph threatens to reveal. With this in mind, the final shot of the film offers a warning but also implicates the viewer in their complicit acceptance of images, control, and their relationship to the past and present.

Melissa Etzler is Lecturer of German and First Year Seminar at Butler University in Indianapolis. She has published book chapters related to her research on author W. G. Sebald and has recently shifted her focus to ecocritical readings of Gothic German texts and films. Her article "Pernicious Plants: Imitation and Uncanny Ecocritical Thought in Gustav Meyrink's *Die Pflanzen des Dr. Cinderella*" appeared in *German Quarterly* (2017). She is coeditor of *Outreach Strategies and Innovative Teaching Approaches for German Programs* (2021) and *Rebellion and Revolution: Defiance in German Language, History and Art* (2010).

Notes

1. See Mike McGranaghan, "*Rammbock* (Berlin Undead)," *The Aisle Seat*, 2011; and Mike Scott, "Suspenseful *Rammbock: Berlin Undead* Kicks Off Horror Film Series on Wednesday," *Nola.com / The Times-Picayune*, 28 May 2013.
2. Chera Kee, "'They are not men . . . they are dead bodies!': From Cannibal to Zombie and Back Again," in *Better Off Dead: The Evolution of the Zombie as Post-Human*, ed. Deborah Christie and Sarah Juliet Lauro (New York: Fordham, 2011), 23.
3. Suzanne Goodney Lea, "Modern Zombie Makers: Enacting the Ancient Impulse to Control and Possess Another," in *Zombies Are Us: Essays on the Humanity of the Walk-

ing Dead, ed. Christopher M. Moreman and Cory James Rushton (Jefferson, NC: McFarland, 2011), 62, 64, 72.

4. "Ich wollte deinen Schlüssel wiederbringen. Ich wollte es halt persönlich machen. Freust du nicht? Du kannst ja nicht nach sieben Jahren wegziehen und es ist aus. Gabi, da geht . . . , Gabi, bitte. Gabi, ich liebe dich."
5. J. L. Austin, *How to Do Things with Words: The William James Lectures Delivered at Harvard University in 1955* (Oxford: Clarendon Press, 1962), 16–17.
6. Ibid., 18.
7. Kevin Boon, "And the Dead Shall Rise—Part Introduction," in *Better Off Dead: The Evolution of the Zombie as Post-Human*, ed. Deborah Christie and Sarah Juliet Lauro (New York: Fordham, 2011), 7.
8. Susan Sontag, "On Photography," in *Essays of the 1960s & 70s*, ed. David Rieff (New York: Library Classics of the United States, 2013), 539.
9. Walter Benjamin, "Work of Art in the Age of Reproducibility [Third Version]," in *Walter Benjamin: Selected Writings*, vol. 4: *1938–1940*, ed. Howard Eiland and Michael W. Jennings, trans. Edmund Jephcott and others (Cambridge, MA: Belknap Press of Harvard University, 2003), 254.
10. Sontag, "On Photography," 539.
11. Ibid., 538.
12. Ibid.
13. Friedrich A. Kittler, *Gramophone, Film, Typewriter*, trans. Geoffrey Winthrop-Young and Michael Wutz (Stanford: Stanford University Press, 1999), 124.
14. See Robert Alpert, "George Romero's *Night of the Living Dead* and *Diary of the Dead*: Recording History," *CineAction* 95 (2015): 16–25.
15. Linnie Blake, "The Horror of the Nazi Past in the Reunification Present: Jörg Buttgereit's *Nekromantiks*," in *The Wounds of Nations: Horror Cinema, Historical Trauma, and National Identity* (Manchester: Manchester University Press, 2008), 26–43.
16. Ibid., 30.
17. Louis-Jean Calvet, *Roland Barthes, a Biography*, trans. Sarah Wykes (Bloomington: Indiana University Press, 1995), 220.
18. Andrés Mario Zervigón, *Photography and Germany* (London: Reaktion Books, 2017), 8.
19. Ibid., 204.
20. Ibid., 8.
21. Annika Blau, "Baudrillard's Instagram: On Social Media and the Hyper-Real," *Sydney Opera House*, 3 July 2013.
22. Ibid.
23. Isabel Cristina Pinedo, "Postmodern Elements of the Contemporary Horror Film," in *The Horror Film*, ed. Stephen Prince (New Brunswick: Rutgers University Press, 2004), 90–91.

Bibliography

Alpert, Robert. "George Romero's *Night of the Living Dead* and *Diary of the Dead*: Recording History." *CineAction Toronto* 95 (2015): 16–25.

Arendt, Hannah. *Eichmann in Jerusalem: A Report on the Banality of Evil*. New York: Penguin Books, 2006 [1963].

Austin, J. L. *How to Do Things with Words*: *The William James Lectures Delivered at Harvard University in 1955*. Oxford: Clarendon Press, 1962.

Benjamin, Walter. "Work of Art in the Age of Reproducibility [Third Version]." In *Walter Benjamin: Selected Writings*. Volume 4: *1938–1940*, edited by Howard Eiland and Michael W. Jennings, translated by Edmund Jephcott and others, 251–83. Cambridge, MA: Belknap Press of Harvard University, 2003.

Blake, Linnie. "The Horror of the Nazi Past in the Reunification Present: Jörg Buttgereit's *Nekromantiks*." In *The Wounds of Nations: Horror Cinema, Historical Trauma, and National Identity*, 26–43. Manchester: Manchester University Press, 2008.

Blau, Annika. "Baudrillard's Instagram: On Social Media and the Hyper-Real." *Sydney Opera House*, 3 July 2013. Retrieved 30 May 2018 from http://web.archive.org/web/20140408040344/http:/ideas.sydneyoperahouse.com/2013/column-baudrillards-instagram-on-social-media-and-the-hyper-real/.

Boon, Kevin. "And the Dead Shall Rise—Part Introduction." In *Better Off Dead: The Evolution of the Zombie as Post-Human*, edited by Deborah Christie and Sarah Juliet Lauro, 5–8. New York: Fordham, 2011.

Calvet, Louis-Jean. *Roland Barthes, a Biography*. Translated by Sarah Wykes. Bloomington: Indiana University Press, 1995.

Cohen, Jeffrey Jerome. "Monster Culture (Seven Theses)." In *Monster Theory: Reading Culture*, edited by Jeffrey Jerome Cohen, 1–25. Minneapolis: University of Minnesota, 1996.

Goldhagen, Daniel Jonah. *Hitler's Willing Executioners: Ordinary Germans and the Holocaust*. New York: Alfred A. Knopf, 1996.

Kee, Chera. "'They are not men . . . they are dead bodies!': From Cannibal to Zombie and Back Again." In *Better Off Dead: The Evolution of the Zombie as Post-Human*, edited by Deborah Christie and Sarah Juliet Lauro, 9–23. New York: Fordham, 2011.

Kittler, Friedrich A. *Gramophone, Film, Typewriter*. Translated by Geoffrey Winthrop-Young and Michael Wutz. Stanford: Stanford University Press, 1999.

Landfair, Alexander. "Facebook of the Dead." *The Missouri Review*, 8 October 2013. Retrieved 30 May 2018 from https://www.missourireview.com/article/facebook-of-the-dead/.

Lea, Suzanne Goodney. "Modern Zombie Makers: Enacting the Ancient Impulse to Control and Possess Another." In *Zombies Are Us: Essays on the Humanity of the Walking Dead*, edited by Christopher M. Moreman and Cory James Rushton, 62–75. Jefferson, NC: McFarland, 2011.

McGranaghan, Mike. "*Rammbock* (Berlin Undead)." *The Aisle Seat*, 2011. Retrieved 30 May 2018 from http://www.aisleseat.com/rammbock.htm.

Pinedo, Isabel Cristina. "Postmodern Elements of the Contemporary Horror Film." In *The Horror Film*, edited by Stephen Prince, 85–117. New Brunswick: Rutgers University Press, 2004.

Scott, Mike. "Suspenseful *Rammbock: Berlin Undead* Kicks Off Horror Film Series on Wednesday." *Nola.com / The Times-Picayune*, 28 May 2013. Retrieved 30 May 2018 from http://www.nola.com/movies/index.ssf/2011/05/suspenseful_rammbock_berlin_un.hml.

Sontag, Susan. "On Photography." In *Essays of the 1960s & 70s*, edited by David Rieff, 529–656. New York: Library Classics of the United States, 2013.

Zervigón, Andrés Mario. *Photography and Germany*. London: Reaktion Books, 2017.

Filmography

Diary of the Dead. Directed by George A. Romero. Los Angeles: Voltage Pictures, 2007.
The Cabinet of Dr. Caligari. Directed by Robert Wiene. Berlin: Decla-Bioscop, 1920.
Nekromantik 2. Directed by Jörg Buttgereit. Berlin: Jelinski Film & Fernsehproduktion, 1990.
The Nightmare. Directed by Achim Bornhak (Akiz). Munich: Koch Media, 2015.
Night of the Living Dead. Directed by George A. Romero. Pittsburgh: Image Ten, 1968.
Rammbock (*Berlin Undead*). Directed by Marvin Kren. Berlin: Moneypenny Filmproduktion, 2010.

Chapter 11

Possible Archives

Encountering a Surveillance Photo in *Karl Marx City* (2016)

Anke Pinkert

A pivotal scene in the 2016 documentary *Karl Marx City* takes the viewer into the quiet space of an archival reading room. Here, surrounded by large industrial shelves lined with document folders, we see the filmmaker Petra Epperlein pore over countless, meticulously catalogued images, which were taken by the Stasi, the East German State Security Service, during street protests in the fall of 1989. Inspecting dozens of these photographs with a magnifying glass, Epperlein attempts to glean evidence about a personal and collective past that over the course of more than two decades has slipped away. What is at stake, amidst these innumerable, anonymous sources, is the past of Epperlein's family, especially her father's suicide in 1997, as well as the vanishing of the German Democratic Republic (GDR), the country in which the filmmaker grew up. After a brief pause, her focus falls on an oversized file containing key photographic documents, which a white-gloved Epperlein handles with care; she wishes to confirm her father's innocence against speculations that he may have collaborated with the Stasi. Incredulously, she does locate her father within a protest photograph and announces this to the camera. Her discovery and gesture emphasize the intersecting role of photography and archives in shaping personal and public memory, which the film sets out to investigate.

Karl Marx City enters a contested field of post-1989 memory politics, linked more than ever with the Stasi and the Stasi Records Agency (BStU)[1]—on its own self-reflexive, nuanced terms. While the globally successful melodrama *Lives of Others* (*Das Leben der Anderen*, 2007)—directed by the West German Florian Henkel von Donnersmarck—never questions the status of the BStU as a stable, permanent repository of truth,[2] codirectors Petra Epperlein's and Michael Tucker's *Karl Marx City* probes the archive as an institution bound up with state power, if not violence. Marketed solely for an international, English-speaking audience, the documentary has been praised by the *New York Times* as a highly personal addition to the growing corpus of distressingly relevant, cautionary tales, which includes George Orwell's *1984* and Hannah Arendt's works on totalitarianism, among others.[3] Such a conclusive, evidentiary reading of the GDR as a totalizing surveillance state appears at first to be supported by the film. Portions of the documentary consist of seamlessly intercut surveillance footage, propaganda films, and Stasi snapshots (which contribute to the viewer's own sense of being watched), as well as extensive sequences shot in the BStU archive in present-day Berlin. These scenes illustrate the Stasi's all-encompassing efforts to document every aspect of people's lives in search of conspiracy. However, not unlike West German feminist documentarians in the late seventies,[4] the film is also invested in self-reflexive artistic modes of performativity and meditation. For example, we see Epperlein throughout the film ostentatiously carrying large headphones and an oversized microphone. Perhaps because Epperlein—who serves as filmmaker and cinematic subject, actor, and protagonist—is close to the history and story that the production team portrays, the film accentuates the mix of sincerity and heightened artifice, peppered with pop cultural sensibilities (i.e., the "camp" style Epperlein and Tucker deployed in earlier documentaries, such as *The Prisoner or: How I Planned to Kill Tony Blair* (2006).[5]

Karl Marx City, I want to suggest, is less focused on exposing the GDR as a surveillance state per se (an interpretation championed by the film's press kit and by reviewers) and more interested in exploring the complex role that photography plays in mediating personal and public memory (as managed by the surveillance archive).[6] In this regard, the film's handling of photographs as intermedial "thinking spaces" is vital.[7] As David Campany and others have suggested, if we were to survey all moments in which cinema deploys photos (and they are countless), we would find that most cases evoke the complex status of the photograph as evidence.[8] Photographs in film are there to "make us see,"[9] and to make us believe. They serve as evidence of an event having taken place. The film comes to a halt while we *look* at the photograph, register it as different from the flow of cinema (and of narrative), and give it the status of ontological truth. Whether in mainstream or avant-garde, modern or postmodern film, the "proof" of photography as memory or history is nearly always at stake.

However, when stripped of their institutionalized context or of any clearly circumscribed relation to an origin, still photographs within the cinematic medium begin to undo what tames them; they begin to produce meanings of their own accord. As *Karl Marx City* demonstrates, the evidentiary status of still photography in the moving image becomes slippery. In the following, the photographic image's indeterminacy in *Karl Marx City* destabilizes the self-same, self-legitimizing, even imperial notion of the Stasi Records Agency (BStU) as sole proprietor of East German life. Considering the (evidentiary) archive through (pensive, self-reflexive) photos and photography casts the archive in a new light. The chapter then turns to the surveillance photo of Epperlein's father at the 1989 protests to discuss the inverse risks of today's excessive investment in mediation in an age of "fake news." Here, the decontextualized, found image needs to be touched—quite literally by hands—to secure its ontological index, its foundational truth.[10] This touch, in turn, links up with the haptics at play in the archive: the dust, the smell, the feeling of the material as evidence that authenticates historical truth.

Finally, through a close examination of the handling and placement of this archival photograph in the concluding scene, it becomes clear how photography can move beyond the evidentiary in the production of personal and public memory. Though it does offer provisional resolution regarding her father's rumored status as a Stasi collaborator and his death in the late 1990s, the photograph Epperlein uncovers also points toward a historical moment that destabilizes established narratives about the GDR and its end in 1989. Rather than a finalized and stored-away past—the Stasi version of the GDR's dictatorial history that the BStU is designed to administer—the film camera scans the photograph for unexposed possible spaces and future temporalities within a history of revolutionary failure.

Unlearning the Archive

Karl Marx City investigates the possibilities of recovering truth in a vanished past. Although the premise of a daughter tracing the story of her father's suicide might promise an interior look into her family, this expectation (in part reflecting the filmmakers' interest in exploring the unknowability of other people's lives) remains unfulfilled. Even the family photographs used in this documentary (i.e., snapshots of Epperlein's socialist confirmation ceremony, a photo album with pictures of the parents at a workplace party, or an image of the parent's weekend home) give little texture to the Epperleins' private past. Mainly, they serve as casual stand-ins for knowledge and experience of life in the GDR. Because these family photos yield little insight into the father's decision to take his own life, the BStU serves the role of supplementing clandestinely collected information in order to assist in disclosing the truth. More than anything it is Epperlein's journey through these archival institutions that shapes the film's storyline of discovery and that holds the promise of eventually exculpating her father from his supposed role within East Germany's oppressive past.

In light of an incomplete familial memory, *Karl Marx City* starts out privileging archives as evidentiary domains above all others. While Epperlein and her family are waiting to receive the Stasi file on her father, which could clarify whether he was an informant, the director visits the BStU in Berlin-Lichtenberg. This institution houses the former Stasi archive—the collection of millions of images, strips of surveillance footage, and thousands of files, ranging from interrogation transcripts and intercepted mail to internal documents on espionage and the GDR's business connections with the West. Throughout this segment, placed toward the middle of the film, Epperlein maintains the slightly performative, self-conscious pose of the documentarian. Carrying her signature oversized headphones and microphone, she roams the stacks and interviews various experts in the field. However, as we begin to follow her through the stark, barren halls of the archival institution, populated by millions of paper files, the film takes on a somber tonality that exposes the GDR as a patriarchal, undead surveillance machine. Framed in long shots down the archival aisles, we see Epperlein pointing her microphone toward the records on the shelves, while we hear overlaid on the soundtrack the muffled voices of countless East Germans, who we can presume were secretly recorded in their workplaces and living rooms. Here, the film animates the GDR state as a totalizing apparatus that oversaw the lives of its citizens by harvesting their interior worlds and forcing an institutional passage of their thoughts from the private realm into a secret archival domain.

Certainly this is a place where people's dreams were cataloged and processed into an archival logic that few could escape. As the soundtrack of diffuse voices slips in and out, we become aware that these archival taxonomies destroyed cultural and social fabrics, silencing people and leaving them wordless.[11] Governed by the surveillance regimes of the

Stasi, East Germans expected that what they said might be recorded and transcribed into an anonymous filing system. Therefore, many learned to censor their speech, until they no longer knew how to speak up. And when a rapidly cut montage of Polaroids captures the work of Stasi staff (in mailrooms, dark rooms, and at the copying bench) with the audible click of a camera shutter, we are further reminded that the Stasi's laborious investment in the archive would not have been possible without the technologies of photographic recording, and the labor of memorization, repetition, and reproduction, which was conducted by human beings, and not just machines.

Here, while focused on the historical violence of the Stasi, Epperlein's and Tucker's film also exposes the violence of the archive itself. In his 1995 book *Archive Fever*, Jacques Derrida calls our attention to the "politics of the archive," that is, to the structures and enactments of governmental authority and privilege, and to the excessive and ultimately gratuitous investment in technologies and procedures, involved in massive document collection.[12] Likening the archive to the accumulation of capital, he writes that there is no political power without the control of the archive, of memory.[13] In fact, *Karl Marx City* navigates the liminal space where the differential, if not imperial, power structure of the BStU comes into view. For instance, the performative interviews with experts who are enlisted and authorized to represent the institution illuminate how the archive that inherited the GDR's Stasi records, post-1989, was established as a "neutral threshold" separating the past and the present, history and politics.[14] The Federal Republic of Germany, the unified German state, has also been considerably invested in the management of public memory, through which the GDR emerges as a totalitarian surveillance system, and as the second dictatorship in the aftermath of the Third Reich.[15]

But the violence of the archive is also mitigated by the content of the collections and their relationship to the lives of the people involved. When protesters stormed the Stasi headquarters in all major East German cities in 1989, Stasi employees left behind tens of thousands of sacks with an estimated 600 million pieces of torn up documents.[16] In 2013, the German government then funded a comprehensive archival project to have these shredded documents digitally reassembled. These material remnants enabled a fantasy of paper-based history, to draw on Ariella Azoulay's formulation;[17] and the emergence of "historical value" from these leftovers has served as major inspiration for the BStU to accumulate and preserve other people's pasts. Notably, Deputy Head Archivist Johanna Schütterle, whom Epperlein also interviews, interprets the total reconstruction of the mangled files as repaying an unsettled debt to society. When we see a female staff member using actual stones, from the beach perhaps, as archival tools to flatten the scraps of shredded paper, the fragmented documents, in turn, become visible as the archive's cherished objects. Although the archive is commonly "envisaged as driven by invisible hands of abstract guardians," and the role of experts is to claim neutrality,[18] Schütterle in the film announces with a sense of responsibility and praise: "we reconstruct records so that at some indefinite point in the future, people will have access to their own files or to those of relatives, and learn something they would have otherwise never known." In searching through the archive for evidence of her father's involvement in the Stasi, Epperlein is also able to access a past (and therefore a future) that she would have otherwise never encountered.

The palpability of the collections also validates their existence and fraught relationship in the construction of historical and personal memory. This relationship is demonstrated during an interview between Epperlein and head spokesperson of the BStU Dagmar Hovestädt, who carefully pulls a set of microfiche out from transparent envelopes. When she runs her fingers over the films, wearing white oversized gloves, she performs the crucial touch that enhances the material's believability as proof of the Stasi's surveillance activity. This touch is already more removed from the indexical, haptic quality of the images on the BStU website that show thick paper folders of the Stasi files. Here, it is as though one can feel the weight, the dust, and the smells that authenticate the Stasi records as historical depositories of truth. After picking up the microfiche, Hovestädt explains to Epperlein, and to the viewer, that the Stasi photographed the envelopes of intercepted mail—which, shown in the documentary as laid out flat with their flaps open, now resemble miniature houses. In a kind of poetic double reflection, these negative filmstrips of thumbnail-size houses allegorize the archive as a domicile for the files.[19] Cast against the largely white mise-en-scène of the archive's clinical interior, these shadow images might also suggest that this place has become a kind of eerie, ghostly new residence for the indefatigable post-1989 archival administrators and possibly for Epperlein as well, who from the beginning of her journey set out to release herself from the "voodoo of nostalgia," from the sense that East Germany was a viable home.

If the multivalent meaning and indeterminacy of photographic images remind us that archives are institutions of mediated, assembled evidence at best and hegemonic institutions at worst, then any indexical, trustworthy handling of the Stasi documents is forfeited. Yet, what if there is something important to be found amid the stored, reconfigured, and revivified wreckage of the files? Having unlearned the archive and exposed its artifice, Epperlein roams the abandoned halls of this temple of truth in an attempt to encounter her own hidden past.

Photographic Contact

Artistically, *Karl Marx City* condemns any simple claims that it is possible to recover truth from a vanished past. If anything, the film's heightened artifice (i.e., Epperlein's mobile recording equipment, the austere black and white cinematography, the graphic intertitles) underscores a focus on mediation that echoes Benjamin's notion of memory work,[20] where any sifting through the past and its residues will also result in random, fruitless searching. Rather than gaining clarity about her father's past through recall and remembrance, we have the distinct sense over the course of the film that Epperlein herself appears to become increasingly caught up in the all-encompassing scopic strictures of the Stasi and the surveillance mechanisms the agency once employed. Together with her, the spectator is drawn into a kind of "spherical dramaturgy,"[21] to borrow Alexander Kluge's term, where a kinetic flow is created by the assemblages of multiple "cinematic streams"—surveillance footage recorded by the Stasi, GDR propaganda film, rapidly sequenced Polaroid freeze frames of the Stasi's clandestine activities, as well as an array of more personal material, including a home video, documentary-style expert interviews, and narrative sequences of Epperlein visiting her family or roaming the ghostly streets of her hometown. The sheer abundance of visual material creates the sense of a larger structure or presence, where presumably nothing escapes an all-seeing eye.

However, devoted to determining whether we can, and should, trust any claims about the father's brush with the Stasi, the final segment seems to break through this web of mediation and remediation to arrive at some kind of evidentiary core of the archive.[22] The Stasi emerges as vital recordkeeper under the purview of the BStU when, right after the last expert interview with deputy head archivist Johanna Schütterle, a scene shows that the father's file has turned up and his reputation is restored. Cutting from the interiors of the archive to an exterior street scene, we see how Epperlein receives a phone call and then announces to the camera, stunned and visibly relieved, that her father did not work as an informer. In a conspicuous affirmation of binaries (which sits uncomfortably with the film's performative artistic style), the documentarian later implies, "Good, he was not one of the bad guys." While we do not hear the voice on the other end (presumably an archivist), the next sequence shows the family poring over copies of the file—Epperlein with her brothers in their apartment, and her mother in her own apartment. Testifying to the Stasi's method of intimate betrayal—or what Wolfgang Thierse and others have described as the banality of a network where informers were "friends, neighbors, and even relatives"[23]—a secret is revealed. Not only was the father *not* a Stasi informer, but he himself was also denounced and spied upon by a family acquaintance, his former boss.

Notably, as the camera pans over typed and handwritten documents while the mother reads the denunciation letter out loud, this dramatized parsing of the written record leaves Epperlein with more questions than answers, especially regarding her father's death. Only by highlighting the discovery of a photograph in the archive and by enlisting its evidentiary power as indisputable proof does the film achieve the emotional closure demanded by the family plotline and the moral reassertion of the father's integrity. As we see Epperlein return to the BStU archive, the voiceover (Tucker and Epperlein's daughter) rather lyrically announces, "The last Stasi report on her father was filed in October 1989, a month before the regime fell. What happened in Karl Marx City in those final weeks? Driven by a nagging sense of the familiar, a misplaced memory, a gap between her own recollection and history, she seeks solace in the files." When the film cuts to the spacious interior of what looks like a public office or reading room in the archive, we see Epperlein equipped with a professional magnifying glass with a compound lens. She is bent over a large industrial desk, closely inspecting a contact sheet of photographic images taken during the protests in the streets of Karl Marx City that were not destroyed by the Stasi in 1989.

Here, the film dramatizes the shifting evidentiary and disclosive capacities of photography in the production of memory most effectively.[24] Given pause by a kind of "tactile looking," to draw on Margaret Olin's term, Epperlein herself takes on the role of the (positivist) archivist, ever so closely related to the production of the original, indexical meaning.[25] Grasping the past meaning of the images through her ocular and manual touch, the film enlists the photographs in a process of authentication, referring to the haptic ability of visual imagery to activate senses other than sight.[26] Once the still photographs expand and fill the film's frame, the tactile, material creases on the surface of the visual records (photographic objects) become visible. They bear the indexical trace of the archivist's handling—or, more likely, of the Stasi's attempt at destruction. At this point, the film slips back into a self-reflexive, meditational register. A rapid montage animates archival stills of the unrest in Karl Marx City's public square, taken by the Stasi in 1989. A mood of risk and danger is created through a sound mix that includes sonic snippets of an approaching helicopter, muffled street chanting, and dramatic music swelling in and out. Not only does this animated still-photo sequence remind the viewer of the historical fact that hardly any film footage existed of these nascent, early protests against the regime until 9 October,[27] it also references the complex relationship between photography and film, between still and moving image itself.[28] Together with the mimetic clicks of the camera shutter, which signal the role of the informers in the demonstrating crowd, *Karl Marx City* creates a sequence of moving images that resembles a photo story. Equally anchored in historical reality and cast through a particular perspective—or multiple distinct perspectives (that of the Stasi, the archival collection, the third-generation voiceover)—we notice how this animated scene is also constructed.

The documentary ends, however, with an arresting scene that makes strong claims to authenticity. In the final two minutes, the entire visual, haptic, and spatial choreography of Epperlein's archival work comes to a standstill. With our visual attention focused on a single still image, we witness a "process of becoming"[29] that belongs as much to memory as to photography, and the magical power ascribed to still images to stand in for the past. The relationship between the perceived authenticity of photography and personal as well as public memory, managed by the archive, is crucial here. What Epperlein reveals from a large archive folder—magnifying glass in hand, and carefully handling the contents with the iconic white gloves (previously shown worn by archival BStU administrator Dagmar Hovestädt, and also by the Stasi)—are two mid-size sheets of paper with faded color photographs. Photographs, after all, belong to the architecture of paper environments such as newspapers, flyers, posters, and, here, the archival record.[30] We briefly see the sheets first from their blank backs and then through an over the shoulder shot, nearly full frame, when Epperlein holding up the second one, looks up from the file, halts in silence (over barely perceptible sounds), and states to the camera, "That's me . . . and my father." With photo in hand, the autobiographical documentarian invites the audience to become a pensive spectator. Epperlein wants to affirm her father's innocence through the existence and veracity of the photograph and the truth afforded to the archive, but this moment of recognition also illustrates the fraught relationship between the archive and photography.

In this final scene, we see on full display how photographs in film provide space for intermedial reflection. Film theorist Raymond Bellour, building on Roland Barthes, describes as "pensive" the "response of the spectator faced with a photograph or freeze frame in a film. Pensiveness is a suspension, a moment of anticipation when things are in the balance. Literally and psychologically, the still image causes a pause."[31] David Campany writes, "Viewing a photograph in a film is very different from viewing it directly. Film tends to overstate the photograph's difference, while presenting that difference as if it were its essence."[32] There are different accounts of time at work in the moving and in the still image. We see the photograph exaggerated by those qualities that distinguish it from film: its stillness, its temporal fixity, its objecthood, its silence—even its deathliness, as if turned to stone.[33] Once Epperlein recognizes herself and her father, the suspension, this gap, this space between (forgotten) memory and history snaps into place, so to speak. The over the shoulder shot, showing them together at a protest meeting in early October 1989, firmly establishes the photo as a piece of evidence for what is presumed to be the father's ultimate resistance to the state: his innocence and integrity.

To a large degree, what we witness in this scene is media and photographic theory in reverse. The closure of the family/Stasi narrative and the intersubjective encounter between the father and the daughter require the photograph to be imbued with the status of a record—that is, with strong indexical certainty and relevance as evidence, and with a physical relation to its original—even if, of course, photography theory since the 1970s, from Barthes to Sontag to Derrida, has increasingly disinvested itself from such claims.[34] And given Epperlein's and Tucker's previous work in contexts rich with media technology, it is safe to assume they are aware of this as well.[35] Although we watch the film in a digital format (which enables us to construct new associative networks of meaning by skipping from scene to scene), the final segment reminds us that contact with the father, across time, is enabled by an analog photograph that left a trace of his physical presence and the idea that something or someone, in that past moment depicted on the photograph, was indeed there. Laura Mulvey, in *Death 24x a Second: Stillness and the Moving Image*, explains this power of the evidentiary: "Whatever their limitations, photographic machines register the image inscribed by light on photosensitive paper, leaving the trace of whatever comes in front of the lens."[36] The irony of discovering the truth about the father in the very archive of the oppressive regime that placed him under surveillance is not lost to the film. As the camera holds the photograph in full frame, the voiceover concludes: "She remembered what she knew all along. She was there in the theater that day, next to her father. Of all the things the Stasi recorded this moment is surely true. The picture was taken as evidence. In another version of history, it would have been used against them. Instead the Stasi unwittingly captured the father she always knew." Then, as if to echo the "violent shutter of the archive" itself, the film promptly cuts to a final, black intertitle, with the dedication "for my father."

Future Memories

Although *Karl Marx City* reinvests in an indexical ontology of the photographic image, there is more at stake in this final contact than meets the eye. In fact, by using cinema to think about the medium from which it ultimately evolved (and by doing so in the mediating context of the archive), Epperlein and Tucker steer the spectator in the direction of interpretive work and toward an open-ended relationality with the image placed at the end of the film. For what is referenced, yet not mentioned here, is the assembly of citizens on 7 October 1989, at Karl Marx City's Luxor-Palast.[37] Undoing the teleology of reunification, the film orients us toward the historical interval of "1989"—the early fall unrest, when people gathered and acted in concert in the streets of Karl Marx City, Leipzig, and Berlin, with no intention to topple the Wall or usher in the capitalist democracy of the West.

The narrative about the inevitability of Germany's reunification is well established in public discourse today, and the revolutionary fall appears to be a closed, distant chapter. The cinematic tendency to dwell on the photograph as a mute and intransigent object from the past is also present in *Karl Marx City* where the photograph's materiality is underscored. Scenes caught by the Stasi photographers nearly three decades ago are rendered on faded color prints, which, in turn, are quite literally trapped under the magnifying glass Epperlein uses to inspect the images. But the documentary moves this photographic moment (and the particular history of early 1989 protest it represents) out from underneath the temporality of self-same archival taxonomies (of what *did* happen) and into the more inchoate, open-ended realm of the future.

The index has a privileged relation to time, to the moment and duration of its inscription, and has a physical relation to its original, for which it is the sign.[38] Yet even as the index is a record of a fraction of time fixed in the photograph when rays of light record an object's presence (remember, the father and daughter were "there" in the theater), they also inscribe that moment of time as henceforth suspended.[39] The film's final frames show in blurry close up the photograph of Epperlein and her father on the upper balcony of the theater. As the material support amplified throughout the scene (lens, magnifying glass, paper, folders, etc.) appears to drop away, the soft tip of the white glove and the now barely perceptible frame of the magnifier stretch into a diffuse outer boundary of the image, a transition that resembles the representational subjectivity of a vignetting effect. With this gesture, the image is eerily brought to life. Almost completely stripped of its material scaffolding, the spectral nature of the image/scene is palpable: the figures in the photograph are still, of course, and the eyes of a younger Epperlein have turned nearly into empty dots in the magnification. Suspended, hanging in the balance, so to speak, the image allows the viewer time to think.

Rather than revealing evidence, then, the final image turns into a space for interpretation. By stopping short with a cut to the poignant dedication intertitle of "for my father," the film incites the spectators to respond to its call to assign it meaning in some way. Bound up in structures of trauma, the photographic image resonates with the metaphors of erasure and self-erasure that are emphasized in earlier chapters of the film with both the fall of the wall ("within weeks every trace of Karl Marx City and the communist past was erased") and with the suicide of the father ("In 1998, much like Karl Marx City, her father set out to erase himself . . . he then secretly collected and burned all his papers and photographs"). Almost like a "floating flash,"[40] the image of Epperlein and her father suspends meaning across time, hovering in the gap between "an abandoned past and an unredeemed future"—language used by the narrative voice early on in the film, when commenting on her walk through the gloomy streets of post-1989 Chemnitz (previously Karl Marx City), a place she refers to as a "city of ghosts."

However, despite this uncanny quality, the enlarged close-up of the young girl and her father alongside protesters of the regime appears rather placid and undersignified in some way. Once Epperlein places the magnifying glass over the image and the extreme close up simulates the aforementioned vignetting effect, we see only the daughter and her father in a kind of contemplative pose in the front row of the audience. Is it, then, precisely because of this silent, quiet desire of the image that it needs to, and can, be heard? Is it because of its amplified stillness that we may want to ask, "What does the picture want?" from us, the viewer? W. J. T. Mitchell addresses this question when he describes the capacity of an image to enthrall and transfix its beholders by renouncing direct signs of desire. Here, the power of the picture to call us to contemplate its meaning comes from "its indirectness, its seeming indifference . . . its anti-theatrical 'absorption' in its own internal drama."[41] We know what motivates the photograph's appearance (in the archive, and in Epperlein's and Tucker's film), but what actually motivated the appearance of the attendees in the theater is less clear. Her father's glance off to the side, outside the frame, is a gesture that seems to invite the viewer into a dialogue and search for other possible archives.

What happened in the theater that day and outside in the streets that Germany's victorious neoliberal narrative of Western victory conceals? The handmade banner reading "Freedom to Travel instead of Mass Flight"[42] recalls the first color photograph that Epperlein slipped out from underneath the transparent sheets in the archive folder and might serve as a sign that can orient us toward the undisclosed spaces within a history of revolutionary failure. According to eyewitness accounts, the organizers of the sold-out event at the Luxor-Palast on 7 October hoped to diffuse any provocations and to establish a dialogue among the citizens and between the populace and the state.[43] The ad-hoc event was also infiltrated by the Stasi. In historical hindsight, the characterization of the GDR as a second dictatorship in the public, post-1989 memory discourse of Germany (let alone in the popular imagination abroad) short-circuits Stasi terror, the oppression of the GDR regime, and the tearing down of the Berlin Wall (which is invoked at the outset of *Karl Marx City* with the iconic footage of East Germans breaking through fences). However, the final photograph of the assembly at the Luxor-Palast in early fall, albeit fleetingly, incites an alternative reading that people indeed constituted themselves as political subjects through the performance of collaborative, embodied action.[44] But rather than a call for toppling the GDR state, these were silent, provisional, heterogeneous gatherings where people acted in concert, not knowing how things would turn out; or, for that matter, what radical shift one could ask for.

Karl Marx City's final photographic reference to an open-ended, unfinalized story of emerging dialogue and self-gathering collaborative action (not aimed from within its own temporality, at the fall of the Berlin Wall, or the ushering in of neoliberal capitalism) may slip through the self-same taxonomies established by an archival lens. Social institutions, including the Federal Republic of Germany's "Federal Foundation for the Reappraisal of the SED dictatorship" (Bundesstiftung für die Aufarbeitung der SED-Diktatur), as well as the Stasi itself, of course, require far-reaching processes of self-stabilization. In order to shape the understanding of personal and collective pasts, they privilege certain interpretations over others by creating the possibility of self-reinforcing dynamics and feedback loops.[45] Taking their cue from Epperlein's personal family story, the directors of *Karl Marx City* invite us to ponder *how* historical memory is constituted in the course of time, and how it is influenced—by the successes and failures of our actions, by the ways in which we perceive, through archives and photography, our conversations with others, and by the institutional networks in which we move.

Although the film was celebrated for portraying the everyday terror of dictatorship and—at least on the surface—for catering to such binaries, *Karl Marx City*, much like the directors' earlier works such as *The Last Cowboy* (1998) and *Gunner Palace* (2004), refuse to give any easy answers. This is most palpable where meditations on photography, memory, and the archive intersect. Here, the art documentary moves beyond films like the blockbuster *The Lives of Others*, which purported a much simpler notion of an archive where the past is "found" rather than being a place where an understanding of the past is "shaped." Like *Karl Marx City*, Henckel von Donnersmarck's movie ends with an iconic scene in the reading room of the BStU. The protagonist, Dreymann, a playwright from the former East Germany, is waiting for his victim file. The camera cuts away, and we see the colossal, by now iconic, stacks, where endless rows stretch out, revealing the vast shelf space tightly packed with files upon files. Eventually, from the recesses of this archive, the staff produces a cart with folders piled up, nearly collapsing under its own weight. As a voiceover reads the reports in the files out loud, the protagonist discovers the code of his informer, HWH XX/7, and finds next to it a red ink-print left behind in the file by the informer's finger—a touch, a haptic sign of truth, an index. Dreymann approaches the archivist in the room, and from an index catalogue the identity of the informer is revealed. To be sure, Donnersmarck's tracking of the archival procedure and technology, while cinematically enhanced, is not false; *Karl Marx City* also includes the naming of the informer who spied on Epperlein's father.

However, ever so powerfully insisting on a kind of performative indexicality of a still photograph,[46] *Karl Marx City* loosens the archive's self-same claims to knowledge, opening into new and possible spaces, where the amassing of information has not yet produced its full ideological truth effect. The larger question of "What do we know and how do we know it" about the past is at stake in the film. Restoring the interpretive authenticity of the photograph, Epperlein and Tucker remind us of the medium's capacity to refer back to an original event while also linking personal memory and collective history, however incomplete.[47] This claim to an indexical ontology may appear out of step in the digital age, where images countlessly proliferate or are altered to produce fake news. But in the end, it is precisely because of this new digital reality and the culture of "post-truth" it fosters, that the final, almost poetic, materially supported protest-image in Epperlein's and Tucker's documentary requests such an emancipatory move. The tangibility of the photograph provides an anchor and a strategy to come to terms with ever-proliferating information, it provides a space to find meaning. Released from indexicality and context, images may generate myriad perspectives and narratives on ever-shifting terrains. The capacity to touch a photograph, however, may allow the photograph to touch us, and, in the process, liberate a memory of the future—here, of a collaborative, radically democratic society Epperlein, her father, and the East Germans in the theatre in 1989 stood for—that became stuck in the past, or was erased.

Coda

Karl Marx City functions as a contemporary project in the digital age, but the film also advances a commentary on digital culture. What drives *Karl Marx City* is not only the particular history of surveillance in the GDR and its aftermath post-1989, but also more topical questions about the nexus of private and public life, mediated through film technology, photography, new media, or the government. Imprinted on the documentary is modernity's enduring fascination with questions of visibility and with the capacity of analog film and photography to track their own shadows and loss, in contrast to digital recordings, where nothing can hide.[48] Mixing quiet, elliptical tonalities with an absurd amount of images (snapshots, family portraits, official ID pictures, etc.), the film poses timely questions about the possibility of knowing the truth about others, or oneself, as this truth is remediated and distributed across our personal, collective, and technological lives. Ultimately, in the era of fake news and digital selves, *Karl Marx City* makes the claim for the performative value of an indexical anchor: we have to better understand our own epistemological frames; we have to devise strategies and understand how to read images.

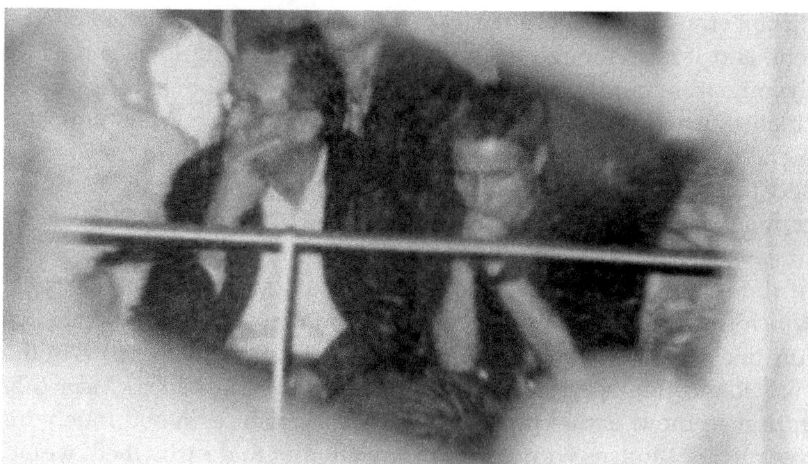

Figure 11.1. *Karl Marx City* (*Karl Marx Stadt*). Directed by Petra Epperlein and Michael Tucker. New York: Pepper & Bones, 2016. Screen capture by Anke Pinkert.

At the end of the documentary, the two modern media—film and photography—converge. Projections of multiple surveillance snapshots, crammed into thumbnail size frames, stream over the screen. Since the emergence of moving images in the late nineteenth century, photography and cinema have often had a strained, even "incestuous," yet also vital relationship.[49] Both media have been caught up in questions of the evidentiary as well as of secrecy and surveillance.[50] Yes, the mechanically reproduced copies of Stasi surveillance footage showing countless ordinary street scenes of East Germans going about their routines seem interchangeable, as they are abruptly switched in and out in a series of rows and columns. The visual grid picks up on an intercepted film shot of a Stasi officer watching multiple television screens and returns the film to its opening scene, where we saw two Stasi officers setting up surveillance equipment. It feels as though we are trapped once more in the surveillance logic of the GDR state, which forced Epperlein to rearrange the postmemory of her father's life and death. But the film actually presents an invitation to zoom out much further, into an expansive ontological large-scale view, and take in the spectacular impassiveness of these running images and their insistence on repeating the same message (or nothing at all).

Here, then, the film echoes the claim of cultural criticism that even today we live in a society of spectacle, surveillance, and simulacra. The distant street surveillance scenes appear fabricated and devoid of content, and it is as though the perpetually proliferating images held by the miniature frames turn themselves into screens, akin to those of calculating machines, such as smartphone computers.[51] While new and social media may have made communication seem more transparent and rational than before, their algorithms also order and distribute commercial and governmental surveillance.[52] At minimum, digital culture enmeshes us in labyrinths of endless image cycles and networked relations; and, just like the computer technology and virtual reality on which they rely, these new media race simultaneously toward the future and the past.[53] Both anchored and mobile, the infinite loops of the surveillance footage in the small frames at the end of *Karl Marx City* appear to move across time and space; they also seem obdurately indestructible, and, as with any idol, any attempt to destroy them would appear in vain.[54] Here, inching toward a dystopian vision, the violence of the archive (embodied in the archive fever of both the Stasi and the BStU, if not today's internet) strikes back. We no longer have agency to house the material in some remote storage place, to access it for our review and contemplation; instead, the material freely, and possibly on its own account, recombines and accumulates, directing us, watching us, and eventually closing us in.

Anke Pinkert is Associate Professor at the University of Illinois at Urbana-Champaign, where she teaches undergraduate and graduate courses on twentieth/twenty-first-century German literature, film, and culture; critical theory; Holocaust representations; and mass incarceration in film and media. Paying particular attention to the aftermath of two turning points in modern German and European history, 1945 and 1989, her scholarship examines aesthetic and political responses to collective feelings of loss and trauma and has appeared in *Seminar*, *The German Quarterly*, and *Studies in Eastern European Cinema*. She is the author of *Memory and Film in East Germany* (2008).

Notes

1. The Federal Commissioner for the Records of the State Security Service of the German Democratic Republic is also known as the Stasi Records Agency. Hereafter, BStU (*Der Bundesbeauftragte für die Unterlagen des Staatssicherheitsdienstes der ehemaligen Deutschen Demokratischen Republik*) will be used.
2. Paul Cooke, "Watching the Stasi: Authenticity, Ostalgie and History in Florian Henckel von Donnersmarck's *The Lives of Others* (2006)," in *New Directions in German Cinema*, ed. Paul Cooke and Chris Homewood (London: Tauris, 2011).

3. A. O. Scott, "*Karl Marx City* Revisits the Everyday Terror of Dictatorship," *New York Times*, 28 March 2017.
4. Judith Mayne, "Female Narration, Women's Cinema: Helke Sander's *The All-Round Reduced Personality/Redupers*," *New German Critique* 24/25 (1981): 155–71.
5. For their early DVD artwork work, see *The Last Cowboy* (1998). Madeleine Casad, "Rescreening Memory Beyond the Wall," *The Germanic Review: Literature, Culture, Theory* 88, no. 3 (2013): 335.
6. Notably, the emergence of photography as modern technology itself has been inextricably bound up with the history of surveillance. See Susan Sontag, *On Photography* (New York: Picador, 1973), 5.
7. David Campany, *Photography and Cinema* (London: Reaction Books, 2008), 95f.
8. Ibid., 95.
9. Carmen Pérez Ríu, "To Make You See: Photography as Intermedial Resource in Theatre and Film Adaptation (*Closer* and *The Winter Guest*)," *Adaptation: The Journal of Literature on Screen Studies* 8, no. 2 (2015): 176–91.
10. For touch as a privileged conduit to reality, see Margaret Olin, *Touching Photographs* (Chicago: University of Chicago Press, 2012), 7.
11. Ariella Azoulay, *Potential History: Unlearning Imperialism* (New York: Verso, 2019), esp. 40–46, 169–79.
12. Jacques Derrida, *Archive Fever: A Freudian Impression* (Chicago: University of Chicago Press, 1995), 1–23, esp. 3, 18.
13. Ibid., 4, 12.
14. Azoulay, *Potential History*, 42, 46. See also, Azoulay, *The Civil Contract of Photography* (New York: Zone Books, 2008), esp. 415–16, 419–21.
15. According to its website, the Stasi Records Agency brands its own political efforts in hegemonic and binary fashion: "The better we understand dictatorship, the better we can shape democracy."
16. Philip Olterman, "Stasi Files: Scanner Struggles to Stitch Together Surveillance State Scraps," *The Guardian*, 3 January 2018.
17. Azoulay, *Potential History*, 169.
18. Ibid., 41–42, 178.
19. Derrida, *Archive Fever*, 2.
20. Walter Benjamin, "Ausgraben und Erinnern," in *Gesammelte Schriften*, ed. Rolf Tiedemann and Hermann Schweppenhäuser (Frankfurt: Suhrkamp, 1972), vol. 4/1: 400.
21. "News from Ideological Antiquity," *Alexander Kluge: Cultural History in Dialogue*, 2006–18.
22. For a discussion of the double logic of remediation, which insists that there never was a past prior to mediation, see Astrid Erll and Ann Rigney, eds., *Meditation, Remediation, and the Dynamics of Cultural Memory* (New York: de Gruyter, 2009), esp. 4.
23. Barbara Miller, *Narratives of Guilt and Compliance in Unified Germany: Stasi Informers and Their Impact on Society* (New York: Routledge, 1999), 9.
24. For the distinction of photography's evidentiary and disclosive modalities, see Kaja Silverman, *The Miracle of Analogy: The History of Photography*, Part 1 (Stanford: Stanford University Press, 2015), 7–11. The former is associated with technology, the index, the copy, and fixity; the latter with the world, with development of discontinuous meaning across space and time, interpretation and analogy.
25. For further discussion of touch and its privileged relation to indexicality, see Olin, *Touching Photographs*, 10–11; For C. S. Pierce's definition of the sign, and his distinction between index and icon, in relation to memory work, see Marianne Hirsch, *The Generation of Postmemory: Writing and Visual Culture after the Holocaust* (New York: Columbia University Press, 2012), 36–37.

26. For the relation of the haptic to other senses, see Robert Rushing, *Descended from Hercules: Biopolitics and the Muscled Male Body on Screen* (Bloomington: Indiana University Press, 2016), 100.
27. Peter Wesnierski, *Die Unheimliche Leichtigkeit der Revolution* (Munich: Deutsche Verlagsanstalt, 2017).
28. For discussions of this relation, see Campany, *Photography and Cinema;* Laurent Guido and Oliver Lugon, eds., *Between Still and Moving Images: Photography and Cinema in the 20th Century* (New Barnet: John Libbey Publishing, 2012); Laura Mulvey, *Death 24x a Second: Stillness and the Moving Image* (London: Reaction Books, 2006).
29. Mulvey, *Death 24x a Second,* 56.
30. Olin, *Touching Photographs,* 2.
31. Campany, *Photography and Cinema,* 96. Here Campany refers to and elaborates on Roland Barthes, *Camera Lucida: Reflections on Photography* (New York: Hill and Wang, 1980) and Raymond Bellour, "The Pensive Spectator," *Wide Angle* 9, no. 1 (1987): 6–10.
32. Campany, *Photography and Cinema,* 96.
33. Ibid.
34. Sontag, *On Photography;* Barthes, *Camera Lucida;* Jacques Derrida, *Copy, Archive, Signature: A Conversation on Photography* (Stanford: Stanford University Press, 2010).
35. Casad, "Rescreening Memory."
36. Mulvey, *Death 24x a Second,* 19.
37. Monika Reum and Steffen Geissler, *Auferstanden aus Ruinen . . . Und Wie Weiter? Chronik der Wende in Karl-Marx Stadt/Chemnitz 1989/90* (Chemnitz: Verlag Heimatland Sachsen GMBH, 1991).
38. Mulvey, *Death 24x a Second,* 9.
39. Ibid., 56.
40. Ibid., 56.
41. W. J. T. Mitchell, *What Do Pictures Want? The Lives and Loves of Images* (Chicago: University of Chicago Press, 2005), 42, 36.
42. "Reisefreiheit statt Massenflucht."
43. Reum and Geissler, *Auferstanden aus Ruinen,* 48.
44. For an elaboration of assemblies as embodied, collective action, see Judith Butler, *Notes Toward a Performative Theory of Assembly* (Cambridge, MA: Harvard University Press, 2015).
45. Andreas Glaeser, *Political Epistemics: The Secret Police, the Opposition, and the End of East German Socialism* (Chicago: University of Chicago Press, 2011), xxiv.
46. The "performative index" indicates that the attempt to create a relationship with photographs depends on the belief in their indexicality but not on what one can see in them (Olin, *Touching Photographs,* 18).
47. For the incomplete, imaginative transmission of memory, especially across generations, and involving photographs, see Hirsch, *Generation of Postmemory.*
48. Silverman, *Miracle of Analogy,* 4, 37.
49. Ari J. Blatt, "Thinking Photography in Film, or the Suspended Cinema of Agnès Varda and Jean Eustache," *French Forum* 36, no. 2–3 (2011): 182.
50. Josh Later, "Surveillance History and the History of New Media: An Evidential Paradigm," *New Media and Society* 14, no. 4 (2011): 566–82.
51. Mitchell, *What Do Pictures Want?,* 26.
52. Siva Vaidhyanathan, *Anti-Social Media: How Facebook Disconnects Us and Undermines Democracy* (Oxford: Oxford University Press, 2018).
53. Wendy Hui Kyong Chun, "The Enduring Ephemeral, or the Future Is a Memory," *Critical Inquiry* 35, no. 1 (2008): 148–71.
54. Mitchell, *What Do Pictures Want?,* 27.

Bibliography

Ash, Timothy Garton. "The Stasi on Our Minds." *The New York Review of Books*, 31 May 2007.

Azoulay, Ariella. *The Civil Contract of Photography*. New York: Zone Books, 2008.

———. *Potential History: Unlearning Imperialism*. New York: Verso, 2019.

Barthes, Roland. *Camera Lucida: Reflections on Photography*. New York: Hill and Wang, 1980.

Bellour, Raymond. "The Pensive Spectator." *Wide Angle* 9, no. 1 (1987): 6–10.

Benjamin, Walter. "Ausgraben und Erinnern." *Gesammelte Schriften*. Volume 4/1: *Kleine Prosa: Baudelaire–Übertragungen*, edited by Rolf Tiedemann and Hermann Schweppenhäuser. Frankfurt: Suhrkamp, 1972.

Blatt, Ari J. "Thinking Photography in Film, or the Suspended Cinema of Agnès Varda and Jean Eustache." *French Forum* 36, no. 2–3 (2011): 181–200.

Butler, Judith. *Notes toward a Performative Theory of Assembly*. Cambridge, MA: Harvard University Press, 2015.

Campany, David. *Photography and Cinema*. London: Reaction Books, 2008.

Casad, Madeleine. "Rescreening Memory Beyond the Wall." *The Germanic Review: Literature, Culture, Theory* 88, no. 3 (2013): 320–38.

Chun, Wendy Hui Kyong. "The Enduring Ephemeral, or the Future Is a Memory." *Critical Inquiry* 35, no. 1 (2008): 148–71.

Cooke, Paul. "Watching the Stasi: Authenticity, Ostalgie and History in Florian Henckel von Donnersmarck's *The Lives of Others* (2006)." In *New Directions in German Cinema*, edited by Paul Cooke and Chris Homewood, 113–29. London: Tauris, 2011.

Derrida, Jacques. *Archive Fever: A Freudian Impression*. Chicago: University of Chicago Press, 1995.

———. *Copy, Archive, Signature: A Conversation on Photography*. Stanford: Stanford University Press, 2010.

Erll, Astrid, and Ann Rigney, eds. *Meditation, Remediation, and the Dynamics of Cultural Memory*. New York: de Gruyter, 2009.

Glaeser, Andreas. *Political Epistemics: The Secret Police, the Opposition, and the End of East German Socialism*. Chicago: University of Chicago Press, 2011.

Guido, Laurent, and Oliver Lugon, eds. *Between Still and Moving Images: Photography and Cinema in the 20th Century*. New Barnet: John Libbey Publishing, 2012.

Hirsch, Marianne. *The Generation of Postmemory: Writing and Visual Culture after the Holocaust*. New York: Columbia University Press, 2012.

Later, Josh. "Surveillance History and the History of New Media: An Evidential Paradigm." *New Media and Society* 14, no. 4 (2011): 566–82.

Mayne, Judith. "Female Narration, Women's Cinema: Helke Sander's *The All-Round Reduced Personality/Redupers*." *New German Critique* 24–25 (1981): 155–71.

Miller, Barbara. *Narratives of Guilt and Compliance in Unified Germany: Stasi Informers and Their Impact on Society*. New York: Routledge, 1999.

Mitchell, W. J. T. *What Do Pictures Want? The Lives and Loves of Images*. Chicago: University of Chicago Press, 2005.

Mulvey, Laura. *Death 24x a Second: Stillness and the Moving Image*. London: Reaction Books, 2006.

"News from Ideological Antiquity." *Alexander Kluge: Cultural History in Dialogue*, 2006–18. Retrieved 25 May 2018 from https://kluge.library.cornell.edu/films/ideological-antiquity.

Olin, Margaret. *Touching Photographs*. Chicago: University of Chicago Press, 2012.

Olterman, Philip. "Stasi Files: Scanner Struggles to Stitch Together Surveillance State Scraps." *The Guardian*, 3 January 2018. Retrieved 25 May 2018 from https://www.theguardian.com/world/2018/jan/03/stasi-files-east-germany-archivists-losing-hope-solving-worlds-biggest-puzzle.

Reum, Monika, and Steffen Geissler. *Auferstanden aus Ruinen . . . Und Wie Weiter? Chronik der Wende in Karl-Marx Stadt/Chemnitz 1989/90*. Chemnitz: Verlag Heimatland Sachsen GMBH, 1991.

Ríu, Carmen Pérez. "To Make You See: Photography as Intermedial Resource in Theatre and Film Adaptation (*Closer* and *The Winter Guest*)." *Adaptation: The Journal of Literature on Screen Studies* 8, no. 2 (2015): 176–91.

Rushing, Robert. *Descended from Hercules: Biopolitics and the Muscled Male Body on Screen*. Bloomington: Indiana University Press, 2016.

Scott, A. O. "*Karl Marx City* Revisits the Everyday Terror of Dictatorship." *New York Times*, 28 March 2017. Retrieved 25 May 2018 from https://www.nytimes.com/2017/03/28/movies/karl-marx-city-review.html.

Silverman, Kaja. *The Miracle of Analogy: The History of Photography*. Part 1. Stanford: Stanford University Press, 2015.

Sontag, Susan. *On Photography*. New York: Picador, 1973.

Vaidhyanathan, Siva. *Anti-Social Media: How Facebook Disconnects Us and Undermines Democracy*. Oxford: Oxford University Press, 2018.

Wesnierski, Peter. *Die Unheimliche Leichtigkeit der Revolution*. Munich: Deutsche Verlagsanstalt, 2017.

Filmography

Gunner Palace. Directed by Petra Epperlein and Michael Tucker. New York: Pepper & Bones, 2004.

Karl Marx City (*Karl Marx Stadt*). Directed by Petra Epperlein and Michael Tucker. New York: Pepper & Bones, 2016.

The Last Cowboy. Directed by Petra Epperlein and Michael Tucker. Potsdam: Nomad, 1998.

The Lives of Others (*Das Leben der Anderen*). Directed by Florian Henckel von Donnersmarck. Munich: Wiedemann und Berg Produktion, 2007.

The Prisoner or: How I Planned to Kill Tony Blair. Directed by Petra Epperlein and Michael Tucker. New York: Pepper & Bones, 2006.

Afterword

TOWARD A *CAMERA LUDICA*

Agency and Photography in Videogame Ecologies

Curtis L. Maughan

On 13 September 2018, *Attentat 1942* became the first videogame featuring Nazi symbols and subject matter to be officially released in Germany. Developed by Charles Games with support from the Czech Academy of the Sciences and Charles University, *Attentat 1942* is a research-intensive, historically sensitive game about the assassination of Reinhard Heydrich and the ensuing Nazi backlash throughout Bohemia. Prior to the game's release, videogames were not eligible for the artistic exceptions in depicting "symbols of unconstitutional organizations" that are often allotted to federally accepted (mostly analog) forms of media that incorporate Nazi imagery.[1] The release of *Attentat 1942*, then, marks a sociopolitical shift in Germany's recognition of the videogame medium's artistic potential—a shift that was reinforced with the January 2020 release of *Through the Darkest of Times*, the first *German*-developed videogame to feature Nazis and Nazi symbols. Much of *Attentat 1942*'s power lies in its engagement with photographs and filmed testimony—cultural artifacts that bring with them a felt historical authority and political urgency. But the gameness of *Attentat 1942* deeply complicates and expands the political–historical status of photography and film by demanding player interaction: in a typical play session, players grapple with photographs as both portals to interactive memories and ludic objects of visual puzzles. Similarly, players exercise their agency by engaging with video testimonies that expand into webs of dialogue hinging on the player's every decision. In the game's world of historical burden and personal trauma, *player agency*—the player's perceived ability to make meaningful decisions in the gameworld—becomes *player responsibility*.

As the player sifts through photographic memories and decides which questions to ask—and which will remain silent—the process of *Vergangenheitsbewältigung* manifests itself in the symbiotic entity of the player-and-videogame. *Attentat 1942*'s historical photographs and filmed testimonies do not exist without the player—in order for these ludic images to be seen, they demand that the player first call them forth and actively engage with them. Still and moving images in *Attentat 1942* gesture to historical gravity and authenticity while serving as a testament to the demands of videogame interactivity. Ultimately the challenge of the game is not reaching one of its several end states; rather, the challenge is working through dozens of testimonies and memories that constitute a tangle of competing personal experiences amid evolving negotiations of national identity. By translating photographs and filmic testimonies into interactive processes, *Attentat 1942* explores and complicates the essential role that analog media continue to play in our ongoing negotiation of (and memories of) the past—while reframing the aesthetics of *Vergangenheitsbewältigung* in Germany and beyond. The nuanced engagement with photographs and film in the game taps into a broader conversation of cameras, perspective, and perception in videogame texts that thrives on intermedial overlap and rupture.

Like photography in German film, photography in videogames has been largely under explored in intermedial scholarship. Sebastian Möring's and Marco de Mutiis' 2014 essay "Camera Ludica," however, provides a striking exception to the dearth of videogame photography research. Rather than focus on photographs as aesthetic objects that appear within videogames, "Camera Ludica" investigates the various—and ever-multiplying—processes of photography that shape gaming culture in and beyond videogame worlds.[2] Indeed, a single gameplay experience could feature a tangle of *photographies*: a player might simulate the act of taking a photograph as a diegetic event in the gameworld; the player could then use a special photography-mode—designed as part of the game's interface—to capture a gameplay moment from a perspective that is both in the game space and removed from the diegesis; and later yet, that same player might grab a desktop screenshot of the gameplay state to document a glitch in the software. In each scenario, the player's photographic act catalyzes further processes, from advancing the game's narrative to sharing a gameplay moment on social media to reporting a design flaw directly to the developer. As Möring and Mutiis are careful to point out, the *visual* layer of the videogame photograph is inextricably entangled with the *performative* layer of gameplay. Though the player-produced image is a static aesthetic artifact, it is teeming with the dynamic potentialities that comprise the algorithmic underbelly of the videogame medium. In this way, "Camera Ludica" emphasizes areas of study—namely, the procedural and participatory essence of photography in gaming—that would provide helpful footholds as photography and film become ever more complicated by digital media ecologies.

Conversely, process-oriented research of videogame photography could benefit from the intermedial analyses offered in the present volume. Considering videogame photography as a site of rupture and affect, for example, unlocks compelling reconfigurations of essential videogame concepts, including player agency and participatory culture. In specific types of games, the player's carefully framed in-game photograph ruptures the steady stream of player inputs-and-machine feedback with a semblance of permanence and personal identity: the affective singularity of the player photo defies the infinitude of potential playthrough permutations, just as it stakes the "here and now" of the personal gameplay experience amid a swath of interchangeable code. The player photo simultaneously ruptures the boundaries of play, as in-game photography provides entryway to online platforms where digital photographs are shared and compared—and player identities are formed through the photographic framing of unique gameplay experiences. Running parallel to player-made still images that capture individual gaming memories, "artistic screenshotting" and "creative photographic interventions" are—according to Möring and Mutiis—modes of videogame photography that treat the gameworld as a medium to "express a particular idea photographically," either through direct manipulation of the game's code or by operating decidedly outside of the game, its story, and its rules.[3] As casual player photographs rupture the privacy of the player's living room with the public politics of online representation, so too *artistic* videogame photography disrupts cultural norms as it recasts "popular entertainment products" as a medium of significant artistic expression.

Based at the Academy of Media Arts of Cologne, media artist Thomas Hawranke works both within and beyond videogame worlds to reflect on the unique perspectives afforded by the game camera. His work, which spans self-playing videogames to fantastical wild animal simulations, has appeared in spaces such as the Neues Museum Nürnberg, Akademie der Künste Berlin, and Filmmuseum Düsseldorf. Hawranke's 2017 photography series titled *OoB* (Out of Bounds) began when he discovered a glitch while playing *Grand Theft Auto V* (GTA V)—suddenly Hawranke fell through a crack in the foundation of the gameworld and found himself looking up at the underside of the game map. The spatial bug in the software (known as a border glitch) inspired Hawranke to modify the game's code and seek out further perspectives of the gameworld from below and beyond its "official" boundaries. Yet in *OoB* Hawranke does not violently pry open the gameworld to confront his audience with a cacophony of deformed images and distorted sounds, as is so often the case with glitch art. Rather *OoB* offers a series of surreal yet serene photographs of the world from a viewpoint slightly askew. The perspective of one such photograph, taken from deep within the gameworld, erases the surface of a mountainside, thus rendering a tree line, clusters of rocks, and a steel lattice transmission tower suspended in the air—a floating constellation of objects that suggests a gentle rupture of the game's boundaries, a subtle rearrangement of the game's code.

Hawranke maintains that the photographs of *OoB* are "deeply cinematic" as they tell the story of a "camera in motion," one that has traveled where it should not and found an impossible perspective from beyond the game's boundaries.[4] Hawranke admits that his fascination with the game camera stems from his earlier career at an animation studio where he worked in 3D modeling, texturing, and rendering, but was especially influenced by his experiences in designing camera motion. Indeed, his interest in camera movement has been a constant thread throughout his work, as Hawranke maintains: "I think it is what you will find in all my pieces: that the camera wants to *move*." When Hawranke takes control of the game camera, he is not interested in stepping back and merely observing the gameworld. On the contrary, he works with and through the game camera to animate the perspectival essence of the game engine—to remind us of the nonhuman way of seeing that is embedded within the lines of code—a perspective that moves in ways a photographer with an analog camera never could. While much of his work appears firmly planted in digital images and spaces, Hawranke is deeply aware of, and continually grapples with, the fundamental and diverse ways in which analog images shape the textures of videogame environments. Reflecting on the simulation of smartphone cameras in mainstream games like *GTA V* and *Watch_Dogs 2*, Hawranke notes the crucial and multilayered role that photography plays in the creation of open world videogames. Photography not only informs the player's perspective—through the game camera and any additional diegetic cameras—but also quite literally constitutes the appearance of so many digital environments. As Hawranke points out: "When you're doing in-game photography actually you are just photographing a collage of other photographies." The player-produced photograph is indeed a "collage" of photographic technologies, from 3D modeling software to photogrammetry to Geographic Information Systems: photographs are the building blocks of not only cinema, but also contemporary videogames.

Hawranke's 2012 installation *FPS* (First-Person Shooter) delves into the digital-material overlap of videogames by interrogating the processes of abstraction and translation that bridge the "real world" click of the mouse with the "virtual" pull of the trigger. Mirroring the complexities of virtual and real coincidence and divergence, *FPS* has the player stand before a PC monitor displaying a first-person shooter; just beyond the monitor, a video camera is trained on the player's face. This digital camera feeds to yet another monitor set up directly behind the player's head, facing away from the player and toward the muzzle of a paint-ball gun trained on the monitor's image of the player's face. Whenever the player clicks the mouse to fire off a virtual gun, the paint-ball gun discharges a round point blank at the live feed of the player's face. With its circular firing squad of cameras and guns, both real and virtual, *FPS* exacerbates the affective potential of the game (gun-)camera while interrogating the conceptual leap ingrained in attributing real-world violence to virtual mayhem. Ultimately, Hawranke's *FPS* poses a visceral and complex response to Germany's conservative track record of videogame censorship, which has included the complete ban of mainstream games deemed unsuitable for German youth. Of course, problematizing culturally conservative tendencies goes hand-in-hand with Hawranke's entire oeuvre, which continually carves out spaces in museums and galleries, bringing digital and analog perspectives into conflict and conversation. Over the past decade and with the bulk of his artistic output, Hawranke's consistent ability to bring videogames into art spaces has coincided with an intensification of debates in Germany concerning questions of aesthetics, representation, memory, and national identity—all in the context of the videogame medium.

While by no means comprehensive, the preceding thoughts link game artifacts to theoretical considerations to artistic explorations—three efforts to interrogate the analog-digital junction, which provides the ground for further study of similar questions posed throughout this volume. The chapters in *Moving Frames: Photographs in German Cinema* compel us to explore the role photographs have played in German films from the Weimar period, through East and West German film, and into the realm of contemporary genres and movements, including heritage films, horror films, and documentaries, as well as the Berlin School. The various approaches to the intersections of still and moving images in this volume attest to the photograph's remarkable ability to disrupt or distort (cinematic) time and inspire sentimental reverie—highlighting the tension between truth and distortion, past and present, and life and death. As the first of its kind to explore the connection between photographs and German cinema, this volume offers insightful readings of both canonical and underestimated films, only touching on what further explorations of the complex intermedial relationship between photographs and German film will articulate. As several chapters of this volume demonstrate, the digital turn has the potential to unlock vast spaces for further exploration, as the process of digitalization has reorganized how still and moving images are constituted, disseminated, and perceived.

Deeply influenced by analog media but born of computer technology, the videogame is not only the site of untold digital futures but also of countless photographic and cinematic afterlives. In videogames, we engage with photographs and film as fluid, ongoing processes that inspire our emotional and mental involvement, while affording—or demanding—our active, haptic input. The interdisciplinary field of Game Studies offers a future avenue to investigate the complex relationship photographs have to rupture and affect within the context of ludic concepts such as player agency. As games like *Attentat 1942*, the writing of Game Studies scholars like Sebastian Möring and Marco de Mutiis, and the works of media artists like Thomas Hawranke continue to spark conversations around national remembrance and identity, it is critical that scholars contextualize and extend these conversations in the complementary and challenging discourse surrounding photography and (German) film. With their interrogation of photography and film in ludic spaces, these intermedial endeavors remind us that videogames—and digital media more broadly—are inseparable from their analog predecessors, just as they are inseparable from the conversations—of rupture and affect, of identify, memory, and representation—that photography and film have long demanded.

Curtis L. Maughan is a Postdoctoral Fellow at Vanderbilt University. His dissertation examines Benjamin's concept of flânerie in the context of open world gameplay and game design practices. He has published on filmmaker Harald Friedl, the German reception of Shakespeare, and the novellas of Thomas Mann and Heinrich von Kleist, and coedited *Violence—Perception—Video Games: New Directions in Game Research* (2019). He managed the Master's program in Game Development and Research at the Cologne Game Lab and currently heads a game development project between TH Köln and the University of Manouba, Tunisia.

Notes

1. Ian Boudreau, "Attentat 1942 wins Berlin gaming festival award, but can't be played in Germany," *PCGamesn*, 5 May 2018.
2. Sebastian Möring and Marco de Mutiis, "Camera Ludica: Reflections on Photography in Video Games," in *Intermedia Games—Games Inter Media: Video Games and Intermediality*, ed. Michael Fuchs and Jeff Thoss (New York: Bloosmbury Academic, 2019), 69–94.
3. Ibid., 74, 83.
4. All quotations from Thomas Hawranke stem from an interview conducted with the artist on 15 March 2021.

Bibliography

Boudreau, Ian. "Attentat 1942 wins Berlin gaming festival award, but can't be played in Germany." *PCGamesn*, 5 May 2018. https://www.pcgamesn.com/attentat-1942/attentat-1942-wins-berlin-gaming-award-censored-in-germany.

Hawranke, Thomas. *FPS* (First-Person Shooter). Kunsthochschule für Medien Köln. 2015. www.thomashawranke.com/FPS.html.

———. *OoB* (Out of Bounds). In Jahresprogramm 2018, NRW-Kultursekretariat, Wuppertal. 2017. www.thomashawranke.com/OOB.html.

Möring, Sebastian, and Marco de Mutiis. "Camera Ludica: Reflections on Photography in Video Games." In *Intermedia Games—Games Inter Media: Video Games and Intermediality*, edited by Michael Fuchs and Jeff Thoss, 69–94. New York: Bloosmbury Academic, 2019.

Ludography

Attentat 1942. Charles Games, 2017.

Grand Theft Auto V. Rockstar Games, 2013.

Through the Darkest of Times. Paintbucket Games, 2020.

Watch_Dogs 2. Ubisoft, 2016.

Index

www.ingramcontent.com/pod-product-compliance
Lightning Source LLC
LaVergne TN
LVHW012046160826
845678LV00014B/2718

* 9 7 8 1 8 0 7 5 8 0 7 3 5 *